Community Writing

Researching Social Issues
Through Composition

Community Writing

Researching Social Issues
Through Composition

Paul S. Collins

LEA

LAWRENCE ERLBAUM ASSOCIATES, PUBLISHERS

2001   Mahwah, New Jersey   London

Lawrence Erlbaum Associates, Inc., Publishers
10 Industrial Avenue
Mahwah, NJ 07430

Cover design by Jennifer Elder

Library of Congress Cataloging-in-Publication Data

Collins, Paul, S.
        p. cm.
Includes bibliographical references and index.
ISBN 0-8058-3834-1 (cloth: alk. paper)
    1. Readers—Social sciences. 2. Social sciences—Problems,
exercises, etc. 3. Community life—Problems, exercises, etc.
    4. English language—Rhetoric. 5. Readers—Community life.
    6. College readers. I. Title. II. Series.
PE1127.S6 C635   2000
808′.0427—dc21   00-062262
                                                              CIP

Printed in the United States of America
10 9 8 7 6 5 4 3 2

Contents

A NOTE TO INSTRUCTORS

How This Book Came About

This book started with the worst teaching experience in my life.

At the tender age of 23, I taught my first composition class in Brooklyn. It was overflowing with students who neither wanted to be there nor quite believed that the quaking young man before them would actually be responsible for their development over the next 14 weeks. I hadn't received any instruction in teaching or on the school's resources; I didn't even know how to fill out the add/drop forms correctly.

My sole source of support was a pedagogy seminar with other newly minted composition adjuncts, all of whom were actually bewildered lit. scholars like myself. In our desperate need to fill class hours, these seminars were spent swapping our latest surefire writing exercises. Strangely enough, the germ of this volume came from one of these besieged sessions.

"What Makes You Angry?" was my colleague's inspired choice of a paper topic. "It works like a charm," she marveled. "After all, they're all angry about something. They were just filling up page after page on that one." I tried it in my class the next day and, sure enough, it was a great hit. In my inexperience I only saw it as one of the better choices in a long series of classroom papers that were unrelated to each other. But what I discovered was the power of a question that allowed students to express their needs and opinions within their own community. They'd found a reason for writing situated within their experiences, and both the quality and volume of our classroom discourse leaped dramatically in response to this.

As I taught more composition courses, I became dissatisfied with the absence of textbooks that could adequately prepare a student to deal with these community issues. Some textbooks spooned out preselected "important social issues" like cod liver oil, without bothering to ask whether students would have a reason to care about them. Others assumed a mercenary rhetoric of arguing an opinion into the ground without having the students first make sure that their opinions were worth arguing for. Even those that had students deal critically with issues within their own community often failed to take into account the bias and deception practiced by many erstwhile sources.

If you've read this far, then you, too, have probably faced many of the same doubts that I did as a composition teacher, and have felt the same lack of a curriculum that would address your needs. This textbook addresses the need for students coming from disparate communities to critically research and act upon conflicts within those communities.

The Theory Behind This Book

This textbook is based on both social-epistemic rhetoric and the pragmatist theories of William James, Charles Peirce, and John Dewey. Pragmatist philosophy underlies these basic educational principles:

- Philosophy is to deal with conflicts generated within one's daily life.
- Provisional philosophies are constructed by individuals as they address conflicts. "Knowledge" is a construct identifying conflicts we have provisionally deemed as solved.
- Given the conflicting arrays of knowledge generated by investigations, education should guide students into methodologies of logic, rather than toward established "facts."
- Educators should strive toward a "continuity of experience," or investigations that build upon the student's previous inquiries.

Given Dewey's emphasis on providing methodology for knowledge making rather than on fixed canons of information, any experience can serve as a starting point for critical thinking. To Dewey, the effective instructor elicits the investigation of a specific conflict or challenge, empowering students to investigate other conflicts in the future.

This holds three implications for this textbook's use of community issues as thematics for critical literacy:

- Because language is used by individuals to satisfy social needs, a pedagogy should find those needs that compel a writer to communicate with others.
- The social construction of knowledge requires that writers be aware of numerous competing perspectives on the issues they are researching.
- If knowledge is dialogic, then an experiential pedagogy employing peer response is essential to a writer's development.

How This Textbook Works

Community Writing guides students into the critical investigation of conflicts within their own communities to encourage local inquiry and problem solving. Each student begins by identifying a community that they belong to, and focusing upon a problem in it. After observing the problem, they analyze possible solutions, construct arguments for them, decide which are likely to succeed, and consider how to initiate action.

This textbook is recursive, with short writing assignments in each chapter building up to longer papers. Each of the assignment questions is accompanied by guides to thinking about and writing the assignment. These are then followed by a short Focus On reading; these provide brief accounts of community activism, media case studies, and notable success stories.

The longer papers are accompanied by in-class peer reading; each successive peer reading attempts a higher level of conceptual critique. By working together throughout the semester, students create increasingly adept peer groups familiar with all the stages of a student's research.

Given the vagaries and schedules of the individuals that the students contact, the timeline behind student assignments may need to become flexible. Some sources will be much more productive than others, of course. Students should be encouraged to allocate their time accordingly, but always after they have at least attempted using each potential source enough to be familiar with the process.

Although this book is structured, there's plenty of "give" in it. If students need more time to cover other chapters, chapter 2 can be skipped. Internet-based assignments can be skipped as well when time or computer access is lacking.

An Overview of the Chapters

Chapter 1. This represents the student's first step toward the ideas of social construction and pluralism. These ideas are couched in the most personal terms of all—the notion that the "self," which most people feel to be profoundly singular and individual, is in fact socially constructed by ourselves among others, reconstructed for literary narrative, and may be defined in a plurality of ways at any time. This plurality of perspectives is then extended to the manifestations of "community." Each assignment coincides with discussions of relevant aspects of interviewing methodology, the description of everyday experience, the inclusion of multiple perspectives, the organization of an introduction in longer papers, and the uses of peer reading and revision.

Chapter 2. This chapter focuses both on the student's account of a community problem and the manner in which media sources portray this problem. The in-class group critique of media articles, which accompanies this, emphasizes the subjectivity of all sources, making clear to students the need for many perspectives when discussing a community conflict. This media research combines with student fieldwork to create a multifaceted portrait of a community conflict. Students critique their own accounts and interviews for forms of bias. This helps establish student research as part of a continuum of writing resources; their everyday experiences are as viable a source as mass media, and are held to the same standards.

Chapter 3. Here students shift their focus from the library to the field, with their research pursuing *solutions* among participants in the community. They use their knowledge of these solutions to evoke reactions and advice from these participants. Students gain experience as critically aware interviewers. As with their research on media materials, they seek "facts" as a social construct. It is important, then, that student writers find as many of these competing points of view as possible. The series of assignments that precede the interviews help them establish where and how these perspectives may be found. This encourages a description and analysis of a variety of solutions in the paper.

Chapter 4. In this chapter, student writers turn from investigation to persuasion. This is done with an ongoing investigation of approaches to persuasion, often by examining logical fallacies and illogical argumentation. Deduction is explored as *one* form of logic rather than *the* form of logic.

Chapter 5. Just as this textbook's papers are recursively drawn from a series of shorter assignments, the final paper for this course is based on the raw material of the longer papers. Students wishing further practice in conventions of research writing may write their final paper in that genre. But since they have already had practice in writing shorter research papers, you may also wish to offer the option of creating a written product that directly addresses a relevant audience in a public format (e.g., brochures, editorials, public service announcements). If the result is much shorter than the research paper format, the students may write an accompanying letter to a representative of the intended media outlet (editor, programming manager, etc.). This letter would provide researched evidence to back up the claims made in the genre writing.

Final Exam. Exams provide an opportunity for reflection. This can be accomplished by asking that the students write a cover letter to you answering questions about their papers. Some of the queries might be:

- Which paper was your weakest, and which was your strongest? Why?
- What's the hardest thing for you to defend in your position papers? Where are you least sure of your opinion? What information would you need to change this opinion?
- How did you prepare to write your papers? Which research resources were especially useful or frustrating? Why?
- If you had to write and research your paper again, what would you do differently?
- Do you have any advice about this course for me? What advice might you give to yourself?
- What grade would you give yourself for this course, and why?

This approach also avoids many of the problems typically associated with exams: The personal subject matter precludes cheating, renders cramming useless, and helps avoid penalizing students who cannot write on arbitrary topics in a timed setting.

Most importantly, it affords you a chance to read about the students' experience in using this curriculum. I've found their responses to be an invaluable help in developing this book. Teaching, like writing, is always a work in progress.

Acknowledgments

All writing is collaborative, but books are especially so. There are a number of people who were essential to this book taking shape in its current form. First and foremost is my wife, Jennifer Elder, without whom this book simply would not have been written.

When I was Ira Shor's student, he was the first person to spark my interest in composition theory; his continued feedback through this book's many revisions was the greatest influence on its pedagogical theory. John Elder of Middlebury College provided valuable advice on its publication. Tom DeWit of Chabot College encouraged me with the very earliest drafts of this textbook, back when it was still little more than haphazard handouts. Many very patient composition students at Dominican College gave vital feedback on each successive draft of the textbook. Online colleagues on the WPA, WCENTER, and FACSUP listservs—either in threads begun by my inquiries or in response to the inquiries of others—provided me with wonderful advice.

Finally, I am grateful to my colleagues in the publishing world, Sonia Nieto and Naomi Silverman, for the guidance and encouragement they have provided.

A NOTE TO STUDENTS

What Is Community Writing?

It is a commonplace that "students are the future." But as a college student, you are not just the future. You are also the *present*. You pay taxes and vote; you might even already be an experienced worker. *Community Writing* addresses you as an active and responsible citizen by helping you to learn about writing within your own community experiences. "Community" can mean any group that you identify with: a neighborhood, a school, a profession, even an entire ethnicity or religion. *Community Writing* asks you to focus on one of the communities that you belong to, to describe an issue that is important to you in that community, to investigate this issue from many sides, and then to propose possible solutions to it.

Everyone in your class will probably be working on different issues and different types of communities. You'll be researching your own individual topic for the entire semester, and in doing so will become the class expert on your chosen topic. The way that you'll be communicating your findings to your instructor, your classmates, and to others in your community is through writing assignments and papers at each stage of your research.

Why Write Papers?

When you enter college, you're entering a **knowledge community**. Like a town, it has its own rules, landmarks, and expectations of its members. At first, like a new kid in town, you might get a bit lost, or try to fit in without much success. But the longer you spend and the more you take part in the community, the better you'll understand the inhabitants. That's why this textbook asks you to try activities like writing research papers or using specialized library resources. Some of these activities may be difficult at first, but that's entirely normal. After all, writing is not about perfection—it is about making mistakes and learning from them.

But why exactly does the college want you to learn these rules and methods? It's because writing is about finding something you care about, looking at it carefully, and then expressing your ideas about it. Once you've learned how to do that in a college setting, it will be much easier for you to do in new knowledge communities—whether town meetings or new jobs. It's like moving to new towns or learning new languages; if you've done it once or twice, you learn to adapt again pretty quickly.

... And Why Write *Research* Papers?

Even after you've joined a community, for your ideas to have credibility they need to be carefully thought out. That's why research papers are emphasized in this course. The point of a research paper isn't to "find the facts" and dutifully report them, because facts don't exist as nuggets waiting to be dug up. They exist between people. In any community, there's my point of view, and there's your point of view—and somewhere in between we can agree that some of our shared observations imply a "fact." As your views and my views change over time, so do the facts. We may even stop agreeing about whether one of our views is a fact anymore. "The sun revolves around the earth" was a "fact" for millennia, until the observations of enough people led them to stop maintaining this as a fact.

When you write a research paper, you're joining in this kind of conversation with other members of a community. When you do research, you're not just absorbing facts. You're entering a debate. You're asking yourself such questions as:

- Do I believe what this person is saying?
- Should what they're saying be important to me?
- Should it change my feelings on the subject?
- Do my own experiences agree or disagree with what they're claiming?

A research paper is the written record of this debate. It's proof that you've carefully thought about these facts, a chance for you to convince readers that your interpretation of the facts is worthwhile, and an opportunity for these readers to join the debate themselves.

For Whom Are You Writing?

Well, there's your instructor, of course. Your instructor will be expecting you to follow certain standards of format (typed and double-spaced pages, for example), citation (where is your information coming from?), grammar, organization (well-written introductions, conclusions, etc.), and logic (how can you prove the claims you've made?) But your instructor's real concern will be in guiding you into learning how to do research and communicate your ideas to *other* people.

What kind of people might they be? To begin with, you're writing for your classmates. You'll be sharing your writings with each other throughout this semester. Since you'll all be writing on different subjects, your research will need to be explained clearly enough that an outsider to your community could understand it. This means that when you use terms or refer to events that only you or members of your community would know about, your papers will have to explain what they mean and why they're important.

And since this course asks you to address a problem in your own community, you may eventually want to spread your ideas to friends, neighbors and colleagues—whether through community organizing, community meetings, editorials, letter writing, or using other types of media. You probably won't want to use your school research word for word; but by having done this research, you'll be able to craft appeals to your peers that have real substance behind them. The facts will be on your side. And if you already have practice in explaining complex problems and solutions to a complete outsider, then it will be even easier to explain them to people inside your community.

Finally, **you** are your most important reader. As times change, so may your beliefs. Maybe you've had the experience of reading an old paper or letter and wondering "What was I thinking when I wrote that?" As you get your ideas down, they give you the chance to reconsider them, to reread them later, to change your mind over time, and to see your own growth. That's why this textbook emphasizes revision and reconsidering your views. If you don't challenge your own beliefs, you can't stand up for them when someone else challenges them.

How to Use This Textbook

This textbook helps you to identify, learn about, and then act upon a problem in your community. It is *recursive*—that is, each assignment relies upon the previous one. Each step needs to be completed before you can go on to later assignments.

There are three types of writing activities in this textbook: assignments, papers, and a final paper.

Your **assignments** (the short papers that you write for class meetings) will serve as the raw material for your **papers** (longer papers incorporating the assignments, peer editing, and a final draft). It's important that you save all of your assignments and papers. Since your **final paper** draws on the previous papers and assignments alike, you'll need them later on!

Finally, this book asks you to listen as much as it asks you speak out. You'll be asked about what issues are important to you, and why—but then you'll be asked to wait before giving your own opinion on what to do about them. This can be frustrating, because in the meantime you'll be learning about everybody else's opinions on the subject, including those of people that you may disagree with. But until you hear out everyone else first, and learn as much as you can about the issue, your opinion won't carry much weight with them.

After you've taken the time to *listen*, then you'll start to learn about how to argue your beliefs—in other words, how to make yourself *heard*. And that's when your writing can really make a difference.

THE FIRST DAY

> **In Class:** Interview a classmate and be prepared to introduce them to your fellow students. Where are they from? What brought them to this school or to the job they're in today? What are they studying here? Why? What are their goals or interests?

The "Plot" of Your Life

Most of our lives don't have a solid "plot," and yet somehow autobiographies almost always do. That's because they're like novels: The writers create themselves as characters and emphasize a few elements of their everyday life.

We construct our own identities the way a writer constructs fiction. Sometimes "nonfiction" even makes an intrusion on the identity that we want to believe in. (Ever avoided an acquaintance from an old part of your life?) Some aspects of our lives we feel are worth emphasizing to others, some we can't even remember, and some we'd rather be rid of.

Today you'll be explaining to a classmate a subject you know intimately—yourself. Research won't be your challenge here so much as deciding what information is worth telling. There are any number of ways that you can present yourself to the world. Which identity have you chosen?

Interviewing a Classmate

The best interviewers aren't always people with the gift of being talkative. Rather, they're people who plan questions carefully in advance, and who know how to set that list of questions aside when a response gets interesting enough to pursue further. Before you start interviewing your partner, take a few minutes to go over the following guidelines to come up with some useful questions.

Basic questions: Have at least three or four questions on hand ready to ask. If one question is a dud, try rephrasing it. If it's still going nowhere, move on quickly to your next question. Don't let it throw you.

Open-ended questions: Ask questions that can't simply be answered with a yes or no. When you find a yes/no question in your list, rephrase it.

Take notes: Don't worry about getting every word. Jot down general notes as the person talks; if a particular sentence is especially good, then do try to write that down word for word.

Go on tangents: Let the person diverge a bit from your questions; you don't have to run through questions like a robot. Good quotes often turn up during a detour in the conversation.

1

Your Community and an Issue That It Faces

DESCRIBING YOUR COMMUNITY

Assignment: Describe one of the communities that you belong to. How would you describe it to a stranger? What misconceptions might people have about your community? What makes it a community to you; that is, what is it that you all have in common? What part do you envision yourself playing in this community in the future?

Defining a Community

"Community" can mean a neighborhood, a school, a profession, even an entire ethnicity or religion—any group bound by a common interest or condition. No matter how small or large this community may be, your own experience of it can become the starting point of worthwhile research.

We all belong to many communities at once, and they may overlap well or conflict sharply with each other. By entering the college community you've already experienced a transition from one distinct community to another. You may also have moved from an old hometown, and perhaps even away from an entire job community or group of peers. In either case, what you're moving into is a new community; the latest of many that you already belong to.

Here are several typical characteristics of a community:

- **Shared History.** There are people, places, or activities that both you and fellow community members would be familiar with.
- **Shared Language or Jargon.** Communities often use specialized words that aren't in common use; for example, when an environmental activist refers to "astroturf" lobbying by industry, a com-

puter programmer refers to a "code compiler," or a drummer uses a "crash cymbal." There may also be slang to refer to things that an outsider would use a more formal term for. For example, someone in England may refer to the Marks & Spencer department store chain as "Marks and Sparks."

- **Shared Standards of Behavior**. There may be an official or an unspoken code of how things are done or not done in your community—how concerns are raised, how problems are dealt with, and how people are expected to act around each other.

Finally, because you're an insider, you'll be knowledgeable about your community in ways that most others aren't. But don't forget the value of "outside" information. Even chance remarks by outsiders, whether compliments or insults, can reveal much about what others think of your community. Sometimes *you've* been an outsider: when you first joined, after you've returned from a long absence, or when the community seemed to turn against you. How did this feel? What were your first impressions of being an outsider in that community?

Freewriting

Do you freeze up when faced by a blinking cursor, or write only a few sentences before obsessing over whether they're any good? One way around this writer's block is freewriting.

Freewriting is exactly what it sounds like: writing freely. Freewriting allows the pure conversational flow of words onto the paper or the screen. That means simply sitting down and writing *as fast as possible*. Don't worry about spelling, punctuation, organization, grammar, or other nagging concerns. The only rule for freewriting is: Go!

Budget yourself 5 to 15 minutes for freewriting. During this time you must write constantly. If you stop to look back at something, you're interrupting the flow of your thoughts. Don't second-guess yourself. (Some people type with the monitor turned off to avoid this temptation.) Write as quickly as possible, and *do not allow your fingers to stop moving*.

Freewriting is a good way of warming up, because it's like stretching out and then running a sprint. You may find your freewriting veering into the argument you had this morning or other things that have nothing to do with your assignment. That's fine. Once you're getting words onto the page, any words at all, you'll be warmed up in a way that makes writing your assignment easier.

Although much of what you freewrite may look like junk, remember that freewriting is for creating raw material. You can always go back and remove paragraphs that go off track and fix misspellings or missing words. Sometimes you'll eliminate everything from a freewriting session but a sentence or two, but those sentences will form the core of your final response, and they're often written more fluidly and honestly than anything you could have written deliberately.

Sample Response

I don't often think of voters as forming a community unto themselves—after all, any adult citizen can vote—but the group of people who actually do vote is small, and it becomes smaller with each election. It's a special experience to me, though, and I can recall election days quite vividly. After being ready to vote in my first election in 1988, I ended up spending election day shivering in bed with the flu; in 1990 I was out of the country, and hadn't thought to file an absentee ballot beforehand. I finally got my chance to vote in the 1992 primary in Pennsylvania; it was held in a drab county services building, and I finished at the voting machine by pulling on an enormous handle. It felt like I was playing the slots at the world's blandest casino. My candidate didn't win, so I guess I didn't hit the jackpot.

By that fall's election, I was living in Manhattan, and I had to vote at a school gymnasium just off Times Square. An ancient man sat on a chair next to the line, waiting for poll workers to help him to the booth and to pull the levers for him. "I voted in every election since '28," he explained to me. "I use a walker now, but by God—I'm here to vote that s.o.b. out of office!" A few people in the line cheered when he emerged from the voting booth. I wonder whether I'll be as dedicated when I'm his age.

In 1994 I was a poll worker myself. I was sent out to a quiet residential neighborhood with a guy who had been let out of a halfway house for the day to work. Our hostess, an elderly Ukrainian woman, fussed over us with cookies and sugary tea while we manned the flimsy polling station set up in her garage. Ironically, because I was sent to a different precinct before the polls opened and was busy until after they closed, I didn't get a chance to vote that day.

I was upset about that, even though friends said it was no big deal. But the greatest misconception about voting is that individual votes don't count. Local elections can be decided by slim margins; here in San Francisco, the construction of a stadium was passed by a fraction of a percentage point. Even in national elections, a sufficient number of votes insures federal financing for a party's next campaign. Not voting for, say, the Green Party or the Reform Party because they "can't win" also prevents them from having a chance in the next election.

There are other deterrents to voting, I suppose. I've heard that voters are disproportionately older, whiter, and wealthier than the population as a whole. I'm not sure whether it's cynicism, apathy, or both that causes this. But there's no reason why the young, the poor, and minorities have to be excluded. Even though voters are an increasingly homogeneous community in decline, it could change in the future. One election is all it would take.

Focus On: The Communities of San Rafael

After all this talk of communities and writing, you may be wondering what exactly this all means when translated into an essay topic. Spring 2000 writing classes at Dominican College, in San Rafael, California faced this question. Looking through some of their term papers reveals a wide range of investigations into student communities:

Affordable Housing—An appraisal of options available to new residents and city planners in the increasingly tight low- and middle-income housing market in Marin County.

Binge Drinking—The problem of binge drinking among college students, particularly in dormitories, fraternities, and sororities.

Police Brutality—An examination of the tension between the police and members of the community in Humboldt County, where a number of environmental protests have been broken up with force.

Maintaining Momentum in Recycling—A discussion of the slowing pace of recycling programs in some towns and cities, and the challenges faced in keeping these programs financially viable.

The Preservation of National Parks—The dilemma faced by national parks in maintaining their ecosystems as budgets are tightened and attendance rises.

School Shootings—The causes of and possible deterrents to mass school shootings.

Balancing Tourism and Residential Planning—A description of the conflict between residential needs and tourist development in a popular area of the San Francisco waterfront.

Water Fluoridation—The debate over the fluoridation of the water supply in a small California town.

Domestic Violence—A discussion of the symptoms, causes, and treatment of abuse by a partner.

Drunk Driving in Africa—The problems facing African countries in preventing drunk driving, and possible solutions drawn from other countries with longstanding anti–drunk driving measures.

MTBE Damage to the Environment—A look at the damage caused by the seepage of MTBE, a gasoline additive, into water supply.

Basque Terrorism—A historical overview of the minority Basque conflict in Spain, as well as approaches that the government and citizens might take to work toward peace.

Only a few of these topics refer to the writer's immediate geographic vicinity, but all the problems discussed had direct effects upon a self-identified community interest of these students. The paper on school shootings came from someone who had been a high school student just a few miles from Littleton, Colorado, when a mass shooting occurred, while the paper on affordable housing resulted from the experience of a student who was struggling to find housing as the semester began. The study of preserving national parks was written by a student who was an avid backpacker; the papers on domestic abuse and binge drinking were also by students with direct interest and experience in their subjects. Even the most seemingly arcane topics—"Drunk Driving in Africa" and "Basque Terrorism"—were by foreign students concerned by worsening developments back home.

Questions to Consider

1. How would you classify the types of communities covered in the above topics? What other kinds of communities might any of these students belong to?

2. What communities do you belong to, or have you belonged to in the past? (Bear in mind that this includes the types discussed above, and not just your immediate neighborhood.)

3. Which of these communities have other members that you can easily contact? If a newcomer to the community could only speak to one or two people to learn about this community, who would you send them to first?

WHAT ISSUE CONCERNS YOU?

> **Assignment:** What issue or problem in your community concerns you or even makes you angry? Give an example of a specific time it affected you or someone you know. Go into as much detail as possible: when and where it happened, your feelings at the time, how you look back at it, and how it's affected you since then.

The Power of Anecdotes

Large-scale news events don't always affect us in large ways, and yet sometimes a small incident can capture our attention easily. While we may follow the sufferings of a single celebrity or a troubled friend, our eyes glaze over at the news of endless foreign carnage or spiraling debts and disease infections.

But this also gives amazing potential to the individual writer. While sanity compels us to shut out overwhelming problems, we can't ignore individuals so easily. An eyewitness account allows the reader to put themselves in your shoes—in other words, to feel empathy. Once that reader starts to care the way you do about a problem, you're closer to getting them to do something about it.

A skilled writer knows this, and uses detailed pictures of relatively minor incidents as clues to some bigger picture. For example, when Malcolm X's *Autobiography* describes the feel of burning lye on his scalp as he tries to straighten his hair, it tells you more about the price of conforming to white standards than any general description of race relations could.

You may find a similar use of everyday details useful in describing an issue. This is because all writers first experience an issue as an everyday challenge in their own lives; it's only later that they become experts with ideas about it. So before we can explain our ideas, first we have to explain the conflicts that they arose from. Without understanding these experiences, readers won't understand why you've had these ideas.

Plagiarism and the Need for Citations

So far you've relied on your own experiences for this class writing, so you haven't had to worry about plagiarism yet. But very soon you will, so you need to know what to look out for in advance.

The *Oxford English Dictionary* defines plagiarism as "The wrongful appropriation or purloining, and publication as one's own, of the ideas ... or the expression of ideas of another." If you plagiarize at school, you violate the honor code against cheating and you make it hard for others to learn more about the subject of your paper.

If you plagiarize on the job, you're liable to get sued for the royalties and credit due to the original author. Take a rash of public plagiarism that occurred in late 1999. Scottish historian James Mackay was caught plagiarizing so many times that in October 1999 his latest publisher, Atlantic Monthly Press, had to recall and destroy all copies of his new biography of John Paul Jones; a *New York Times* writer had discovered multiple plagiarisms in the text. In August 1999 Nixon biographer Monica Crowley published a piece in the *Wall Street Journal* that lifted entire sections from a 1988 *Commentary* article by Paul Johnson, which a sharp-eyed reader of the paper immediately detected. And earlier that summer, the *Indianapolis Star* fired a television columnist who had plagiarized from another columnist. In each case, the writer's career was badly damaged or destroyed by carelessness and a lack of ethics in citation; all for a shortcut that may have only saved an hour or two of actual work.

It wasn't always this way. Shakespeare lifted the titles, plots, and characters' names from other people's work in order to write "his" versions of *Romeo and Juliet* and *King Lear*. This was all quite normal. But printing presses made libraries grow more complex, and authors saw profits being reaped by publishers. Authors wanted to make a living on this market of ideas, and readers needed ways to track down the huge numbers of new sources these presses were generating. By the 18th century our modern notions of copyright and plagiarism began to form, and they're still evolving today; the Internet has raised a whole new set of questions about who owns what!

Here are some basic ways to avoid plagiarism:

Cite Your Sources. In the longer papers for this course you'll include a Works Cited page and citations within your text. (Look for more on how to do this in our next assignment.) They're essential if your readers want to learn more about the subject, how recent your information is, how reliable it is, and what kind of biases your sources may have.

Acknowledge Assistance. There is nothing wrong—unless your instructor has explicitly forbidden it—with getting assistance on your paper from friends, family, tutors, or classmates. But if they contribute an important idea or significantly alter part of your text, you should acknowledge it in your Works Cited page with a brief note; for example: "Edward Gomez provided editing help and ideas on the employment statistics used in this paper."

Don't Recycle. Believe it or not, it is possible to plagiarize yourself! Don't turn in work written for other courses, past or present, without your instructor's permission. Some schools will punish this as if it were plagiarism. The same is true outside school; for example, according to the October 1999 issue of *Brill's Content*, one third of an article historian Alistair Horne had submitted to the *New York Times*, comparing the war in Kosovo to the World War I Battle of Verdun; had been lifted from a 1991 *Times* article he'd also written comparing the Iran–Iraq War to Verdun. As a result, the *Times* refused to pay Horne. Not to be outdone, the following February another *Brill's Content* reviewer discovered that the respected sociologist Neil Postman had recycled 15 pages from a previous book of his in his "new" book *Building a Bridge to the Eighteenth Century*. The revelation did not exactly enhance Postman's reputation.

Check Your Notes. Often we forget ideas from other people, and then remember them as if they were our own original thoughts. This happens to all writers, so after you've finished your paper, read it over and then quickly skim your research sources. This will help you catch any plagiarism that you may unwittingly have committed.

Sample Response

As a voter, I'm disturbed by the fundraising in most political campaigns. Enormous amounts of money are required for a modern campaign, and with each election spending records are broken. Much of the money in these campaigns seems to come from wealthy individuals, companies, and interest groups who then expect that these contributions will buy them extra pull with elected officials. Joe Public with his $40 contribution won't get the time of day from anyone, but captains of industry with bulging wallets can expect all sorts of luncheons, golf retreats, and events where they can plead their case to a senator or a representative.

Even when a candidate won't take money from such people, all is not necessarily well. In the 1998 and 2000 elections, I was dismayed by the huge amounts of money spent by multimillionaire candidates like Steve Forbes, Al Checci, and Darrell Issa; each seemed determined to buy his way into government. Checci and Issa, running in California, both spent millions of their own money on TV ads, even though neither seemed interested in debating or spelling out his beliefs very clearly on paper. If you have enough money, they seemed to think, you can just buy enough TV coverage to drown out any meaningful questions about your qualifications. Fortunately, voters proved these millionaires wrong; all of them lost in the primaries. But perhaps it's only a matter of time before such blatant tactics start working. Money-driven campaigns that are only slightly more subtle have already landed many candidates in office.

Perhaps elections are becoming the preserve of millionaires and their desperate political friends. The millions spent in some campaigns shut out potential candidates—decent, everyday people who don't earn six- and seven-figure salaries—who either lack rich friends or are unwilling to be the sort of wheeler-dealers who can make such connections.

Focus On: "Granny D"

On April 21, 2000, tourists in the Rotunda of the U.S. Capitol were treated to an odd sight: a woman standing up to begin reciting dramatically from the Declaration of Independence. And then, stranger still, there was the sight of Capitol police hustling this apparently harmless old woman off in handcuffs, to spend the rest of the day in jail. The charge? Illegally demonstrating on the Capitol grounds. "I am glad we were only reading from the Declaration of Independence," she snapped at a judge when she appeared in court on May 24th. "I shudder to think what might have happened had we read from the Bill of Rights."

The arrest of Doris Haddock (aka "Granny D") was more than a fluke in the daily routine of the Capitol. It was the culmination of one woman's determination and of her 3,200-mile walk across the United States. Haddock, appalled by the country's dire need for campaign finance reform, had spent 14 months walking all the way across the country—a 3,200-mile journey.

Haddock is 90 years old.

She had been playing with the idea of a cross-country walk for reform for years, but it was not until she was encouraged by other members of her senior ballet class that she decided to go through with it. At the age of 88, she undertook a 9-month regimen of training so that she could walk the 10 miles a day that her journey would require.

This was not the first time Haddock had been involved in social activism. During the 1930s she appeared in feminist plays, and in the 1960s she protested in Alaska against a proposal to carve out a new harbor along the coast by exploding a nuclear weapon. But not only was the scale of this latest protest much bigger than before, so was the publicity surrounding it. Haddock was rarely alone on her 3,200-mile journey; people that she met on the road often joined her for miles at a time, and two Oberlin College students stuck with her for a 140-mile stretch. But the one constant was Haddock herself. In her 14 months on the road she wore out three pairs of running shoes, encountered rattlesnakes in the desert, and braved weather of every variety. Often she had no clear plan for where she would be staying at the end of each day, but each time someone would take her in.

As she neared Washington, press coverage became more intense, bolstered in part by presidential candidate John McCain's own insistence on campaign finance reform. By the time she reached the Capitol on February 29, 2000, she had thousands of supporters there cheering her on, and was accompanied on her final steps by four members of Congress. Standing on the steps of the Capitol, she lashed out at the senators inside who "turned this headquarters of a great and self-governing people into a bawdy house ... If I have offended you speaking this way on your front steps, that is as it should be. You have offended America and you have dishonored the best things it stands for.... You have somewhere on your desks, under the love letters from your greedy friends and coconspirators against representative democracy, a modest bill against soft money. Pass it."

"Granny D" has gone on to speak across the country for her cause. She gets admiring comments that someone of her age could accomplish so much—but she feels that this misses the point. If she can do something about an issue that concerns her, Haddock points out, anybody can:

> I live on Social Security and I do not have a television show or a political action committee, but I knew that if I walked far enough, at my age, people would care to know what is worth this effort of mine. My walk was difficult and it was painful. But I did not care for the difficulty or the pain because I valued what I was doing, and, by doing, I valued the life I had re-created for myself, even after so many years. It is for all of us, I am sure, to engage the world with our deepest values. I think that is why we are here.

Sources

Baldauf, Scott. "Granny D Goes to Washington." *Christian Science Monitor.* 30 Jun. 1999: 3

Gabrielli, Betty. "Two Oberlin Students March with Granny D for Campaign-Finance Reform." Mar. 2000. <http://www.Oberlin.edu/news-info/00mar/grannyd.html>.

Glod, Maria. "'Granny D' Takes a Walk for a Purpose; Students Get a Message Carried Across Country." *Washington Post.* 24 Feb. 2000: 3

"Granny D. Home Page." Granny D. 8 Jun. 2000. 11 Jun. 2000. <http://www.grannyd.com>.

"Praise the Pilgrim Protester." *Christian Science Monitor.* 1 Mar. 2000: 8

"Protester, 90, Arrested in Capitol Rotunda." *New York Times.* 22 Apr. 2000: A9

Ruane, Michael E. "The Mission Is My Passion"; At Age 90, Woman Walks Across the Country on a Crusade to Change Campaign Finance Laws." *Washington Post.* 29 Feb. 2000: B1

Wallsten, Peter. "Backers Hope Presidential Race Confers Front-Burner Status on Campaign Finance Overhaul." *CQ Weekly.* 4 Mar. 2000: 463

Questions to Consider

1. What makes Haddock, a woman with no formal training in politics or public relations, a compelling advocate for campaign finance reform? Conversely, who might have a harder time reaching out to American voters?

2. How did Haddock leverage a small amount of funding and experience into something much larger? How would she have had to prepare for this?

3. Haddock started as a concerned citizen, and was initially overwhelmed by the extent of the problems that she saw. What problems in your community seem so difficult that people who want to help simply get overwhelmed by them? What might keep them from giving up?

COMPARING NEWS ACCOUNTS

Assignment: Find two news accounts of the problem that you've written about, or on a similar problem in another community. Summarize the basic points of the articles, and include Works Cited references for both of them. Compare the articles with your own experience. How are they similar? How are they different?

Finding Sources

You'll need to locate two articles for today's writing. Much of the most useful information on your topic may be found in journals, magazines, and newspapers. Books take years to go to press, while periodicals are often more up to date. They also have the advantage of brevity. Don't shy away from asking a reference librarian about where and how to look for these sources. Here are a few starting places:

Electronic Databases—These have rapidly taken over as the fastest and most comprehensive way to search for articles; you can then print out full texts of articles or e-mail them to yourself to read at home later. Most databases will search thousands of magazines and journals, but each has a somewhat different selection, so it doesn't hurt to do the same search on more than one database. Their interfaces are becoming increasingly standardized, so once you've learned how to use one, you'll have largely learned the others, too. Ask your library which databases they have available, and which one would best suit your topic.

New York Times Index—This is the preeminent source for national and international news, though not as useful for local issues. Many libraries have a *New York Times* print or CD-ROM index.

Local Paper Index—Your city's newspaper may publish an index of its stories. This will be especially useful for detailed local stories that the national press might not cover. Ask the librarian if such an index exists, or call the newspaper directly.

Newspaper Morgue—Local papers may not publish an index, but they'll have back files ("the morgue") of clippings. Call the newspaper's office; if they allow public access, you'll find it useful for specific local issues.

WWW Newspaper Sites—You can find these through a search engine (e.g., Yahoo) or from newspaper links at sites like the Drudge Report (drudgereport.com). These newspaper sites often only archive very recent articles, although some will cover years of back issues.

Article Dossiers—Library reference sections have issue summaries like *Facts on File*, or article clippings like SIRS (*Social Issues Resource Series*, in print and CD-ROM).

Online Library Catalogs—Online catalogs typically allow you to search by author, title, subject, or keyword. Jot down all the possible search terms beforehand, because not all searches are successful: Several perfectly reasonable sounding search terms may turn up nothing before one of the terms on your list gets a response. On the other hand, such searches can also be too successful; you may end up with thousands of responses. Often you can narrow your search by combining keywords with terms like *and, or, but,* etc. For example, *Photography* may bring a flood of matches, but *Photography and War* will bring a much more focused group. And computers can be quite unforgiving: Make sure that you spell your search terms correctly!

Card Catalogs—While most library catalogs are online now, some libraries still maintain card catalogs. Even libraries that have extensive online catalogs may not have cataloged their entire collection, so you'll need to use both to cover their entire holdings. Ask the staff whether this is case. Card catalogs are organized alphabetically for author, subject, and title. For example, you can find *The Noam Chomsky Reader* under three different card catalog entries:

Chomsky, Noam

The Chomsky Reader

United States—Foreign Relations—1945 –

Authors are listed alphabetically by their last name. To determine the alphabetical order of title, ignore *A, An,* or *The.* The above title, therefore, would be filed under *C.* And while you might guess at some relevant subject headings, you can also look them up in the *Library of Congress Subject Headings* (LCSH). It's usually available at the reference desk.

Citing Your Sources

In this paper you'll include a Works Cited page and citations within your text. This is essential if your readers want to learn more about the subject, how recent your information is, how reliable it is, and what biases your sources may have. Citing your sources also guards against plagiarism.

So when do you need to cite something? Here are some guidelines:

Direct Quotes—Any time you use the exact wording from someone else's written or spoken work, whether it's a phrase or an entire paragraph, you need to cite it.

Paraphrasing—If you rework someone else's original wording into a new sentence, even if you've changed every word but kept the same basic idea, you need to cite it.

Someone Else's Original Idea—If you adopt a form or approach that is unique to another person, even without quoting or paraphrasing their work, you need to cite them.

Statistics and Graphics—Unless you use a mathematical fact (e.g., the value of pi) or a common symbol or geometric figure, any time you give figures in your writing you have to say where they are coming from.

The Exception: Public Domain—If something is common knowledge (e.g., "Canada borders the United States" or "Jefferson was our third president") or you use a common quote that has no clear source, then you do not need a citation.

Citing With the MLA Format.   This textbook uses the MLA (Modern Language Association) format for citation; it's one of a number of different formats used by schools and other organizations, so always ask your instructor which format to use. While you'll find this format explained here and in appendix 3, the most complete reference work on the subject is the *MLA Handbook for Writers of Research Papers.* It's available in bookstores and at the reference desk of most libraries.

The following (entirely fictitious) paragraph shows how to cite a paraphrase from a web page, a quote, and a quote where you've already mentioned the author's name. (In this last case, you previously cited Zimmerman's article.)

> The owners of the Plunket Company avoided takeover by offering to buy shares from any and all shareholders (Plunket Company Page). They knew that the philosophy behind the Widget Company's growth has been described as "the voracious and unceasing acquisition of competitors" (Zimmerman C2). At least one financial analyst believes that "the Plunket family lost itself more money in this 'rescue' than the takeover would have cost them"(C2).

Now that you've made your citations in the text, you also need to give information on your sources in a separate Works Cited page at the end of your paper. Note that the entries are listed in alphabetical order by their last names. Here are what the entries would look like for a web page, a book, a magazine article, a book with two authors, a personal interview, a phone interview, and a newspaper article:

Works Cited

Carvell, Tim. "I Was Alan Greenspan's Roadie." *Timothy McSweeney's Worldwide Fondness.* 6 Jan. 2000. Timothy McSweeney's. 11 Apr. 2000 <http://www.mcsweeneys.net/2000/01/06greenspan.html>.
Eggers, Dave. *A Heartbreaking Work of Staggering Genius.* New York: Simon & Schuster, 2000
Friedman, Robert I. "Land of the Stupid." *New Yorker.* 10 Apr. 2000: 40–49
Lake, Brian and Russell Ash. *Bizarre Books.* London: Pavilion Books, 1998
Vowell, Sarah. Personal interview. 30 Jun. 2000
Wallace, David Foster. Telephone interview. 24 Jun. 2000
Weber, Bruce. "Plan Your Family Reunion in Rehab." *New York Times.* 11 Apr. 2000: B1

Sample Response

I often get the feeling that I'm in a shrinking community of voters. As reported in the *New York Times,* research by the Committee for the Study of the American Electorate found that nationwide turnout in the most recent primaries was a mere 17 percent of eligible voters; in 10 states, turnout sank to record lows, despite the use of such innovations as "Motor Voter" registration. As committee director Curtis Gans noted: "The problem we have is not procedural but motivational" ("Voter Turnout Drops" A18). Even with registration gimmicks, there's an underlying apathy among Americans.

My suspicion is that this apathy stems in part from the vast sums of money involved in campaigning. Press coverage of campaign finance and its reform doesn't give much immediate hope for a solution. The *New York Times* article "Campaign Finance: The Lateral Pass" explains the curious phenomenon of how members of Congress can talk about reform without actually getting anything achieved. Here's how it's worked eight times in the last 19 years: Every couple of years, one chamber (either the Senate or the House) will pass a campaign finance reform bill with the tacit understanding that the other chamber will defeat it (Clymer 6). This pattern has occurred under both Democratic- and Republican-controlled congresses. This way, the parties can claim that they "passed finance reform" without having to turn it into a law. Occasionally this cozy arrangement is laid bare: " ... in 1992 House Speaker Thomas Foley only got a bill passed by assuring wavering Democrats that President Bush would veto it" (6). Sure enough, that is what happened. Even when both sides of Congress do pass a finance reform, it's with the knowledge that nothing substantial will result from it.

The president's tacit collusion in stifling reform has changed little in the last decade. As the *Christian Science Monitor* notes, neither candidate in the 2000 election has any serious commitment to campaign finance reform:

> These two guys have been throwing fake punches, because neither is really in a position to do a lot. Both benefit mightily from the system as it is. From a mere 65 people, a group of donors called "Pioneers," [George W.] Bush had raised $4.4 million by the end of 1999 .... And Gore too has a club. The 13 people in his inner circle have raised about $1.5 million as of January 1.
> (Chinni 9)

It's sad to think that were it not for the strident denunciations of fundraising made by failed candidates John McCain and Bill Bradley, the issue would probably never have come up at all; Bush and Gore, like most political insiders, wouldn't even have had to pretend to care about it.

Works Cited

Chinni, Dante. "Throwing Fake Punches in Campaign Finance Reform." *Christian Science Monitor*. 16 Mar. 2000: 9

Clymer, Adam. "Campaign Finance: The Lateral Pass." *New York Times*. 9 Aug. 1998: Review 6

"Voter Turnout Drops in 1998 Primaries." *New York Times*. 30 Jun. 1998: A18

Focus On: Stephen Glass

Still not sure why you should always list your sources? Then consider the case of Stephen Glass, a brilliant young reporter whose career flameout in mid-1998 was a classic case of flimsy or nonexistent sources catching up with a writer. The 25-year-old Glass was a rising star, having written for the *New*

Republic, George, Harper's, Rolling Stone, and NPR. His stories were memorable: coke-fueled young conservatives running amok at a convention, an account of work as a phone psychic, a church that worshiped George Bush, and a Lewinsky-inspired "Monicondom."

Too bad that they were faked.

Glass's deceptions unraveled in May 1998, when an online editor for *Forbes* magazine contacted the *New Republic;* in following up a story by Glass about a teen hacker working for a software company, *Forbes* couldn't find sources that checked out. Glass hurriedly created a Web site for the company and gave editors his brother's cell phone number as the company's voice mail. But it emerged that not only was this article faked, but that most and maybe all of his articles were.

Glass himself had worked as a fact checker for the *New Republic.* He knew that if he turned in stories late and insisted his sources were confidential and didn't want to be contacted, he might get away with it. And so he did—for a while.

Aside from Glass's insisting on the "privacy" of his sources, there were other warning signs. In January 1997, the Center for Science in the Public Interest (CSPI) responded to an unflattering Glass profile by pointing out a number of inconsistencies in Glass's work; they also noted a number of unattributed quotes and near-quotes by Glass from an earlier *Detroit News* article on CSPI. But these charges didn't deter the *New Republic*—which had previously been burned by another young plagiarist, Ruth Shalit—from using its new star.

Fudging facts cost Glass his job and it cost him money. In October 1998, the antidrug group D.A.R.E. filed a $10 million libel suit against Glass for false allegations in the *New Republic* and *Rolling Stone;* several months later the group settled for an undisclosed sum of money. Even after Glass tried to begin anew in 1999 by enrolling in Georgetown University's law school, his past misdeeds caused him to be passed over for a position on the school's law review journal.

In the meantime, other news organizations underwent similar humiliations. The *Boston Globe* discovered that columnist Patricia Smith had been inventing quotes and people. Soon there were accusations of bias (Smith is African American), because dubious stories by a veteran white columnist, Mike Barnicle, had not been scrutinized. When his articles didn't check out, and when one column was found to have been plagiarized from the George Carlin book *Brain Droppings,* Barnicle was also let go. Later, in December 1999, while working for the New York *Daily News,* Barnicle was snagged yet again—this time for self-plagiarizing an old Christmas column he'd written for the *Globe,* which itself bore a suspicious resemblance to one written in 1967 by *Chicago Daily News* columnist Mike Royko.

After over a year in professional exile, Patricia Smith was hired in 2000 as a columnist by *Ms.* magazine—which, an editor there stressed to a *New York Times* reporter, does have a fact checking department. But despite Smith's seeming rehabilitation, other unwary papers continue to get into themselves into similar messes. In the summer of 1999, the *Arizona Republic* fired a columnist for inventing her sources. And the *Chicago Tribune* was embarrassed by a June 1999 story by Gaby Plattner claiming that she'd witnessed a pilot on Air Zimbabwe leave the cockpit in midflight to use the bathroom, lock himself out, and then get back into the cockpit by smashing down the door with an axe. A reader wrote in to say that he'd heard this story before as an urban legend; on investigation it turned out that Plattner had invented the whole episode. One phone call to check the facts could have punctured the whole lie: Air Zimbabwe doesn't even carry axes on its planes.

TV news didn't fare much better. In June 1998, CNN broadcast allegations that in Vietnam the United States had used nerve gas on its own soldiers in "Operation Tailwind." They hadn't checked their facts properly, and soon retracted the account—but by then newspapers and TV stations nationwide had repeated the false charges. Long afterward, CNN quietly paid a retired army general to settle the defamation that he suffered.

The CBS show *60 Minutes* also tripped up when it aired a faked segment on drug runners in Colombia and London. Although the documentary, which originally ran in Britain under the auspices of Carlton TV, had long ago been debunked by the British press, apparently no one at *60 Minutes* bothered to check up on this.

Research can't be considered much more than interesting anecdotes unless it is verifiable. Ideally, that means that it should have:

- A byline (that is, the name listed) of the reporter or researcher
- Named sources for all quotes and figures
- Locations (i.e., city, even a street address) for any organization mentioned
- Independent verification by a competing news organization or a fact checker

Magazines and newspapers don't list their sources the way college papers do. But reporters provide such lists to an editor or a fact checker. The reason is the same: They give insight into bias; they allow verification of sources; and they prevent libel suits, copyright suits, or damage to reputation. In the end, listed sources are the only real guarantee of reliability.

Sources

Barringer, Felicity. "*Boston Globe* Columnist Resigns Over Authenticity of 1995 Story." *New York Times*. 20 Aug. 1998: A1+
"CNN Settles Lawsuit Over Nerve Gas Report." *New York Times*. 16 Apr. 2000: 21
Dowd, Ann Reilly. "The Great Pretender: How a Writer Fooled His Readers." *Columbia Journalism Review*. Jul./Aug. 1998: 14–15
Gillard, Michael Sean and Laurie Flynn. "*The Guardian*: Special Reports: The Fake Connection." *The Manchester Guardian*. 9 Jun. 1998. 7 Dec. 1998. <http://reports.guardian.co.uk/papers/19980506-37.html>.
Goldman, David. "Storyteller: Stephen Glass Makes Fact From Fiction." *Biography*. Oct. 1999: 22
Kuczynski, Alex. "Media Talk: *Ms.* Is Ready to Give Ex-*Globe* Columnist Another Chance." *New York Times*. 24 Jan. 2000: C11

Manners, Jane. "Can't Keep a Good Man Down." *Brill's Content*. Apr. 2000: 82–85

McLain, Dylan Loeb. "Media Talk: Scandals Don't Much Harm an Already Bad Reputation." *New York Times*. 19 Oct. 1998: C4

Pesca, Mike. "Barnicle Recycles." *On the Media*. National Public Radio. 25 Dec. 1999

Pogrebin, Abigail and Rifka Rosenwein. "Not the First Time." *Brill's Content*. Sept. 1998: 120–123

Pogrebin, Robin. "Rechecking a Writer's Facts, A Magazine Uncovers Fiction." *NewYork Times*. 12 Jun. 1998: A1

"Prize Winning Documentary Was Faked, Investigators Say." *San Francisco Examiner*. 7 Dec. 1998: B14

Reliable Sources. Cable Network News (CNN). 5 Sept. 1999

Shanahan, Ed. "A Travel Tale's Crash Landing." *Brill's Content*. September 1999: 16

Stamler, Bernard. "Anti-Drug Group Sues Writer Who Made up Some Sources." *New York Times*. 5 Oct. 1998: C11

Tullis, Paul and Lorne Manly. "Slipping Past the Fact Checkers: How Magazines Do Not Check Their Stories." *Brill's Content*. July/August 1998: 30

"What's New—CSPI Press Releases." Center for Science in the Public Interest. 7 Jan. 2000. <http://www.cspinet.org/new/newrepb.html>.

Questions to Consider

1. Why do you think that retractions and corrections usually receive much less space and smaller headlines than a new but inaccurate story?

2. If someone reported false information about the issue that you are writing about, could it be damaging to your community? How?

3. Do you know for certain that I haven't just made up the characters of Stephen Glass, Patricia Smith, and Mike Barnicle? If you wanted to verify the truthfulness of this story, what steps could you take?

INTERVIEWING A COMMUNITY MEMBER

> **Assignment:** Interview someone else who has been affected by the issue that you've described. Ask them the same questions that you used on yourself, as well as any others that you can think of. In what ways are your experiences similar and different?

Getting Your Interview

One of your most powerful tools as a writer is your own eyewitness account. "I know because I was there" is an argument that is very difficult for others to dismiss. But when you can confirm or widen your experience by combining your account with those of others around you, your work becomes exponentially more powerful. So for this assignment you'll have to interview someone—either in person, by phone, or by e-mail. If you're shy, this can sound like a nerve-racking assignment. But as you'll discover, most people actually like being interviewed; it's not often they get to talk about themselves and their ideas while having someone intently scribbling it all down.

Here are a few pointers to start you out:

Refresh Your Memory: Glance over the tips you used in "Interviewing a Classmate" at the beginning of this textbook. These will come in handy for any interview.

Explain yourself: In Hollywood, "high concept" refers to movies whose premise can be explained in one sentence. Be ready to explain your project quickly: You don't want an awkward silence when someone asks why you're calling.

Make an appointment: If someone's impatient with you it doesn't mean that they don't want to be interviewed—they may just be busy at that moment. Be courteous and always ask what would be the best time to speak.

Get a referral: Even if someone can't help you, they may still be a useful lead. Ask them if they know who would be able to help. You'll get a lead *and* your foot in the other person's door: Now you can say "So-and-so sent me."

Quoting and Paraphrasing

If you want to use someone else's ideas or words in your writing, you have two options: quoting or paraphrasing.

Quoting is simply using someone else's exact words in your own writing. You indicate their words by using quotation marks:

According to the chief of police, "murders are at a 40-year low."

You can leave out unnecessary words by leaving an ellipsis (…) in their place. Three dots indicate that you've jumped over words within one sentence, and four dots indicate that you've jumped between sentences:

As Chomsky points out, "We have the right of free expression, though some can shout louder than others, by reason of power, wealth, and privilege.... We readily understand why the powerful and the privileged often rise to the defense of personal freedom, of which they are the chief beneficiaries in practice"(189).

Use the term *sic* to indicate an error in your source. That way you can quote accurately, but without the reader thinking that you made the mistake:

In his essay, Charles claimed that "The city guvernment [sic] is in severe fiscal crisis."

Paraphrasing is when your restate someone else's idea in your own words. If the original quote is poorly worded, too long, overly complex, or simply more (or less) detailed than you need, your paraphrase can digest it into a few words (or expand it) so that your reader can use and understand it. It's important stylistically, too. If you use too many direct quotes, your paper may start sounding more like a grab bag of other people's thoughts than your own thinking about these ideas. Mixing paraphrase and quotation lets you vary the flow of the paper enough to keep it from becoming repetitive.

Most importantly, a paraphrase allows you to add information or commentary that wasn't in the original quote. It is this type of added context that will make your paper become more than the sum of its sources; it will start to become your own synthesis of source material and original analysis.

One danger of paraphrasing, though, is that you'll twist the original quote's meaning into something different from what the author intended. This may be quite accidental on your part, especially if you don't fully understand the quote to begin with. Before paraphrasing, make sure you understand all the words in the original quote. If you don't, look them up in a dictionary.

Substituting a few words but otherwise keeping the general wording or construction of an original quote is not paraphrasing. It's a half-baked quotation, and liable to get you charged with plagiarism if you're not careful. Some words don't have synonyms, though; or sometimes there isn't really a good way to rephrase the original quote's wording. You may employ a directly quoted phrase or sentence within a paraphrase, however, if you place quotation marks around these phrases. If you're only directly quoting one or two words, it's not necessary to use quotation marks—unless that word or usage is unique to the original author. Using quotes in this case will show the reader that it's your source making an unusual use of wording, and not you.

Sample Response

Ted Loewenberg has been a neighbor of mine in Haight-Ashbury for the last three years. An advisor with IBM's research division, he and his wife have lived here since 1989; recently, they opened a neighborhood B&B. He's active in organizing the monthly meetings of our block's neighborhood association, and so I guessed—correctly, as it turned out—that if anyone on my block was committed to the civic duty of voting, it would be Ted.

> I first voted in the 1970 midterm elections. As he recalls: And I remember that it felt like—"At last! I'm finally getting to do this." I'd been politically active even before that. That year, though, it felt especially significant. The Vietnam War had expanded into Cambodia, and Attorney General John Mitchell had decided not to go after the National Guard for [the massacre at] Kent State. My vote was based partly on candidate stances towards those events.

Even in these early years of voting, Ted noted the civic cohesion that resulted from the shared experience of voting.

> I had a sense of neighbors meeting at the polling place. With all the isolation of people in their cars and off their porches, that's important. Today, with all the use of absentee ballots, or the mail-in voting that they're trying in Oregon, I think you lose a lot of that. People don't have a chance to change their mind before the final day .... It takes away a window of time where events can influence the outcome.

Campaign financing is even more troubling to him: "We basically leave government to the highest bidder. When we see the communications industry invited to write their own deregulation legislation, the system is corrupted and completely broken." He points out that this corrupting influence seeps down to the local level. "You can't run for city supervisor now without a quarter of a million dollars handy." This tilts elections in favor of the well connected, who in turn are usually incumbents.

As a result, he looks askance at the pleas of national political parties for citizen contributions, because he views them as a cynical play on naiveté about who really pulls the strings. "They should outlaw private money in elections. Otherwise, the $20 you contribute is just a quaint gesture."

Thanks in part to his master's degree in history—something that I hadn't even known about before the interview—Ted also had an interesting historical perspective on the problem. "Bought candidates aren't new. Look at Warren Harding in the 1920 election. But it's become so much worse in recent years. While special interests have always been part of politics, what has changed is that they now dominate it."

The attention lavished on these deep-pocketed special interests can literally separate politicians from their citizenry.

> I've seen every presidential candidate in person since 1960—I even made a point of seeking out Nixon! Except I never saw Bush. He was too busy talking at $1,000 a plate dinners ... and really, without interacting with your public, these politicians never have to explain their views or have them challenged.

Despite (and perhaps even because of) the flaws in the election system, he remains convinced of the importance of voting. "The biggest mistake is to think that 'My vote doesn't make a difference.' It's been shown time and time again to not be the case. It's the one lever that we all have as citizens."

Works Cited

Loewenberg, Ted. Personal interview. 21 Dec. 1998

Focus On: Studs Terkel

Mention the word *interviewer*, and people often think of Barbara Walters or Larry King, that is, interviewers who are rich and famous from talking with the rich and famous. But hidden in the country's heartland, Chicago radio host Studs Terkel has made a career out of interviewing everyday people about everyday experiences.

After graduating from law school in 1934, and playing villains and tough guys in stage and radio plays, Studs began working as a sportscaster and radio announcer in Chicago. His nightly *Studs Terkel Show*, on the air on WFMT since 1948, features interviews with a wide variety of actors, artists, and activists. Over the years he's interviewed Martin Luther King Jr., Bertrand Russell, and reclusive personalities like Marlon Brando and Marlene Dietrich. Unlike many talk show hosts, he always reads his guests' latest works before interviewing them.

Despite his work with well-known guests, Studs gained a national reputation by wandering around the country with a tape recorder and interviewing the unknown public. In his book *Working*, he explores workplaces not by citing economists and captains of industry but by interviewing actual workers: people like Dolores Dante, a waitress who's worked 23 years in the same restaurant, or Joseph Lattimore, a black insurance salesman. Most historians write about wars in terms of generals, leaders, and weapons. But in *The Good War*, Terkel creates a portrait of World War II by interviewing common soldiers. "It's history written from the bottom," he explains, "rather than history written by the generals."

Terkel's approach to interviewing is conversational. He may go into an interview with a set of questions in mind, but he's ready to set them aside or create new ones in order to chat with his interviewee. It's an approach that he often likens to jazz—he'll start with a simple theme, but then he'll improvise off of it, or let a guest take a long solo. Sometimes Studs himself will interrupt the interview to tell an anecdote of his own. By not always sticking to the script, he often gets his subjects to be far more open and friendly than they might be in a more formal interview. And even when he interviews someone with offensive views—as when Studs, who is Jewish, talked with a Ku Klux Klan leader—he gives readers and listeners the chance to judge the person for themselves.

Now 88 years old, Studs continues working as a radio host in Chicago and on a weekly show on NPR. His 1993 book *Race* won a Pulitzer Prize, and in 1997 he donated 9,000 hours of interview tapes to the Chicago Historical Society, representing decades of field research with thousands of everyday Americans. Long after our "famous" talk show hosts have been forgotten, future historians may still be turning to the oral histories of Studs Terkel for the inside story of what it was like to be an American in the 20th century.

Sources

Albin, Kira. "Studs Terkel: An Interview with the Man Who Interviews America" *Grand Times*. 5 Jan. 2000. <http://www.grandtimes.com/studs.html>.

"An Interview with Studs Terkel." Narr. David Barsamian. *Alternative Radio with David Barsamian*. Public Radio International. KALW, San Francisco. 4 Jun. 1998

Marks, Peter. "Angst of Working Stiffs From Mason to Waitress." *New York Times*. 22 Mar. 1999: B5

Sklar, Robert. "The Interviewer." *New York Times Book Review*. 26 Sept. 1999: 28

"Studs Terkel: The Ancient Mariner." *National Times*. Nov./Dec. 1996. 24 Dec. 1998. <http://www.nattimes.com/tntissues/il196/studs.html>.

Terkel, Studs. *American Dreams: Lost and Found*. NY: New Press, 1999

———and Ronald Grele. *Envelopes of Sound: The Art of Oral History*. 2nd ed. New York: Praeger, 1991

———.*The Good War: An Oral History of World War II*. 1984. New York: New Press, 1997

———.*My American Century*. New York: New Press, 1998

———.*Race*. New York: Anchor, 1993

———.*Studs Terkel's Chicago*. Narr. Studs Terkel. Videocassette. Home Vision, 1994

———.*Working*. 1974. New York: New Press, 1997

Questions to Consider

1. People can spend much of their lives without being interviewed about their family, what they do for a living, or their experience of situations like racism or war. If someone could interview you at length, who or what would you want to tell them about?

2. Can you think of anyone else who interviews "ordinary" people, that is, people who wouldn't normally be considered famous or powerful? How do these interviews differ from those with the rich and famous?

PAPER:
DESCRIBE YOUR COMMUNITY AND AN ISSUE IT FACES

> **The First Draft:** Describe a community that you belong to, and a problem that it has. How has this problem affected you? How has it affected others in the community? Have other communities had similar problems? What might happen if this problem is mishandled in your community?

Writing a Rough Draft

First of all, don't despair—writing a rough draft is a process that all writers go through! Don't worry too much about getting your ideas down in full sentences or with correct grammar and spelling: That can come later. Focus more on combining and reworking the raw material from your previous assignments into an introduction, body, and conclusion. Material from previous assignments may be left out, left in, or explained more fully, and some parts may raise questions that you'll have to address with new material altogether.

While some teachers recommend a quiet, concentrated workplace to write in, actual composing can be very different. I almost always listen to music, or write in coffeehouses where I'm surrounded by passersby and other tables in loud conversation. While silence brings more intense concentration, I don't like it much—it takes all the joy out of my work.

Life's too short for self-punishment, unless it's absolutely necessary; write in whatever environment you feel most comfortable and productive. Similarly, whether you tend to procrastinate or overplan, learn to adapt your work habits to the strengths and weaknesses of your own personality:

Read smarter, not harder. You don't have time to read everything in the library. Skim the beginnings and ends of long articles, and perhaps the beginning of each paragraph, to quickly dig up information. In longer works, check the index for sections that relate directly to your topic. If the article looks particularly promising after you've skimmed it, then read it in full.

Start with your most promising sources first. If you run out of time you'll still have the best material at hand.

Don't get overwhelmed. Any learning experience can seem overwhelming at first glance. Break your work down into manageable steps.

Don't overorganize. Your opinions on a subject may change as you learn more, so give yourself time early on to simply gather information without thinking of how exactly it will fit into your paper or "prove" your theory.

Keep your notes concise. Don't waste time copying articles and whole paragraphs word for word into your notes when a short paraphrase or a few comments will do. Taking notes on index cards often forces your notes to stay concise.

Give yourself time to write. Give yourself time to write your paper, along with an extra day to revise any mistakes that you didn't catch while you were writing it. If problems appear, you'll have the time to find more information to address them.

Don't erase lengthy deletions. Thinking of getting rid of a sentence or paragraph? Move it to an extra page at the end of paper, just in case you do need it later.

Don't feel obliged to write "in order." Are you stuck at the beginning? Then don't start there! You can easily rearrange your paragraphs later, especially if you write on a computer.

Introductions

You may have heard that the introduction to a piece of writing "states a thesis," thus making its goals clear right at the start. Read a magazine article or anything other than a textbook, though, and chances are that it doesn't clearly state a thesis at the beginning. In fact, not all writing begins by stating a thesis, and not all papers that do are terribly interesting. There are actually many different ways of introducing a piece of writing:

Chronological Order—Begin at the beginning! What happened first?

A Question—Direct a question at a reader or at yourself; your paper should then work toward finding the answer.

Anecdote—A brief story that humorously or dramatically illustrates the subject is one of the best ways to pull a reader in.

Description of Characters—Before describing an event or a subject, start with its participants: "Once upon a time, there was a king with three lovely daughters .... "

Description of Setting—Focus on the location of your paper's subject: a general description of the place, or a specific object that says a lot about the surroundings.

General Statement of a Thesis—Begin with a belief or "thesis" that you plan to explain and define. Back this up carefully, or it will look like you carelessly generalized about your subject.

Describe the Past—Describe how things used to be before current or future conditions. This is useful if readers aren't familiar with how the past led to a current situation.

Quote—Open with a provocative quote on your subject. A response to this quote can create an opening for the paper.

Dialogue—A variation of quotation, this involves opening with a conversation between people that is relevant to your topic.

Contrast—Compare two or more apparently unlike things that, in fact, both relate to the topic.

If You're Still Stuck ...   Still having a hard time writing your introduction? Then don't write it! Many writers make the mistake of assuming that they have to begin at the beginning. The finished paper needs to start with your introduction, true, but your composing process doesn't have to. Start with whatever part of your essay comes most easily to you. It's a little bit like arranging a jigsaw; once you set a few pieces down, they make it easier to figure out where the other pieces should go. If you start somewhere in the middle, for example, this writing will dictate that only one of a few types of introductions will fit with what you've already written down. The same is true of any part of your essay, whether you're stuck at the beginning, middle, or end. Simply skip that section and go back to it later. Once you have more of the rest of your essay written, it will be easier to figure out the parts you skipped.

Some writers also muddle about before cutting to the interesting material. That's fine, as long as you get rid of the muddling at some point. Try this: Take out the first few lines of your introduction, or even the entire paragraph. Does the essay still make sense? Does it still convey the same knowledge? Then leave it that way.

Sample Paper

I don't often think of voters as forming a distinct community unto themselves—after all, any adult citizen can vote—but the group of people who actually do vote is small, and it becomes smaller with each election. And as one of this ever shrinking group of voters, I'm disturbed by the fundraising process of most political campaigns.

Election days themselves are always a special experience, though, and I can recall them quite vividly. After being ready to vote in my first election in 1988, I ended up spending election day shivering in bed with the flu. I finally got my chance to vote in the 1992 primary in Pennsylvania; it was held in a drab county services building, and I finished at the voting machine by pulling on an enormous handle. It felt like I was playing the slots at the world's blandest casino. My candidate didn't win, so I guess I didn't hit the jackpot.

By that fall's election, I was living in Manhattan, and I had to vote at a school gymnasium just off Times Square. An ancient man sat on a chair next to the line, waiting for poll workers to help him to the booth and to pull the levers for him. "I voted in every election since '28," he explained to me. "I use a walker now, but by God—I'm here to vote that s.o.b. out of office!" A few people in line cheered when he emerged from the voting booth. Voting is more than just a vote—it's a shared civic experience among neighbors that makes you feel like a citizen with a stake in the country's success. (Loewenberg)

In 1994 I was a poll worker myself. I was sent out to a quiet residential neighborhood with a guy who'd been let out of a halfway house for the day to work. Our hostess, an elderly Ukrainian woman, fussed over us with cookies and sugary tea while we manned the flimsy polling station set up in her garage. Ironically, because I was sent to a different precinct before the polls opened and was busy until after they closed, I didn't get a chance to vote that day.

I was upset about that, even though friends said it was no big deal. But the greatest misconception about voting is that individual votes don't count. As

Ted Loewenberg, a neighborhood activist with an academic background in American history, notes: "The biggest mistake is to think that 'My vote doesn't make a difference.' It's been shown time and time again to not be the case. It's the one lever that we all have as citizens." Local elections are sometimes decided by very slim margins; in San Francisco, the construction of a stadium was passed by a fraction of a percentage point. Even in national elections, a sufficient number of votes insures federal financing for a party's next campaign. Not voting for, say, the Green Party or the Reform Party because they "can't win" also prevents them from having a chance in the next election.

There are other deterrents to voting, I suppose. But the *New York Times* recently reported research by the Committee for the Study of the American Electorate, which found that nationwide turnout in primaries was a mere 17 percent of eligible voters; in 10 states, turnout sank to record lows, despite the use of such innovations as "Motor Voter" registration. As committee director Curtis Gans noted: "The problem we have is not procedural but motivational" ("Voter Turnout Drops" A18). Even with registration gimmicks, there's an underlying apathy among Americans.

My suspicion is that this apathy stems in part from the vast sums of money involved in campaigning. Enormous amounts of money are required for a modern political campaign, and with each election spending records are broken. Much of the money in these campaigns seems to come from wealthy individuals, companies, and interest groups who then expect (not surprisingly) that this money will buy them extra pull with their elected officials. Jane Public with her $20 contribution won't get the time of day from anyone, but captains of industry with bulging wallets can expect all sorts of opportunities to plead their case to a senator or a representative. "We basically leave government to the highest bidder," Loewenberg complains. "When we see the communications industry invited to write their own deregulation legislation, the system is corrupted and completely broken." He points out that this corrupting influence seeps down to the local level. "You can't run for city supervisor now without a quarter of a million dollars handy." This tilts elections in favor of the well connected, who in turn are usually incumbents.

Even when a candidate won't take money from such people, all is not necessarily well. In the 1998 and 2000 elections, I was dismayed by the huge amounts of money spent by multimillionaire candidates like Steve Forbes, Al Checci, and Darrell Issa; each seemed determined to buy his way into government. Checci and Issa, running in California, both spent millions of their own money on TV ads, even though neither seemed interested in debating or spelling out his beliefs very clearly on paper. If you have enough money, they seemed to think, you can just buy enough TV coverage to drown out any meaningful questions about your qualifications. Fortunately, voters proved these millionaires wrong; all of them lost in the primaries. But perhaps it's only a matter of time before such blatant tactics start working. Money-driven campaigns that are only slightly more subtle have already landed many candidates in office.

I can't help wondering whether elections are becoming the preserve of millionaires and their desperate political friends. The millions spent in some campaigns shut out potential candidates—decent, everyday people who don't earn six- and seven-figure salaries—who either lack rich friends or are unwilling to be the sort of wheeler-dealers who can make such connections. And without these ordinary citizens among our elected officials, the politicians and their wealthy supporters start looking awfully similar: rich, male, probably white, and probably not very ethical. What's more, the attention lavished on these deep-pocketed special interests can literally separate politicians from their citizenry. As Loewenberg notes:

> I've seen every presidential candidate in person since 1960—I even made a point of seeking out Nixon! Except I never saw Bush. He was too busy talking at $1,000 a plate dinners—and really, without interacting with your public, these politicians never have to explain their views or have them challenged.

Press coverage of campaign finance and its reform doesn't give much immediate hope for a solution. The *New York Times* article "Campaign Finance: The Lateral Pass" explains how members of Congress can talk about reform without actually getting anything achieved. Here's how it's worked eight times in the last 19 years: Every couple of years, one chamber (either the Senate or the House) will pass a campaign finance reform bill with the tacit understanding that the other chamber will defeat it (Clymer 6). This pattern has occurred under both Democratic- and Republican-controlled congresses. This way, the parties can claim that they "passed finance reform" without having to turn it into a law. Occasionally this cozy arrangement is laid bare: " ... in 1992 House Speaker Thomas Foley only got a bill passed by assuring wavering Democrats that President Bush would veto it" (6). Sure enough, that is what happened. Even when both sides of Congress do pass a finance reform, it's with the knowledge that nothing substantial will result from it.

The president's tacit collusion in stifling reform has changed little in the last decade. As the *Christian Science Monitor* notes, neither candidate in the 2000 election has any serious commitment to campaign finance reform:

> These two guys have been throwing fake punches, because neither is really in a position to do a lot. Both benefit mightily from the system as it is. From a mere 65 people, a group of donors called "Pioneers," [George W.] Bush had raised $4.4 million by the end of 1999.... And Gore too has a club. The 13 people in his inner circle have raised about $1.5 million as of January 1.
> (Chinni 9)

The strong influence of such groups has long been a part of American politics, according to Ted Loewenberg: "Bought candidates aren't new. Look at Warren Harding in the 1920 election. But it's become so much worse in recent years. While special interests have always been part of politics, what has changed is that they now dominate it."

Works Cited

Chinni, Dante. "Throwing Fake Punches in Campaign Finance Reform." *Christian Science Monitor.* 16 Mar. 2000: 9

Clymer, Adam. "Campaign Finance: The Lateral Pass." *New York Times.* 9 Aug. 1998: Review 6

Loewenberg, Ted. Personal interview. 21 Dec. 1998

"Voter Turnout Drops in 1998 Primaries." *New York Times.* 30 Jun. 1998: A18

Focus On: Community Gardens

Walk down the 200 block of East 3rd Street in Manhattan, and you'll find yourself hearing poetry on one side of the street and facing a garden on the other. The poetry comes out of the Nuyorican Poet's Cafe, one of the homes of the poetry slam. The garden is the Brisas del Caribe Garden, started in 1986 by Mary and Angel Aponte. This couple, tired of living next to an abandoned lot that was covered with trash and frequented by drug addicts, cleaned it up and invited the neighbors on their primarily Hispanic street to join them in planting everything from tomatoes to roses. Their neighbors may not have been used to congregating together as a single community, or to having others from their neighborhood ask them about their ideas and needs, but they quickly warmed to the project. Soon squirrels and birds also found the spot, turning it into a tranquil place for urban life and wildlife alike.

For over 20 years, New Yorkers have been turning abandoned lots into community gardens. Often their neighborhoods have been abandoned by supermarket chains, so the gardens are an important source of fresh food. But more importantly, the gardens help neighborhood residents to work together toward a common goal: a green space in the urban landscape where parents and children can work and play in safety, and even learn about nature in the process. These gardens, in turn, help attract new residents and drive down the crime that otherwise would thrive on abandoned and misused land.

Sometimes getting a garden started takes as little as an abandoned lot and motivated neighbors. But cities often have funds for starting these community gardens, and some can recommend specific lots that are ready for renovating. Tools and seeds can be donated by neighbors, purchased with city support, or donated by local hardware stores and plant nurseries. With hard work, these gardens can reward their members with fresh vegetables and fruit; just as often, this fresh food is also shared with poor families and senior citizens.

Thanks to the New York City Garden Coalition, newcomers can draw on the tools and experience of other members to start their own gardens. The coalition is a powerful voice in having their efforts recognized and preserved. Nor is New York City the only success story. Groups like the National Gardening Association and the Public Land Trust have encouraged gardens nationwide and abroad. Melody Chavis recounts how she led a group of teens in Berkeley, California, to create a community garden. Parts of Berkeley had "liquor stores selling overpriced milk and overripe bananas as their only produce. We decided to start a garden." After finding a lot available through a local senior center, Chavis and youth supervisor Shyaam Shabaka were able to bring teens and senior citizens together to grow crops for the community. In Seattle, land that was too steep for building on was transformed by a community gardening program into a lush series of terraced gardens. Montreal also has a city garden program, as do San Francisco and Los Angeles.

Even the Environmental Protection Agency has shown an interest in community gardens, in particular those created on the rooftops of buildings; their studies indicate that such gardens help cool down the high temperatures of urban areas, thus resulting in less electricity used for air conditioning. As a result, the EPA too has undertaken an effort to encourage rooftop community gardens.

One pitfall with community gardens is that once a lot has been improved through gardening, the owner may sell the land or build on it. While this can be seen as a step in the revival of formerly abandoned lots, it can still be disappointing. In 1999, New York City nearly auctioned off over 100 lots being used as gardens; it was only with lawsuits and the financial intervention of environmental groups and celebrities like Bette Midler that a sellout was averted. But community gardens are increasingly being recognized as playing a continuing role in the revitalization of neighborhoods, and not just a first step.

Sources

"American Community Gardening Association." American Community Gardening Association. 3 Jan. 2000. <http://www.communitygarden.org>.

Barry, Dan. "With Bette Midler's Aid, A Rescue for Gardens." *New York Times*. 13 May 1999: A27

Chavis, Melody. "Strong Roots." *Sierra*. May/June 1997: 48. EBSCO. Online. 19 Feb. 1998

"Community Gardens Growing Nationwide." *In Business*. Mar./Apr. 1998: 6

Corley, Cheryl. "Rooftop Gardens." *All Things Considered*. National Public Radio. KALW, San Francisco. 29 Nov. 1999

Hassler, David and Lynn Gregor (eds.). *A Place to Grow: Voices and Images of Urban Gardeners*. Cleveland: Pilgrim Press, 1999

Herzenhorn, David. "Garden Lovers Sue New York." *New York Times*. 8 May 1999: A15

Huff, Barbara. *Greening the City Streets: The Story of Community Gardens*. New York: Clarion, 1990

Hynes, H. Patricia. *A Patch of Eden*. New York: Chelsea Green Publishing Company, 1996

Irvine, Seana. "Community Gardens and Sustainable Land Use Planning." *Local Environment*. Feb. 1999: 33

"The New York City Garden Coalition." The New York City Garden Coalition. 3 Jan. 2000. <http://www.nycgardens.org>.

"San Francisco League of Urban Gardeners." San Francisco League of Urban Gardeners. 3 Jan. 2000. <http://www.slug-sf.org>.

"Seeds of Hope ... Harvest of Pride." Ohio State University's Urban Gardening Program. 30 Nov. 1999. 3 Jan. 2000. <http://www.bright.net/~gardens/>.

Walker, Andrea. "A New Garden Is Only Part of a Neighborhood's Greening." *New York Times*. 20 Apr. 1997, 14:8

"Welcome to the Green Guerrillas Website." Green Guerrillas. 30 Jul. 1999. 3 Jan. 2000. <http://www.users.interport.net/~ggsnyc/>.

Questions to Consider

1. Would a community that you belong to benefit from a garden? Why or why not?

2. If you were writing about the Brisas del Caribe Garden, who could you interview? Which community members would be involved in or affected by the creation of a garden?

3. Try paraphrasing and direct quoting from any sentence of the preceding essay. How might you use an ellipsis (...) to quote it accurately but more briefly?

PEER READING

> **In-Class:** Read and respond to the papers written by your class-mates.

Working With Others

Revision means "seeing again." After working this long on a project, it's hard to see your own weaknesses; and the explanations that seem obvious to you may not to other readers. That's why you need the perspective that an outsider brings. Getting the opinion of a reader can improve your work tremendously.

As your writings progress and change, so will the questions that you ask your readers. But there are a few guidelines to keep in mind whenever you work with other readers:

Don't monopolize the conversation. Let your readers speak: You already had your chance to explain yourself in the paper! If you feel the need to explain things further, then that's a sign that you should include that information in a revised version of your paper.

Don't nitpick. Don't get caught up in inefficient debates over a single word or phrase; such things are typically more a matter of style than of substance. Focus on ideas and organization: Do your explanations make sense? Does the paper flow in a sensible manner?

Don't be quick to take offense. Everybody has their own style of working with others: some are no-nonsense and impatient, while others joke around or strain to be polite. But remember that the object of the conversation is your paper, and not you personally. Even a clod can see where a boat's sprung a leak; don't let someone else's tactlessness distract you from the good advice that they may be giving.

Stay positive. Speak to others as you would like them to speak to you. Don't pick on them personally ("You messed this up"); instead, analyze their papers ("What about this paragraph? It threw me a bit."). Suggestions are also friendlier when they're phrased in terms in improvement ("It might help to … "), and not as criticism ("This is awful").

Relax. Gossiping or just being sociable isn't a waste of time. It's essential for the kind of trust and familiarity found in most successful partnerships.

Equal Time. While it's typical for some people to be more talkative than others, let everyone in a group have their say. Encourage quieter members to explain their opinions in more detail. Unequal time can build up resentment over who is or isn't pulling their weight.

Offer questions instead of statements. Instead of saying "This sentence doesn't make sense," ask "Could you explain what you mean in this part?" Giving writers a chance to explain themselves to you is less confrontational than their having to defend what they've written.

Praise. We all need it. Even if a paper seems like a disaster to you, it's not likely to improve if you can't give the writer some encouragement!

Peer Reading in Six Steps

1. Gather into groups and find a partner to assist you.
   Your draft is raw material. To help refine it, you'll be listening to and commenting on each other's papers.

2. Read your writing out loud to your group.
   Nobody can interrupt you. You'll hear how it sounds out loud, and you may catch mistakes on your own. This also gives the group a feel for how the essay works as a whole, so they'll make more informed comments the next time around.

3. Read it out loud again.
   This time, the group can interrupt you with suggestions and questions. Be ready to scribble in corrections or notes to yourself as you're reading.

4. Your partner takes notes.
   Their job is to make sure the group considers each question on the Peer Reading Worksheet carefully. If the group gets stuck, your partner should try prompting them by rewording the question, or skipping it and coming back to it later. When your partner reaches the last question, that partner should pass the worksheet back to you.

5. Each group member comments on your paper.
   You'll be writing down their comments, so don't interrupt. Most of your readers won't have you there to explain things, so this is your chance to hear exactly what they'd be wondering about.

6. Discuss their comments and questions.
   Once step 5 is finished, you may respond in an open discussion. Write down any last ideas you have for revising the paper.

Peer Reading Worksheet: Paper #1

Writer:

Partner:

What unfamiliar terms or assumptions weren't explained?

What kind of introduction did they use? Did it make the subject clear or draw you in as a reader? How might it be improved?

Is anyone quoted in the paper? Do they seem like a reliable source? What else might you want to ask them?

Overall, how might the writer improve this paper?

REVISING YOUR PAPER

> Revise and print out a new version of your paper. Then add it to a folder that includes your first draft, your Peer Reading Worksheet, and the shorter assignments.

Revising for Content and Style

Remember that revision isn't simply a matter of fixing grammar and tweaking a paragraph or two—it's literally looking again at your entire writing process. Here are a few ways that you might get a fresh view of your work:

Look at Your Peer Comments: Don't feel obliged to make all the changes that your peer group suggested; not all advice is good advice. Still, you should consider it carefully, especially if more than one person has made the same suggestion.

Reread Your Paper: Ideas that seemed perfectly connected when you wrote them at 3 A.M. can look pretty jumbled after you've had some time away from them.

Go to Another Reader: While you've already got some feedback from your class group, don't hesitate to consult friends, family, or your instructor. Another member of your community might help, because they can point out both factual errors and details worth adding.

Cut and Paste: Take an extra copy of your paper and rearrange the order of your paragraphs; it may turn out that having one paragraph before another makes more sense. Perhaps an anecdote or detail from the body of your essay actually makes a compelling introduction. This rearranging can be done easily on a computer or physically with scissors and paste.

Make an Outline: Not only do outlines help with rough drafts, they can also help with revisions. You can even work backward: Describe each paragraph in an outline, noting what purpose it serves in the essay. If you can't think of one, it needs fixing or removing.

Put Yourself in the Reader's Shoes: Would *you* find this essay interesting? What would make it more compelling? The assignment questions are only a starting point, so don't be afraid to go off on some more interesting tangent. The more you like the subject, the more your readers will.

Find More Material: Often the best way to revise is to dig deeper for the details of people and places that you've already found. Revisit sites and write down every detail you can think of; call back your interviewees with further questions or try a new interview altogether. Most rough drafts already have the makings of a solid piece of writing—it's just a matter of finding which parts work best and developing them as much as possible.

Simplify Your Language: Writers often get stalled adding words until they get a thought down just right. There's nothing wrong with this, but remember to eventually pull down this scaffolding. If you can chop a word or phrase out of a sentence without changing its meaning, then you probably should.

Use Your Senses: If you mention a physical object, your senses can turn it from an abstract idea into something your reader can see and hear. Think of the difference implied by "an old playground" as opposed to "a weedy playground of rusty swings and chirping crickets."

Explaining Thoroughly

Once you've been researching a subject for a while, it's easy to forget that not everyone is as familiar with it as you are. Your paper may have assumptions about events, people, or processes that many readers won't be familiar with. Try reading a draft of your paper to a friend who isn't familiar with the issue. Take note of when they get confused or stop you for further explanation, and remember to add this information when you revise the draft. Be particularly careful with abbreviations or acronyms; for example, not everyone knows that AFDC means Aid to Families with Dependent Children. The same is true of jargon or slang that is specific to your community.

Whenever possible, provide a specific explanation. Don't just call something "short"—say how short. Don't just say that something costs a lot of money—say how much money. Don't just describe vague "people" or "groups" involved in an issue—name them. It is possible to take this too far, of course. Unless you're writing about sports or nutrition, an interviewee's height probably won't matter to the reader. But if specific information does help give the reader a better idea of the situation, then include it.

Focus On: Sweatshops

The United States has stringent workplace safety regulations, but this was not always the case. In 1911 a fire broke out at the Manhattan factory of the Triangle Shirtwaist Company. Hundreds of women garment workers were trapped inside the 10-story building; as the fire roared to life among tons of fabric, panicked employees discovered that exits were locked, a measure taken by management to keep workers at their machines. The fire department, with ladders that only reached six stories up, were unable to reach the upper floors of the building, and many women died jumping to their death on the street below. Those who stayed behind were suffocated or burned. Within 15 minutes, 146 women were dead.

Some people continued to argue for the right of business owners to run factories however they saw fit, and the families of the dead received little or no compensation. But outrage over the tragedy helped bring about workplace safety regulations. By the end of the 20th century, though, American garment companies began moving their operations offshore to countries where wages were cheaper and labor laws were once again loose or even nonexistent.

Strangely enough, the rise of expensive logo clothing has contributed to the problem. According to the Canadian activist Naomi Klein, in the words of the *New York Times*, "As companies' marketing budgets become more and more lavish, they maintain profit margins by farming out manufacturing to sweatshops in the poorest corners of the globe."

Activists wanting to pressure companies to stop such behavior often find that hitting them in the wallet is the best way to get their attention—and that means calling for a boycott. In recent years, manufacturers like Nike, Guess, Reebok, and the Gap have faced boycotts for their alleged use of sweatshops; and in response to the bad publicity generated by these protests, they have slowly begun to rectify some of the worst abuses. College students play a crucial role, too, by boycotting sweatshop manufacturers of campus logo clothing. The impact of college action was underscored when, angered that students had persuaded the University of Oregon simply to monitor the source of its clothing, Nike chairman Phil Knight canceled a planned $30 million gift to the university stadium. Just days later, Nike also canceled a multimillion dollar licensing deal with the University of Michigan, in a move that was widely seen as being in retaliation for the university's intention to join the same sweatshop monitoring group.

Ultimately, these boycotts focus as much on the responsibility of consumers as on corporate responsibility. As Adam Yauch, a boycott activist better known as a band member with the Beastie Boys, explained to a *Village Voice* reporter:

> Right now I think we're all kind of seduced by Nike and things like that. But it's too easy to just demonize corporations as this monster .... What we have to remember is the corporations are created by all the individuals that work at them and all the consumers that buy from them. We're as responsible for those corporations as much as anyone.

When describing an issue facing your community, it is often all too easy to fall into an adversarial stance of us versus them, or wrongdoers versus the righteous. And yet we all bear responsibilities for some of the problems facing our society. One typical though utterly illogical response is to think that if everybody's guilty, then nobody's really guilty. Just the opposite: *Everybody* has a responsibility to work toward fixing the problems facing their communities—or, at the very least, to try not to contribute further to those problems. Even if you feel that some of your own "wrongs" are justified, keep in mind that you are probably someone else's troublemaker. When you see someone as an opponent, remember it could just as easily have been you in their shoes.

Sources

Applebaum, Richard and Peter Dreier. "The Campus Anti-Sweatshop Movement." *American Prospect*. Sept./Oct. 1999: 71

Bernstein, Aaron. "Sweatshops: No More Excuses." *Business Week*. 8 Nov. 1999: 104

Brooke, James. "Canada's Anti-Corporate Crusader." *New York Times*. 3 Apr. 2000: A6

Ferguson, Sarah. "Boycotts 'R' Us." *Village Voice*. 8 Jul. 1997: 44

Greenhouse, Steven. "Nike's Chief Cancels a Gift Over Monitor of Sweat-shops." *New York Times*. 25 Apr. 2000: A12

———."Students Urge Colleges to Join New Group Against Sweatshops." *New York Times*. 20 Oct. 1999: A23

"Guess Boycott Home Page." Guess Boycott. 27 Jan. 2000. <http://www.guessboycott.org>.

Irwin, Jim. "Nike Drops Deal With University of Michigan." *San Francisco Chronicle*. 28 Apr. 2000: A15

Jackson, Kenneth (ed.). *The Encyclopedia of New York City*. New Haven, CT: Yale University Press, 1995

Kennedy, Randy. "Using Every Trick in Fighting Sweatshops." *New York Times*. 9 Dec. 1999: B2

Klein, Naomi. *No Logo: Taking Aim at the Brand Bullies*. New York: Picador USA, 2000

Lazaroff, Leon. "Garment Workers' Union Revolts Against Sweatshop Abuse." *Christian Science Monitor*. 20 Aug. 1999 : 3

"Making Kathie Lee Cry." *Wall Street Journal* (Eastern Edition). 29 Sept. 1999: A22

Sweatshop Watch. 27 Jan. 2000. <http://www.igc.apc.org/swatch/>.

"Sweatshops Made in USA." *Multinational Monitor*. Jan. / Feb. 1999 : 4

Varley, Pamela and Carolyn Matiesen (eds.). *The Sweatshop Quandary: Corporate Responsibility on the Global Frontier*. Washington, DC: Investor Responsibility Research Center, 1998

Questions to Consider

Sit down and make out a mental list of every illegal or questionable activity you've ever engaged in. Include minor things like jaywalking or copying software.

1. Who have you inconvenienced or potentially endangered?

2. If caught, would you have been labeled as part of a social problem? How?

3. What problems do you continue to be a part of? Are there any problems that you contribute to through your choices as a consumer?

2

Media Views
of an Issue

ANALYZING ARTICLES ON AN ISSUE

Assignment: Analyze a newspaper or magazine article written about your issue. This is less about the issue itself than about how journalists report it, so focus on how the article is constructed. Who gets quoted, and what kind of role do they play in the issue? What kind of people involved in this issue don't get quoted? Are there any types of bias apparent in the article? Judging from the advertisements and articles in this periodical, what kind of audience is it aimed at?

Bias in the Media

All writing has a bias of some kind; it frames some questions, answers, ideas, or people as being more valid than others. To determine bias in a piece of writing, there are three basic questions you need to ask: At whom is the writing aimed? Who is and isn't quoted? Where and to what extent are they quoted?

At Whom Is the Writing Aimed? What age group is it aimed at? Is it aimed at residents of a particular region? Members of a specific profession? People with a certain level of income? Members of a political group? Followers of a particular religion?

Some of these questions may be easy to answer. The *San Francisco Chronicle* is aimed at a particular region, and the *Journal of the American Medical Association* is aimed at health care professionals. But sometimes titles can be misleading; the *New York Times* is read nationally, for example, and the *Christian Science Monitor* has a wide readership outside of the Christian Science faith.

In some cases, you may be able to tell the publication's political stance by the writers it features and the editorials it runs. If you see Pat Buchanan and William Kristol editorials in the *Weekly Standard*, for example, and then articles by Ralph Nader and Susan Faludi in the *Nation*, and you're familiar with their political reputations, then you might guess (correctly) that the first magazine is conservative and the second is liberal.

But the most telling indicator of a magazine's real audience is in the ads it runs. Most magazines create their content with a very specific set of readers in mind—they have to, because when they sell ad space to advertisers, they need to be able to tell them whom they'll reach with their ads. When you see lots of ads for mutual funds and brokerages in the *Wall Street Journal*, but ads for hemp products and expensive eco-friendly products in the *Utne Reader*, it's no accident. The intended readership of the *Journal* is investors, while the *Utne Reader* is aimed at upwardly mobile liberals.

Who Is and Isn't Quoted in the Article?   Sit down and create a list of everybody connected with your issue. For example, let's say you're writing about homelessness in your neighborhood. Such a list might include homeless people, local residents, business owners, the police, social workers, the mayor, the board of supervisors, employees of the homeless shelter, and so forth.

Now go through the article and make a list of the people who are quoted or given as sources. When you're done, ask yourself: Is there a wide range of opinions given here? For example, an article on homelessness that only quotes business owners and the police, but not social workers or the homeless themselves, is more likely to have a bias toward the viewpoint of business and law enforcement.

What kind of people from these sources are getting quoted? To use the above example, are you only quoting a police spokesperson and a chain business owner, or are you quoting a cop on the beat and a counter clerk? You're likely to get very different perspectives and details depending on which people you asked.

Note how many people are quoted. An extraordinary number of newspaper articles, particularly in lower-quality papers, will have only one source, or one type of source (e.g., two members of the same business or organization), with the result that the article is heavily biased toward that source's point of view.

Finally, and most important of all, who *isn't* getting quoted? When you tally up the potential sources left out of a story, suddenly it can look very biased indeed. What effect might their absence from the reporting have on the story? Why do you think the writer didn't use them as sources?

Where and to What Extent Are They Quoted?   People don't typically read every word of a magazine or newspaper. They may read only the headlines of some stories, the first paragraph of others, and the first page of still others. Writers know this, and will usually front-load information so that the most crucial material comes at or near the beginning of an article.

The flip side of this is that material coming later in the article is much less likely to get read. Whenever you have to turn pages or go to the back of a paper—which in the trade is known as a "jump"—you lose some readers. So any material placed after a jump or deep into an article is, to use the writers' jargon, "buried." An article that quotes a homeless advocate extensively in the beginning, and then a police chief just as extensively near the end, is more likely to be perceived by readers as being from the perspective of the homeless advocate.

There's also the simple matter of tallying quotes. If the homeless advocate is quoted six times, and the police chief just twice, then this is also more likely to bias the article toward the advocate's perspective. Keep in mind that this tally is not a sure/fire method of detecting bias: Some of the quotes may be very short, and the writer may only be including them to then shoot them down.

The Politics of Selected Periodicals

All publications have a certain political slant or self-interest involved in their writing. Some even have long-established reputations for liberalism or conservatism. Just because a publication has an overall tendency to be conservative or liberal doesn't mean that every one of its articles is too, but it helps to know which side their editors favor. Periodicals are also liable to change over time; the *New Republic* and the *Atlantic Monthly*, for example, are both formerly liberal publications that have pulled significantly to the right in recent years. Don't be fooled by appearances, either: A flashy and erstwhile libertarian "tech" magazine like *Wired* contains a deeply conservative admiration for industry and wealth, while a "community" paper like the *Village Voice* is, in fact, nationally recognized as a liberal publication.

Below is a guide to the bias of selected publications. It's quite subjective and liable to change, because journalistic bias is notoriously difficult to pin down and quantify. Magazines with strong leanings to the left or right are denoted with an asterisk. Centrist publications, with an occasional leaning to the left or right, are noted by an (L) or (R).

LEFT / LIBERAL	CENTER	RIGHT/CONSERVATIVE
The Nation*	Newsweek	The Weekly Standard*
The New Yorker	Time (R)	American Spectator*
The American Prospect	Rolling Stone (L)	Money
Harper's Magazine	The Atlantic Monthly (R)	Forbes
The New York Times	World Press Review	Fortune Magazine
The Boston Globe	The Economist (R)	U.S. News & World Report
Utne Reader	Brill's Content	Business Week
The Advocate	Wired (R)	Reader's Digest*
Ms.*	Los Angeles Times	Inc.
Village Voice*	USA Today (R)	New York Observer

Mother Jones*	The Washington Post (L)	New York Post
Z Magazine*	Vanity Fair (L)	The Washington Times*
Color Lines	The New Republic (R)	National Review*
The Christian Science Monitor	Associated Press	Financial Times
Progressive*	Esquire	The Wall Street Journal
Emerge	Chicago Tribune (L)	The Times (London)

Once you've examined the arguments from different sides of the issue that you're studying, it also helps to ask yourself how these sources portray opposing ideas and advocates. Who are the "extremists" or "fringe" members on either side of your debate? How have they been labeled, and are they left out of the debate? Why? What are their ideas, and why exactly are these ideas considered unusable? What phrases do both sides use? Do they both mean the same thing? What do they mean? Are they accurate?

Sample Response

"When Liberty Is Not So Sweet" appeared in the British magazine the *Economist* in the same week that the U.S. House of Representatives, in the unnamed reporter's words, "buried campaign finance reform" (26). The article points out a number of polls showing that while Americans continue to strongly support free speech, a wide majority also supports campaign finance reform. The article characterizes the American Civil Liberties Union as a major opponent of this popular position; given its purist view, its members are officially, though not unanimously, against any restriction of advertising or other forms of political speech. The writer then extends this counterpopulist purism to other ACLU positions against popular measures like public housing searches and teen curfews. The ACLU's "rights first" stand, the author argues, was appropriate in more restrictive eras like the 1950s and the 1960s, but is now counter to the desires of the people it claims to protect.

The *Economist* itself is clearly aimed at an international audience. Headquartered in London, it includes prices for many different countries on its cover. Both its title and its articles indicate an emphasis on business and investing, and its ads are predominantly for large investment concerns, business travel, and expensive consumer products (e.g., Rolex watches). Its target audience, then, might be defined as wealthy (or would-be wealthy) adult business people and investors with an interest in international news.

The article itself has a noticeable anti-ACLU bias. The *Economist* does not quote the ACLU or its positions at all; the closest it comes is with a rebelling former ACLU legal director, Burt Neuborne, who now calls the organization "anachronistic." An article by two members of the Chicago Law School attacking the ACLU's "purism" is also quoted approvingly; the article ran in the conservative *Atlantic Monthly*. Neuborne and the *Atlantic Monthly* articles are cited at length. Earlier in the article, there are briefer quotes and citations from the conservative former House speaker Newt Gingrich and from polls by conservative news organizations like the *Wall Street Journal* and Fox News.

The only break from this pattern is one paragraph summarizing the results of a poll commissioned by a First Amendment foundation, Freedom Forum. Overall, though, there is strong emphasis on perspectives from conservative publications in general and from lawyers opposing the ACLU in particular. No current member or representative of the ACLU is quoted. Nor are any citizens, voters, or campaigning politicians. The resulting bias is conservative and anti-ACLU—though the assumption underlying the article, in contrast with that of some conservative politicians, is that campaign finance reform is a desirable thing.

Works Cited

"When Liberty Is Not So Sweet: Campaign Finance Reform Has Been Stifled at Birth by Defenders of Free Speech." *Economist*. 4 Apr. 1998: 26

Focus On: Joey Skaggs

Have you heard about the Portofess, a wheeled confessional booth on-the-go for busy New Yorkers? How about the Solomon software program, designed to replace fallible human juries? Or how about the "Cathouse for Dogs," a canine brothel where your pet can get lucky? The first two stories ran on CNN, while the third was the subject of an Emmy-nominated documentary by WABC.

If you've read or watched any of these stories, then you've unwittingly witnessed the work of Joey Skaggs. Skaggs is, by his own description, a performance artist. Most would call him a media hoaxer. In any case, Skaggs has successfully fooled major media outlets for over 30 years into spreading outrageous misinformation—often on the basis of nothing more than a phony press release, an answering machine, and a rented mailbox.

Beginning in 1968, Skaggs got the *New York Times* to cover a supposed "hippie bus tour"—not the usual busload of tourists gawking at hippies in Greenwich Village, but rather a busload of hippies touring the suburbs and snapping photos of people mowing their lawns and washing their cars. In 1976 his "dog bordello" hoax was staged so successfully that it resulted in Skaggs being hauled in by NYPD Vice on suspicion of pimping. His Solomon software hoax, staged in the wake of the 1995 O. J. Simpson trial, landed "Joseph Bonuso, a computer scientist affiliated with NYU Law School" on CNN and in the pages of the *San Francisco Chronicle*. It might have gone undetected, except that N.Y.U. lawyers called CNN to complain that no such person existed on their faculty.

Skaggs has staged dozens of hoaxes over the years, some of which were reported as fact in hundreds of newspapers; often, no retraction was ever made. This is a serious problem for the media outlets, even when there is no intent to deceive. Faulty research findings from sociologists and education researchers often make for a sensational initial headline—that a single woman over 40 has a better chance of getting killed by a terrorist than of getting married, say, or that a woman's standard of living plunges 73 percent after a divorce—which is rarely followed up on when, as in both of these examples, subsequent scrutiny of the statistics show them to be completely miscalculated. Imagine, then, the reluctance of some media outlets to admit that their incorrect stories were caused not just by bad research but by a thinly disguised prankster.

Skaggs has even appeared on the same news programs several times over—most famously on *Good Morning America*— in different disguises, all without being recognized from previous escapades. When *Entertainment Tonight* requested an interview with Skaggs himself as part of a piece on media hoaxing, he sent a friend with no visible resemblance to him to be interviewed as "Joey Skaggs." *ET* never checked out this man's claim that he was the "real" Joey Skaggs, and so the segment on hoaxing was itself the victim of yet another hoax.

As amusing as this is, the reason why Skaggs is so successful so often says much about the perils of reporting. Namely, these journalists never sought independent confirmation; that is, they failed to vary their sources. In their rush to publish a hot story, they relied solely on the images and words that Skaggs and his accomplices fed them. Had they checked to see whether his various fictitious personas and businesses were recognized in public records or by professional colleagues, they would have realized that something was amiss.

Nor is this a failing limited to the American press; foreign papers have also carried stories floated by Skaggs. One of the most embarrassing hoaxes in recent memory didn't involve Skaggs, but it might as well have: The Agence France-Presse reported that NASA had been conducting zero-gravity copulation experiments, based on an official-looking "research" report that had landed in their hands. Too bad they didn't bother to call NASA before running the story.

Similarly, some papers will reprint stories that were never even intended to be taken seriously. *The Onion*, a newspaper parody based in Madison, Wisconsin, (motto: "You Are Dumb") and perhaps the preeminent online humor Web site, discovered that its spoof story "Winners Occasionally Use Drugs"—in which a supposed new study led the DEA to recall video games with a "winners don't take drugs" public service announcement—was reprinted as factual material by the *Times* of London. Later, *Forbes FYI* reprinted in total an *Onion* story titled "Neighbors Remember Serial Killer as Serial Killer," a blatantly satirical inversion of the crime reporting cliché about shocked neighbors recalling a homicidal maniac as a quiet but friendly fellow.

And so what about Joey Skaggs; does he have another hoax planned? He isn't saying. But it's sure to involve little more than a catchy idea, a fake name, and a rented voicemail box. And as likely as not it will show up as a "fact" on one of your major news sources.

Sources

Alba, Lourdes. "Joey Skaggs—Media Hoax Artist." *Aloha From Hawai'i*. 8 Jan. 2000. <http://www.aloha-hawaii.com/4issue/skaggs.html>.

Cohen, Patricia. "Oops, Sorry: Seems That My Pie Chart Is Half-Baked." *New York Times*. 8 Apr. 2000: A15

Hough, Robert. "America's Most Gullible." *World Press Review*. Oct. 1992: 36

Kimbro, Ellen. "Journalism Class' Experiment Aims to Teach a Lesson." *Daily Beacon*. 18 Apr. 1995. University of Tennessee. 27 Nov. 1998. <http://beacon-www.asa.utk.edu /issues/v68/n63/fake.63n.html>.

"Opinion Feedback." *New Scientist*. 11 Mar. 2000: 100

Skaggs, Joey. "Joey Skaggs." 8 Jan. 2000. <http://www.joeyskaggs.com>.

Tierney, John. "Falling For It." *New York Times Magazine*, 17 Jul. 1994: 16

Umansky, Eric. "*The Onion*, Misunderstood." *Columbia Journalism Review*. Apr. 2000: 12

Questions to Consider

1. Why might few publications retract their stories, even after they're aware of a hoax?

2. A follow-up story might have shown that Skaggs's supposed events never occurred. Why do you think so few publications ever try following up on their initial stories?

3. Why exactly were these reporters fooled so easily? What steps can a researcher on any subject take to avoid being misled?

COMPARING BIAS IN DIFFERENT ARTICLES

Assignment: Find an article on your issue in a publication that has a significantly different political viewpoint from the publication you've previously analyzed, and apply the same questions to it. What are the similarities and differences between the two articles?

Keep in mind some basic questions worth asking when comparing and contrasting items: In what ways are they similar or connected? In what ways are they different or divided? How might one group or side respond to another? Does one set a pattern that the others follow? Does it imply some larger trend? Are these differences/similarities significant? Why? Are any of these differences or similarities more or less important than others? Why?

The Alternative Media

What Is News?   There's an important distinction between an event and news. An event happens in our lives or other people's lives; it may be daily, intermittent, or unique. But it is only the knowledge of a few witnesses until an editor or news director makes the crucial decision to turn it into news. News is a commercial product that purports to summarize the "important" events of the day.

So who gets to decide what is important for you to know? Editors and news directors do; and above them, the publishers and executives of an increasingly small number of conglomerates and wealthy families. No news organization will deny the facts of an event; rather, they will deny that it is "news"—it is "not important."

Most people won't consider my broken arm to be national news, even though it is an event in my household. This distinction becomes less apparent, though, when relatively privileged editors and publishers are exercising their criteria of importance over political and social events that do in fact affect a number of people outside of their social and economic circle. If Donald Trump breaks his arm, it becomes news—even though this is of less direct importance to most people's lives than, say, changes in the tax code or in the inspection procedures used on the food they eat. This bias toward the following the news of the rich, famous, and powerful may seem entirely natural to an equally rich and powerful media elite.

More self-interested motives can also come into play here. Stories that challenge this elite's values or beliefs, that threaten a parent company's finances, or that pull in less affluent viewers than those the advertisers want—these are all less ethical reasons for an event to be judged too "unimportant" to be "news."

This is compounded by the fact that news is a form of entertainment, intended to fascinate you enough or make you feel so good that you also notice the advertising. As the profit motive becomes more important in such news organizations, so does the motivation to select only those events that don't challenge or disturb the audience's or advertiser's values. This accounts for the explosive growth of "soft news" over the last two decades; stories about celebrities, natural disasters, sordid local crimes, and "feel-good" interests like cooking and fashion. These stories are cheap to produce and are unlikely to make anyone's purse strings draw shut.

Pack Journalism.   If you read a national paper and a local paper on the same day, you'll get a sense of déjà vu. The articles may be shorter or longer, appear on different pages, and have different headlines and pictures, but somehow they feel ... *exactly the same.*

It's not your imagination. Papers boost their content by buying stories from wire services (e.g., The Associated Press and Reuters) and from a few agenda-setting national papers (e.g., the *New York Times*, *Washington Post*, *Wall Street Journal*, and *Los Angeles Times*). This is "pack journalism": Once one of these big dogs catches a scent, the runts of the litter all follow. You'll find these news outlets cited at the beginning or end of the article, sometimes simply as "AP" (Associated Press). If an article from the *New York Times* is reprinted in a local paper, chances are that it appeared in that day's or yesterday's *Times*. If the article is important to your research, you should track down the original version.

Why? Because of the inverted pyramid approach in newspaper writing. Many articles start with broad opening paragraphs that give four of the "five Ws" (who, what, where, when). Later paragraphs explain "why" and quote sources. Because the reporter isn't sure how much space editors will give the story, the article is designed to be cut at the end of any paragraph. There's no firm concluding paragraph. Local papers often whittle down the long articles that national papers publish. In a local paper's version, you may literally get only half the story.

Finding Alternative Media.   Given the dominance of a few pack journalist news leaders, how can you get information from outside the echo chamber of the mainstream press? Nonprofit and government sources are a good place to start. It's a bit much to follow all or even a few of these media sources, but trying to follow at least one or two on a regular basis is a good start.

Public Broadcasting—The largest and best-known alternative media sources are PBS television (www.pbs.org) and National Public Radio (www.npr.org). They often follow the same pack journalism as the commercial outlets, but just as often they'll go into much more detail.

The Internet. There are a number of news sources that operate solely through the Internet. The reliability of these sources can vary wildly, but some of the better established online sources include Slate (www.slate.com), Salon (www.salon.com), and Alternet (www.alternet.org). These web sources are often more up to date and more willing to go out on a limb than mainstream news sources.

Foreign Press—Most libraries stock at least one English-language newspaper published abroad. Better yet, many of these newspapers also have Web sites.

These papers have stories that don't get covered in the U.S. press (including, strangely enough, events happening in the United States) and stories written from a different perspective than those in the U.S. press. Here are a few of the better English-language online papers; those with site search engines for older stories are indicated with an asterisk:

* The Independent (England). www.independent.co.uk
* The Times (England). www.the-times.co.uk
* The Daily Telegraph (England). www.telegraph.co.uk
* The Globe and Mail (Canada). www.globeand mail.com
South China Morning Post (Hong Kong). www.scmp.com
Buenos Aires Herald (Argentina). www.buenosaires.com
Jerusalem Post (Israel). www.jpost.com
Daily Mail & Guardian (South Africa). www.mg.co.za/mg/
Sydney Morning Herald (Australia). www.smh.com.au
Asahi Shimbun (Japan). www.asahi.com/english/english.html
The Times (India). www.timesofindia.com
The Straits Times (Singapore). www.straitstimes.asia1.com.sg

There's also the magazine *World Press Review* , available online (www.worldpress.org) and in most libraries, which excerpts translated articles from across the world. Some NPR stations also carry news programs by the BBC World Service (British Broadcasting Corporation, available at http://news.bbc.co.uk), the CBC (Canadian Broadcasting Corporation, available at www.cbc.ca), and Radio Deutsche Welle (www.dwelle.de). Their respective Web sites also feature these news stories and other English-language web broadcasts.

Community Media—Student radio stations and public-access TV, while less polished than their commercial counterparts, often give a broader array of viewpoints. Contact your college or your local cable provider for where and when to find these.

Community Newspapers—Some weekly newspapers, such as the *Bay Area Guardian* (www.sfbg.com) and the *Village Voice* (www.villagevoice.com), make a point of covering news that mainstream daily papers ignore or whitewash.

Signs of Bias

If a source has the signs of bias listed below, then you may want to balance it with perspectives from differently biased sources.

Fake Trends—"More and more" all the "experts say" the "latest trend" among "us" is happening. Strangely enough, the article has no solid numbers—maybe an estimate, at best—and only quotes one or two self-styled "experts"!

We and Us—Are your beliefs being lumped in with a governmental, political, or economic point of view? Some reporters take it upon themselves to describe the way "we" feel about an issue; they label you as a group so that "most of us" feel a certain way. Is this a group or view that you would choose to be represented by?

Loaded Language—Coverage may divide the sides taken on an issue into that of "moderates" or "the mainstream" (us) versus that taken by "extremists" (them). The assumption is that we (the majority) are right. Keep in mind that most of the rights and beliefs we take for granted today were once minority views.

Who's Getting Quoted?—Think of every person involved an article's topic. Then pick apart the article to see who gets to speak and who doesn't. Is there a difference between the professional, economic, or political status of those quoted and the status of those who aren't?

All Experts and No Participants—Many reporters always go to the same phone list of political, corporate, and academic "experts" to comment on issues. Do ground-level participants get to speak at length, or does the report rely on outside "experts"?

Unidentified Sources—Stories that rely on "sources [who] tell us" and insiders who "asked not be identified" should be regarded with great suspicion. You simply have no way of knowing if such sources are reputable or impartial.

Sample Response

The *Nation* magazine article "Free Speech and Campaign Myth," written by Ellen Miller and E. Joshua Rosenkranz in April 1998, details the opposition of Senator Mitch McConnell to campaign finance reform. According to the authors, McConnell has argued that restrictions on campaign advertising are counter to the First Amendment guarantees of freedom of speech. Miller and Rosenkranz claim that while McConnell quotes selectively from Supreme Court decisions to back his views, he ignores free speech concerns when they apply to art and political protest. As they note, "McConnell's First Amendment applies only to the wealthy special interests who finance campaigns."

The *Nation* is well known for its liberal editorial viewpoint, and both the selection of columnists (e.g., Katha Pollitt, Alexander Cockburn) and the topics that they cover evince the magazine's focus on the progressive, liberal side of American politics. The relatively few ads in the magazine are for liberal political forums in New York City, politically oriented publishers, and progressive companies like Working Assets, a long distance service. The audience appears to be primarily highly literate and politically active urban liberals.

Unlike many publications, The *Nation* does make a point of identifying the professional and political affiliations of its writers. Ellen Miller is identified as "executive director of Public Campaign," while E. Joshua Rosenkranz is the "executive director of the Brennan Center for Justice at N.Y.U. law school." This article is written, it seems, from the perspective, it seems, of two proreform urbanites, both of whom are experienced in law or politics themselves. (Public Campaign is based in Washington, DC, while New York University is in Manhattan.)

Senator McConnell is quoted extensively throughout the article, although his quotes are always parried by the authors. Miller and Rosenkranz do not appear to agree at any point with McConnell; not surprisingly, they also always get the last word. There are no quotes from voters, organizations opposed to reform, or from anyone else on McConnell's side. There are no other sources quoted in the article, although a couple of Supreme Court decisions are paraphrased.

The continual focus of this article is on Senator McConnell, although by extension the authors are attacking other opponents of campaign reform. In the opening paragraph there's a comparison of McConnell with a chicken; strutting around the Senate "like the cock of the walk ... pecking to death the latest (and most modest) of campaign finance reforms .... " (22) This personal animus against McConnell may be justified, but the article abandons any pretense to objectivity. Given the partisan audience that the magazine is aimed at, perhaps the writers felt no need to downplay their opinions. But it is noticeably less diverse in its sources than the *Economist*'s article, relying instead more on close legal argumentation. It should be noted that both the *Economist* and the *Nation* assume the basic necessity for campaign finance reform. The *Nation* points its finger of blame at a conservative senator and his cronies, though, while the *Economist* blames liberal legal advocates at the American Civil Liberties Union.

Works Cited

Miller, Ellen and Joshua Rosenkranz. "Free Speech and Campaign Myth." *Nation*. 27 Apr. 1998: 22–25

Focus On: Noam Chomsky

Noam Chomsky is an influential professor of linguistics and philosophy at the Massachusetts Institute of Technology (MIT), but he has gained his greatest fame as a critic of the media and American politics. His lectures sell out quickly, and his speeches have been included on the B-sides of records and CDs by a number of rock bands. But he's not a media critic in the sense of writing reviews of movies and TV shows. His concern is how the media and government constrain the range of thinkable thoughts in political debates. "Common sense" and "practicality," he points out, shape the ideas we can have. My ideas may seem opposite to yours, but they're both in a small band of a broad spectrum of possibility:

> There's a complicated system of illusions and self-deception that are the given framework for most discussion and debate. And if you don't happen to take part in that system ... [then] what you say is incomprehensible. (*The Chomsky Reader* 19)

> Adherence to the party line confers the right to act in ways that would probably be regarded as scandalous on the part of any critic .... This freedom from the requirements of evidence or even rationality is quite a convenience. (37)

Ideas outside of this narrow band are labeled extreme, seditious, or just crazy.

Conservatives often take great umbrage at Chomsky's views; when Columbia University awarded him an honorary doctorate in 1999, the *Wall Street Journal* fired off an editorial titled "A Dishonorable Honorary Degree." But Chomsky disdains his supposed liberal allies as often as he does his conservative foes. He sees little difference between Democrats and Republicans; to him, they simply engage in personal attacks on each other rather than on corruption within the political system, and disagree on cosmetic issues while ignoring fundamental inequalities and government excesses. He rejects the claim that idealism on such matters is in any way unrealistic:

> We are not condemned to live in a society based on greed, envy, and hate. I have no way to prove that ... but there are also no grounds for the common belief that [this] must be wrong.
>
> The burden of proof rests on those who insist that there are some fundamental conditions of repression, exploitation, or inequality that are inescapable. To say merely that things have never been otherwise is not very convincing. On these grounds, one could have demonstrated, in the eighteenth century, that capitalist democracy is an impossible dream. (192–193)

If you're interested in learning more about Chomsky, the documentary film *Manufacturing Consent* is a fine place to start; numerous Web sites have now also taken up Chomsky's work.

Sources

Chomsky, Noam. *The Chomsky Reader*. Ed. James Peck. New York: Pantheon Books, 1987

Cogswell, David. *Chomsky for Beginners*. New York: Writers & Readers, 1996

The Essential Chomsky: Political Writings of Noam Chomsky. Monroe Maine: Common Courage Press, 2000

Hellman, Peter. "A Dishonorable Honorary Degree." *Wall Street Journal* (Eastern Edition). 19 May 1999: A22

Herman, Edward and Noam Chomsky. *Manufacturing Consent*. New York: Pantheon Books, 1988

Lyndes, Cathy and David Lyndes. "Noam Chomsky." 5 Jan. 2000. <http://www.hal-pc.org/~clyndes/political-chomsky.html>.

Manufacturing Consent: Noam Chomsky and the Media. Dir. Peter Wintonick and Mark Achbar. Zeitgeist Films: 1992

"The Noam Chomsky Archive." *The Noam Chomsky Archive*. Z Magazine. 5 Jan. 2000. <http://www.zmag.org/chomsky/index.cfm>.

Questions to Consider

1. What events have happened where you realized afterward that your reaction was based on not getting the full story?

2. When have you felt left out of media discourse, felt that the points of view of people like you weren't even being considered in a debate?

3. Are there any situations locally or nationally that you feel receive insufficient coverage in the press? Why do you think the press doesn't cover them?

4. When was the last time that you heard about developments in Kuwait? Somalia? Panama? The Falklands? Grenada? Why are they no longer "news"?

ONLINE REPRESENTATION OF AN ISSUE

> **Assignment:** How is your issue represented on an online site? How is it similar to or different from your other media sources? If you had created this site, is there anything would have done differently? Why?
>
> If you don't find a Web site on your issue, analyze why there isn't one. What might such a site look like? What kind of people are involved with your issue, and are they likely to have the resources or the inclination to make a web page? Given the web's demographics, is there an audience for your issue on the web?

Finding Sources Online

So how do you find items online? If you already have some web addresses handy, they may provide enough related links to keep you busy. But at some point in a serious research project you'll have to use a search engine, which is a site programmed to search the web for you.

These engines tend to work the same way library catalog searches do. By using search terms—the more specific, the better—you'll dredge up a number of related (and often completely unrelated) WWW sites. If you get many responses but aren't finding any useful sites in the first screenful or two, try searching using more specific terms, related terms, or synonyms.

Here are just a few of the search engines available on the web; ask your librarian for other useful sites:

> www.lycos.com
> www.excite.com
> www.metacrawler.com
> www.altavista.com
> www.yahoo.com
> www.hotbot.com
> www.askjeeves.com
> www.northernlight.com
> www.go.com
> www.alltheweb.com
> www.google.com
> www.looksmart.com

Metacrawler is of particular interest because it harnesses the search abilities of many of these engines at once. Some search engines, like Yahoo, also include reviews and ordered searches by increasingly narrowed choices.

Joining Online Groups.   For serious research, your best resources may turn out to be mail lists and Usenet newsgroups.

Mail lists. Listservs are e-mail lists sorted by interest, and they exist on virtually every subject. They're one of the oldest and most effective of the Internet communities, partly because of their simplicity (i.e., you send an e-mail to a central address, and it goes out to everyone else interested), and because having messages land in your e-mail, as opposed to a chat room, newsgroup, or Web site, means that you're involved every day. There's no better way to immediately reach out to hundreds or even thousands of experts. Of course, it can also mean that your e-mail gets clogged! Some lists get up to 50 messages a day, while other lists may only a post a few messages a month.

It can be surprisingly difficult to find these listservs, but if there's any topic that you really care about, then it's well worth your time. Here are some of the best sites for looking for listservs:

> L-SOFT: www.lsoft.com/lists/listref.html
> LISZT: www.liszt.com
> TILENET: http://tile.net/lists/

And finally, if you can't find an e-mail group, you can always make your own. Topica.com offers both a listserv search engine and free e-mail group hosting.

Usenet newsgroups.
Usenet newsgroups are electronic bulletin boards labeled by subject. For example, alt.music.yes is the newsgroup for fans of the rock band Yes. The first word in the names of newsgroups will give some clue to their general emphasis: alt (alternative/informal), comp (computer), news (current events), rec (recreation), sci (science), and soc (social issue).

One of the fastest and easiest ways to find Usenet newsgroups is by searching archived postings with a WWW search engine, some of which (such as www.metacrawler.com) allow you to specify a search of newsgroups.

To quickly see whether a newsgroup has already created a FAQ (Frequently Asked Questions) that will bring you up to speed with the rest of its subscribers, try this Usenet archive:
> www.cis.ohiostate.edu/hypertext/faq/usenet

Netiquette.   Before you venture into online research, particularly in newsgroups and listservs, you need to know the net's etiquette:

Label your inquiry clearly and stay on one point. The series of responses that an inquiry generates is known online as a thread. Fellow members often decide by their title and maybe the first post, whether to look into these threads, so keep them clear and focused.

Be easy on the eyes. In electronic text, people read by the screenful: If your paragraphs extend much further than that, you'll lose some readers.

Don't Flame. That is, don't spout abuse or insults, even if you feel mightily tempted. It jams up the flow of conversation and can escalate in a nasty way. Mature users will ignore or gently correct those who run afoul of them.

BEWARE OF THE CAPS LOCK KEY. People who use all capital letters sound like they are SHOUTING online. If you want to emphasize a word, put *asterisks* around it.

Learn when not to talk. When you first join an online group, it's tempting to spill out all your opinions and questions at once. Hold off for a while. See how threads develop so that you can get a feel for what they look like, what people will or won't respond to, and what topics may already have been covered. Your group may put out a FAQ that covers much of what you'd ask about. And don't feel that you have to respond to every question that others pose: Most members "lurk" and only respond occasionally.

Read through the thread before responding. Before you hit the reply button, make sure that someone else hasn't already made your reply irrelevant.

Analyzing Web sites

How Reliable Is the Site?   Since few Web sites have factcheckers or editors in the same way that other media do, there is nothing to prevent web pages from presenting information that is false, misleading, or just plain crazy. The Internet is a breeding ground for misinformation, uncited data, and assorted urban legends. Just because you see the same information or claims at a number of sites or newsgroup postings doesn't guarantee that it's true—or that's it not all coming from the same one or two people.

Similarly, there are a number of anonymous authors and those with aliases on the web. If you claim to be a medical doctor, or part of the president's reelection campaign, it's hard for anyone else to prove it untrue. A verifiable web page will have links from the sites of established groups or institutions, references to print articles, and a phone number or address for further information.

Here are a few things to look for when examining a Web site:

Are There Links?—Are they linked to related sites? Do the links work? A true research site will often feature such links as a way for users to further their knowledge. Commercial-oriented sites, though, are more interested in keeping you on their page than in giving you access to anyone else's.

Are They Responsive?—Does the site give you an e-mail address to send questions or suggestions to, in case the page itself doesn't give you all the information that you want? Or is it a case of "what you see is what you get"?

Are There Citations?—Do they cite the sources of their facts and figures? Do they suggest any books or articles where you can find out more information?

Who's Talking?—Is the author identified? If there are quotes, who is it that is being quoted? Are there people involved in the issue or in the creation of this page who aren't being acknowledged?

Is It Current?—Does the site indicate how current it is by listing the date of its last update?

Is It Invasive?—Does the site ask you to enter any personal information or to "register" with them? Is this required or not to use the site? This kind of consumer information is often used in creating mailing lists and in creating demographic profiles of a target audience.

Who Is the Audience?—At whom does the page appear to be aimed? How would it appeal to them? Is the audience addressed by this site expected to be unfamiliar with its subject, or are they assumed to be knowledgeable already?

Is It Biased?—Does the site have a sponsoring organization? How might it bias the content of the site?

How Is the Site Designed?   Web designers know that most people don't like reading more than a few minutes at a time on a computer screen. Flashy graphics and lots of short documents often give issue coverage that is more gloss than substance. There's no technical reason that a Web site can't have detailed documents and statistics. But in practice, Web sites often act more as advertisements than as adequate reference works in their own right.

The resulting design of a web page can give subtle cues about its content:

Background Colors and Text—Does the page's background color or intrusive imagery make it difficult to read? Is splashy appearance given more importance than usable information?

Lots of Images—Does the heavy use of images chew up far more download time than the actual text? This is also a sign that appearance is being valued over textual substance.

How Long Is the Text?—Quantity does not equal quality, of course. But is the site's information arranged in a way that allows you to read at length (for more than a few minutes) about a topic? Or can all the pages be read in a minute or two?

Are the Images Useful?—Do the images contain information that adds to the text (e.g., an illustration of condition, charts and graphs), or are they more ornamental in function? If these images weren't there, would you know any less about the issue?

Is It Exclusive?—Does this site accept only users with certain high-end capabilities (e.g., audio applications, video capabilities, etc.) and exclude all other users? This may indicate that the Web site is primarily interested in a higher-income audience, even if it means shutting some people out.

Is It Easy to Use?—Does the site have many distracting errors? How attractive is the page? Does it look professionally designed or more like a personal project? Why? Did you find it easy or difficult to navigate around the site?

Sample Response

Public Campaign is a Washington, DC-based political organization supporting campaign finance reform, and its Web site's "org" suffix indicates that it is not a commercial operation. The page has a sprawling but easily readable layout, with professional-quality logos and icons for press releases, web links, and programs sponsored by the group. The opening page is highly responsive: It includes a street mailing address for their headquarters, telephone and fax numbers, an e-mail address for "comments and questions," and a separate e-mail address to report problems with the site.

Beginners to this issue can peruse a straightforward list of "20 Things You Can Do." Newcomers can browse an "Organizational Profile" that describes Public Campaign's origins and aims. Bios and e-mail addresses for all the staff members are also provided. For those who are convinced enough there is then a "Join Public Campaign" page with a registration form.

The site does include other points of view via web links, though these links are largely to other proreform groups. The opening page features icons leading to an alphabetized list of campaign finance groups in every state, as well as to a list of national groups like Common Cause. There are a few links to nonpartisan governmental agencies like the Federal Election Commission, as well as to both the Democratic National Committee and the Republican National Committee.

The site is quite current, as the opening page includes links to four different campaign finance related press releases from the last two weeks, the most recent of which was published today. An archive page compiles press releases from as far back as April 1997. The press releases—most of which are attributed to Public Campaign president, Ellen Miller—are overwhelmingly in favor of campaign finance reform. For example, one news article is titled "New National Survey Shows Robust Support for Clean Money, Public Financing of Elections." The press releases themselves are based on Public Campaign's own studies and analysis, and the few outside quotes tend to come from politicians (usually Democratic) supportive of Public Campaign. For example, the press release for September 23, 1998, "The Color of Money," is supported by quotes from Ellen Miller (director of Public Campaign), John Lewis (a Democratic Congressional representative from Georgia), and Luis Guitierrez (a Democratic Congressional representative from Illinois). No Republicans, campaign funders, or opponents to reform are quoted. These releases are meant to provide a proreform slant on the news, presumably to readers who are already inclined to such ideas.

Perhaps the most unusual feature of the site is its listing of major financial supporters: the Stern Family Fund, the San Diego Foundation, the Kohlberg Foundation, the Steven and Michele Kirsch Foundation, the Blum-Kovler Foundation, the Florence & John Schumann Foundation, The Open Society Institute, and the J. Roderick MacArthur Foundation. For a page that is so strongly biased toward campaign finance reform, perhaps they thought it only fitting that they should reveal their own sources of funding.

Works Cited

Press Release: New National Survey Shows Robust Support for Clean Money, Public Financing of Elections. Public Campaign. 3 Apr. 2000. 13 Apr. 2000. <http://www.publiccampaign.org/press_releases/pr4_3_00.html>.

"Press Release September 23 1998: The Color of Money." Public Campaign. 23 Sept. 2000. 13 Apr. 2000. <http://www.publiccampaign.org/pr9_23_98.html>.

"Public Campaign: Organizational Profile." Public Campaign. 13 Apr. 2000. 13 Apr. 2000. <http://www.publiccampaign.org/who.html>.

"Public Campaign: Real Campaign Finance Reform." Public Campaign. 13 Apr. 2000. 13 Apr. 2000. <http://www.publiccampaign.org>.

Focus On: The Drudge Report

At times, it's difficult to turn on a TV or read a newspaper for long before running into Internet journalist Matt Drudge and his "Drudge Report" Web site. Drudge single-handedly broke stories like Jack Kemp's selection as a vice presidential candidate, Connie Chung's firing from CBS, and Bill Clinton's affair with Monica Lewinsky. In a 1-month period during Clinton's admission of an affair, Drudge's site logged over 13 million hits.

Drudge never attended college and, before beginning his own Internet gossip column in 1995, had never worked in journalism. His last known job had been in the gift shop at the CBS Studio Center. But by 1997 his column was one of the most popular news sites on the web, and had been picked up for distribution by Internet behemoth America Online (AOL). By 1999 Drudge was a commentator and panelist for Fox News.

Part of his success is due to the frequency with which "establishment" journalists visit his site. It is very efficiently designed, with links to dozens of columnists, every major American and British news organization, and a variety of foreign press agencies. But it's his scoops that have gained him the most fame and notoriety. He lets readers send in leads by e-mail, resulting in an avalanche of hundreds of messages a day. And while these often help Drudge to break sensational stories, just as often they lead him astray.

In August 1997 Drudge reprinted allegations by *Mother Jones* magazine that Republican consultant Don Sipple abused his wife. This was an example of the double standard, Drudge wrote, because court records and unnamed sources had also revealed Democratic White House aide Sidney Blumenthal as a spouse abuser. One day later, Drudge retracted this story.

Blumenthal responded by slapping Drudge and AOL with $30 million libel suits. Not only were there no such court records, but Drudge's claim that he tried to verify the story with Blumenthal also appears to be untrue. Drudge's supporters claim he's being persecuted by media colleagues who sneer at him as an untrained rumor/monger. Drudge often criticizes these journalists for being cozy with the powerful people that they write about. As to his own integrity, Drudge insists paradoxically: "I have an incredible level of credibility." But in a November 1998 article reviewing 51 of Drudge's on-line "exclusives," media magazine *Brill's Content* found that only 31 were in fact exclusive; of these, one third (10 stories) were not true.

Drudge likens himself to Revolutionary War pamphleteer Thomas Paine. Paine, who certainly had no aversion to writing viciously about his enemies, was nonetheless concerned with far-reaching issues of religion, governmental power, and the destiny of democracy. Drudge prefers hot-breaking stories of scandal and sensation to any nuanced discussion of policy or ethics; rather than a new Thomas Paine, he is more like a new Walter Winchell.

From the 1930s through the 1950s, Winchell was the most powerful newspaper columnist and radio broadcaster in the country, and a master of political and showbiz gossip. He cloaked tidbits in slang and innuendo, protecting himself from libel suits—a precaution missing from the Blumenthal story. But even Winchell couldn't last forever. His relentless self-promotion and vindictiveness eventually lost favor. By the time he was skewered in the movie *The Sweet Smell of Success,* he was already on his way out.

Drudge has himself become increasingly part of the very media that he criticizes, as a regular commentator on the conservative television show *Fox News.* But a rebellious attitude does not excuse reporters from keeping their facts straight. Drudge is an example of the Internet's potential for anyone to make themselves heard—and a cautionary tale in its abuse.

Sources

Barringer, Felicity. "What Hath Drudge Wrought? Partisan Web Sites Gain Some Media Credibility." *New York Times.* 8 Mar. 1999: C10

Conanson, Joe. "*Salon*/Media Circus: Outlaw Justice." *Salon Magazine.* 19 Jan. 1998. 6 Jan. 2000. <http://www.salon.com/media/1998/01/19media.html>.

Drudge, Matt. "Drudge Report 2000." Drudge Report. 6 Jan. 2000. 6 Jan. 2000. <http://www.drudgereport.com>.

Jurkowitz, Mark. "The Drudge Report's Scandalous Scoop." *Boston Globe.* 22 Jan. 1998: E1

Kraw, George. "Intellectual Property, November 1997—A Drudge Report." Nov. 1997. *IP Magazine.* 6 Jan. 2000. <http://www.ipmag.com/kraw.html>.

"Matt Drudge Information Center." Center for the Study of Popular Culture. 7 Jan. 2000. <http://www.cspc.org/drudge/mdinfo.html>.

McClintock, David. "Town Crier for the New Age." *Brill's Content.* Nov. 1998: 113–127

Purdum, Todd. "It Was Something He Said: The Dangers of Dishing Dirt in Cyberspace." *New York Times,* 17 Aug. 1997, sec. 4: 3

Richtel, Matt. "From Drudge Report to Drudge Retort." *New York Times.* 27 Aug. 1998: G3

Questions to Consider

1. What are the advantages of news delivered by the Internet? What are its disadvantages? How might these differences manifest themselves in coverage of your issue?

2. How might Drudge have avoided the libel suit, or the frequent occurrence of other untrue stories on his Web site?

3. If you find information on a Web site that lacks a clear source or any corroborating stories in the mainstream media, how should you make use of this information?

INTERVIEWING COMMUNITY MEMBERS ABOUT THE MEDIA

Assignment: Interview community members about the issue that you've been researching. What are their direct experiences with this issue? How do they get news about it? How does what they see on the news compare with their own actual experience of the issue? What kind of misconceptions do they think journalists—or anyone else—have about the issue? Are there any news accounts that have struck them as particularly accurate or inaccurate? How do they think the issue could be better covered?

Arranging an Interview

For this assignment, you'll have to interview a fellow member of your community. If you're nervous, remember that most people appreciate attention! Many people like being interviewed; they rarely get the chance to talk about issues that affect them, or about their areas of expertise. Interview sources can include authors of the works or articles you've read, someone mentioned in your readings, or simply a friend or acquaintance.

You may have to call a number of times before finally reaching your interviewees. Have a "script" ready before your call: This should include a brief explanation of your project and of why you'd like to talk with them. You don't have to read from it by rote, but it helps to have it near by when you start grasping for words. Don't be discouraged if they're a little hesitant initially; emphasize that even 10 minutes of their time would still be a big help. Set up an interview date as soon as is convenient, but be ready to schedule an interview many days in advance if necessary.

There are a few important steps you can take before the interview happens:

Review your notes. Find out as much as possible about your subject before the interview. This will help you come off as more serious about your topic and it may inspire more specific questions for the interview.

Prioritize Your Questions. Arrange your questions in order of importance. If your interview is interrupted, you'll at least have covered the major points.

Think of Open-Ended Questions. Be creative in coming up with questions that can't simply be answered "Yes" or "No." Here are some examples:

- What is the hardest part of your job/role?

- What are the most common misconceptions about this issue? Why are they inaccurate?

- How did you wind up here or involved in this issue?

- What's the most important advice that you can give to people new to this issue or situation?

- What direction do you see this issue heading toward in the future?

- Can you describe an experience that affected the way you think about this issue?

- Are there any other contacts or sources that you can recommend?

- Is there anything I haven't asked about that you think is important?

Think of Open-Minded Questions. Remember that you're still forming a tentative hypothesis; the purpose of your interview is to get into their perceptions, not to impress them with yours.

Conducting the Interview

Arriving at the Interview. Arrive on time; remember, they're doing you a favor! When you arrive, you should have a notebook or legal pad and several pens and pencils. Have your questions written down and prioritized.

During the Interview. **Keep notes brief.** You don't want your notetaking to take up too much of your interview time, so abbreviate as much as you can. You don't have to write their responses word for word—just paraphrase most of what they say, and only directly quote anything that seems especially striking. The more you can keep eye contact, and the fewer pauses you need to scribble things down, the more it will be like a normal conversation—and the more sincere and in-depth their answers are likely to be.

Be a listener. Don't be afraid of pauses. Give them space to think and the opportunity to go off on tangents. If your respondent mentions some interesting detail, be ready to improvise a question that will take advantage of this unexpected insight.

Know when to leave. Be ready to stand up, thank them, and leave at the end of the meeting—especially if it's someone that you don't know. Don't wait for your respondent to end the meeting, because they may let it drag on out of fear of seeming impolite. Thank them for their time, and make sure you have their name and affiliation (if any) spelled correctly.

Recording the Interview. If you like, you can bring a tape recorder to the interview; ask before you meet for the interview whether this is okay with your interviewee. Remember that many people freeze up when they know they're on tape, especially if they're not used to being interviewed. If you think this may be the case, then don't use a recorder. Relying on your memory and notes may be difficult, but it often results in a more relaxed and open interview.

Recording does leave you free to put your pen down; even so, afterward you'll still want to jot down your visual and personal impressions of the interviewee, since these can't be captured on an audio tape.

If you do record your interview, make sure you have fresh tape and batteries. As soon as you're away from the interview, play back your recording. It may be that the recorder didn't work, the batteries were too weak, or the microphone was placed so as to make the conversation inaudible. If that's the case, take notes about the interview immediately! You don't want to discover a blank or unusable tape days after the interview, when your memories have faded.

Phone Interviews. Often you'll find that in person interviews aren't practical: Your phone sources may be in a different state, and Internet respondents may be in another country altogether. If you're interviewing by phone, call from your home—you don't want your boss or those in line for a pay phone to be interrupting you. Find a room with little background noise. If possible, turn off call waiting or any other phone options that could interrupt you.

If you have the interviewee's permission, you can tape your phone interview. Most electronics stores carry telephone jack-to-⅛" (or RCA plug) adapter cables; this will allow you to plug a tape deck into a phone jack.

Internet Interviews. If you're eliciting responses from people on the Internet, make sure you use a "RE:" subject line in your replies so that they can follow your conversation. Also, if you question them further about one of their previous responses, make sure that you cut and paste in the relevant sections of their response; that way they won't have to rack their memory for exactly which quote from yesterday or last week you're referring to.

When asking a newsgroup or a listserv group for respondents to a question, or for people to interview, make your inquiry as specific as possible. Newsgroups get "I'm a student, please enlighten me" pleas all the time; rarely do they answer such broad inquiries. Where, as a group member, would you even start to answer such a question? Instead, start with one of the specific aspects of your issue, or one of the interview questions that you've already come up with. You don't even need to inform people that you're a student, because it's probably irrelevant. No one is a student online, everyone is a colleague.

After the Interview. One technique I often employ is to write only a few direct quotes during the interview, along with whatever names, acronyms, or numbers that interviewees they may give—things that I'm likely to forget quickly otherwise. Then, as soon as I'm out the door I sit down and frantically scribble down paraphrases of all their answers during the interview. You have to do this while it is still fresh in your memory, or the accuracy of your notes may suffer. But this method allows the best of both worlds: A relatively smooth flow of conversation during your interview, and detailed notes taken immediately afterward.

Finally, if your interviewee isn't a friend or acquaintance already, write or e-mail them after the interview to thank them for their time.

Sample Response

Despite the strong opinions that politics elicits from my friends, Melissa Ehman is the only person I know who has actually run for public office. Although Melissa today attends grad school at U.C. Berkeley to study public health epidemiology, in the past she ran for mayor of San Francisco (1987), then for state assembly in a special election (1988), and again in the regular election (1989). At the same time, she chaired the Peace and Freedom Party in San Francisco. The party, founded nationwide by antiwar activists and the Black Panthers in the 1960s, is still active in socialist and leftist politics in California.

Ehman faced many obstacles common to third-party candidates. "To qualify for the mayor's race, you pay a fee or get enough signatures. We didn't have the money, so we collected 10,000 signatures." While her later run for assembly was simpler—she qualified as the candidate of a recognized party—she found that campaign less open.

> The mayor's race was more open to the full range of candidates than the assembly race. It [the assembly race] was really shameful at times; at one point the League of Women Voters held a candidates' debate, and they just shut us out. And we were on the ballot! So we picketed them.

Ehman relies on a variety of sources for news: *Harper's* magazine, the *New York Times*, BBC World Service radio, National Public Radio, and the online Pacific Islands Report. She remains wary of the outsized influence of the *New York Times*.

> It's accurate, but what they choose to cover isn't necessarily representative of what's happening in the world. That's what makes foreign media sources important—they'll give a different perspective than what you get from the *Times* or other American sources.

Similarly, Ehman didn't encounter difficulties with accuracy in the local press as she campaigned; it was more what they chose to cover and how they covered it. "A lot of the coverage of the smaller [mayoral] candidates, when there was any, was 'That wacky San Francisco race!' Even CNN used that angle. When they showed third-party people, they'd pick the crazy ones."

The local media coverage that Ehman encountered is a good example of how a publication's editorial policy doesn't always equate directly with its coverage.

> Conservatives were often nicer to me than the supposed liberals. The worst interview I had was with the *Bay Guardian*, a weekly newspaper that's supposed to be liberal, alternative. The editor who interviewed me was mean, condescending … a real bastard. That was an eye-opening experience.

Her experience with the *San Francisco Examiner*, a more conservative daily paper, was different. "It wasn't like their writer was going to vote for me, but he respected my beliefs and what I was trying to do. He was a really nice guy."

Ehman found that the best coverage came from local public radio stations KGO, KQED, and KPFA. Outside of these appearances, she relied on community meetings to get the word out. But without the money to buy advertising, she and other third-party candidates were in a catch-22: They lacked the money to get well known, and they weren't well known enough to get money. The media did little to help this situation. "If the media took itself seriously, they'd give equal time to every candidate. The media decides to narrow it down early on—but why shouldn't everyone get equal time?"

This selective lack of coverage also affects people's perceptions of campaign finances, in her view.

> People are becoming aware that, say, one candidate with a pile of money can unfairly drown out another. But people don't extrapolate to third-party candidates. Third parties don't get elected because they don't get the money and don't get heard. Without media coverage, you're marginalized. Third-party candidates are considered not legitimate, or just crazy. People are so dead set on the two-party system, and they'll say "Why are you bothering to run? You know you can't win." And yeah, I knew that. But I was trying to build something for the future.

Works Cited

Ehman, Melissa. Telephone interview. 24 Dec. 1998

Focus On: Internet Panics

The reports were shocking:

> Mr. President, Georgetown University Law School has released a remarkable study conducted by researchers at Carnegie-Mellon University. This study raises important questions about the availability and the nature of cyberporn .... The university surveyed 900,000 computer images. Of these 900,000 images, 83.5 percent of all computerized photographs available on the Internet are pornographic.

These congressional remarks by Senator Grassley on June 26, 1995, were typical of the blowup after *Time* magazine ran a "cyberporn" cover story. Starting with the generalization that "Sex is everywhere these days;" the article appeared to claim that a Carnegie-Mellon University study had found that a majority of material on the Internet was pornographic. Moreover, as the story's headlines proclaimed, it was "ubiquitous," "immensely popular," and "a big moneymaker."

This would have been strange news to anyone who used the Internet. But the study, directed by student researcher Marty Rimm, had also made some strange assumptions. It only looked at a few Usenet newsgroups that specialized in visual erotica, while the vast majority of Usenet is text based. It assumed that a posting was the same as a download, that is, that just because something was available people were viewing it. It used a very short period of time to study Internet traffic. And finally, the sample of Internet users was drawn from the predominantly male engineering students at Carnegie-Mellon.

None of this seemed to bother Rimm or *Time*—they had a scoop. They denied other experts a chance to review the report, a standard procedure for any accurate scientific study. When Dr. Brian Reid—a member of Digital Equipment Corporation's Network Systems Lab, and the designer of the software that Rimm used—finally got a copy of the study, he was horrified. "I am so distressed by its lack of scientific credibility that I don't even know where to begin critiquing it .... The writer appears to me to not have a glimmer of an understanding even of basic statistical measurement technique .... "

But it was too late. The article was out, complete with sensational artwork of a man humping his computer, and senators demanded that something be done. This culminated in the Communications Decency Act. The "83.5 percent" figure was trumpeted throughout the press, even though buried in *Time*'s article, and implied by Rimm's own figures, was a more accurate figure of perhaps .5 percent.

Colorful information also emerged about Rimm himself. Despite his moralizing, he had previously published *The Pornographer's Handbook: How to Exploit Women, Dupe Men, and Make Lots of Money.* With its credibility falling apart, *Time* printed a partial retraction near the back of its magazine three weeks later—but insisted that it had all been in the service of a "more important debate about hard-core porn on the Internet."

Will the press now be more careful? Maybe not. In June 1998, newspapers reprinted a similarly flawed online survey by MSNBC. The poll was neither designed by a statistical professional nor accepted by any professional journal. After sensational front-page headlines, the *San Francisco Chronicle* buried one statistician's contention that MSNBC's work was "scientifically worthless" on a back page, 25 paragraphs into a 30-paragraph story.

The press stumbled yet again just months after the MSNBC poll debacle, when another study emanating from Carnegie-Mellon University—this time from Professor Robert Kraut—purported to show that the more time one spent online, the greater the likelihood of social withdrawal and depression. The results were featured in virtually every major news outlet, and Kraut himself was interviewed uncritically by such prestigious sources as National Public Radio. After this flurry of attention, though, only a few publications bothered to run follow-up stories demonstrating that, once again, the study was statistically worthless. For starters, Kraut had no control group—that is, no observations of people not using the Internet. And rather than using a random sampling of the population, or even a random sampling of likely Internet users, Kraut had gathered volunteers from high schools, a group that could skew the results of a study on social interaction and depression. As statistician Donna Hoffman complained to the *New York Times,* "Speaking as an editor, if this had crossed my desk, I would have rejected it."

Unlike the headline-grabbing attention given to the initial reports on Kraut, this follow-up was buried in the *New York Times* in the middle of the business section, once again leaving most readers with faulty reporting on the Internet still stuck in their minds. And it wasn't even as if journalists didn't know what the Internet was. A March 2000 *New York Times* article revealed that polling data had shown that while only about 20 percent of professional journalists used the Internet on a daily basis in 1995, over 60 percent were using it by late 1998. By early 2000, the figure had topped 80 percent.

At major media outlets, this percentage is probably even higher. But even with the near-universal use of the Internet at major newspapers, scare stories still flourish. In February 2000, after Professor Norman Nie of Stanford University conducted a survey on Internet use and loneliness, he bypassed the usual academic peer-review process—that is, a critical reading of his data and conclusions by other experts in the field—in order to trumpet his results directly to the media via a press release. He claimed to have found that even relatively modest amounts of net usage resulted in people "attending fewer social events" and "spending less time with family." What Nie did not proclaim as loudly was that he had found that this statement only applied to about 7 percent of his respondents—meaning that the vast majority did not suffer from some vague net-borne social malady.

Christopher Weare, a professor at the U.S.C. Annenberg School for Communications, complained that "the press release is replete with numerous other omissions, distortions, and questionable inferences, exactly the types of problems that peer review is designed to weed out." While net may be made to look bad in such stories, on closer inspection the newspapers look even worse. "If there was any discovery from this survey worthy of front-page coverage," adds Weare, "it is the gullibility of reporters."

Sources

Caruso, Denise. "Technology: Critics Are Picking Apart a Professor's Study … " *New York Times*. 14 Sept. 1998: C5

Elmer-Dewitt, Philip. "Fire Storm on the Computer Nets." *Time*. 24 Jul. 1995: 57

———"On a Screen Near You: Cyberporn." *Time*. 3 Jul. 1995: 38

———, et al. "How *Time* Fed the Internet Porn Panic." *Harper's*. Sept. 1995: 11

"The Ethics of Marty Rimm and CMU." Electronic Freedom Foundation. Jan. 1997. 10 Jan. 2000. <http://www.eff.org/~declan/rimm/>.

Hafner, Katie. "Questions About Sex on Line Raise Questions About Survey." *New York Times*. 11 Jun. 1998: D3

"Hotwired Pornscare Index." *Hotwired*. 30 Oct. 1995. Wired Magazine. 10 Jan. 2000 <http://www.hotwired.com/special/pornscare/>.

Kraut, Robert. "Robert Kraut." Carnegie-Mellon University. 10 Jan. 2000. <http://www.cs.cmu.edu/afs/cs.cmu.edu/user/kraut/www/kraut.html>.

Markoff, John. "A Newer, Lonelier Crowd Emerges in Internet Study." *New York Times*. 16 Feb. 2000: A1

"Smut N' Stuff" [A Rimm Critique]. SunSITE USA. 10 Jan. 2000. <http://sunsite.unc.edu/smut.html>.

Swartz, Jon. "'Sex' Called Most Wanted Word on Net." *San Francisco Chronicle*. 10 Jun. 1998: A1

Weare, Christopher. "Internet Statistics Unsound: Media Reporting on Internet Studies Misses Fundamental Problems." 25 Apr. 2000. Online Journalism Review. 28 Apr. 2000. <http://www.ojr.usc.edu/content/story.cfm?request=370>.

Questions to Consider

1. How might newspapers or researchers have avoided being misled by Rimm's or Kraut's studies?

2. How could you check these studies against the experience of actual Internet users? What questions might you ask them?

PAPER:
HOW IS THIS ISSUE PORTRAYED IN THE MEDIA?

> **Assignment:** How has your issue been portrayed in various forms of the media? What are some of the biases or problems you found in their coverage? Compare the coverage given in print and Internet sources. How do you and members of the community respond to this coverage?

Organizing the Body of Your Paper

Using Your Notes.   Go back over your notes regularly—all of them, or in sections. Since your knowledge of a subject changes over time, you may make connections or have insights that wouldn't have occurred to you back when you wrote these notes down. For many writers, one of the best ways to write a rough draft is by reading through notes once or twice, setting them aside, and then writing the draft without referring to them. You'll tend to remember the really good material, and forget the miscellaneous information that would only get in the way. In other words, if it's interesting enough to remember, then it will probably be interesting enough for someone to want to read. Once you're done writing, go back and track down the documentation (names and page numbers) as needed.

Developing a Narrative.   Even with all your notes at hand, you still need to organize this data into the narrative body of your rough draft. A few of the approaches listed below are similar to the *introductions* described previously; that's because many introductions flow so logically into the body of the paper that it's hard to separate the two! Remember that the approaches below can be combined—in fact, most papers are not based purely on one method of narrative development. But one of these approaches usually typifies a paper's body:

Chronological Order—Lay out important events and details as they happened, from beginning to end. Weave other people's views or comments into this narrative, even if they contradict your accounting of events or anyone else's.

Spatial Order—Describe a conflict in a geographic line (e.g., house by house, street by street, region by region) or according to physical size (e.g., the smallest manifestation to the largest).

Compare and Contrast—Compare coverage in two or more different sources, or in the same source at different times in its history. You can describe one source before moving on to the next, or note specific details of each source in alternating paragraphs:

Introduction
Source A
Source B
Conclusion

OR

Introduction
Point 1 about Source A versus Source B
Point 2 about Source A versus Source B
Point 3 and so on
Conclusion

Known to Unknown (and vice versa)—Begin by closely describing the known facts and reports of an issue, and move to describing the parts that are still poorly understood or underreported. Make an educated guess as to why there are unknown aspects to this problem.

Individual to Community—Begin with a detailed description of a specific person, place, or event, and expand into a discussion of the broader picture that this example typifies. This is common in human interest news stories, but don't place too much weight on any one account, even if it's your own. Find at least one or two other examples, and try to find news research that makes it clear whether any of these are typical of some broader problem or solution.

Process—Explain your subject step by step as a process. Make sure that you include enough detail for your readers not to get lost; don't assume that they're familiar enough with all the terms or background knowledge.

Classification—Some topics lend themselves to being broken down into categories or separate eras.

General to Specific—Begin with some broad description of a topic, and then funnel down to specific details or incidents that relate to it.

Transitions

Even if you've figured out how to develop the body of your essay, your reader needs to know why you are shifting from one paragraph to another. Otherwise your essay won't flow smoothly; it will jump from idea to idea without any apparent connection, and it may be hard to follow your reasoning. Sometimes all you need to do is ask yourself "Why am I following with this paragraph? How do the two relate?"—and then begin your paragraph with a sentence explaining this relation.

If you're stuck, try using a transition. A transition is a word or phrase that connects different ideas or examples; they're often used between examples and between different parts of an essay (introduction–body, or body–conclusion). Transition terms include: *however, nevertheless, for example, on the other hand, despite the evidence, as* [name here] *notes, and, in addition, also, in fact, as a result, yet, similarly, for instance, although, after, next.*

If you use these terms too often, your essay may sound contrived—as if you're just plugging in words without giving them any real thought. Don't simply slap these words on: Make sure that you understand what they mean, and make sure that they express some relation between the two paragraphs that the reader needs to know. If one paragraph already flows from the next logically without needing any of these terms, then don't use them. If you do use them, try reading the sentence without that word. If it still makes sense, leave it out.

On the other hand, there may be almost no relation between your two paragraphs except that they both relate to the overall subject of your paper. In this case, try skipping a line and starting a new subsection. Title it in bold face so that your reader knows that you've shifted your focus significantly for this part of the paper. These section or chapter divisions are especially useful in long research papers, where an otherwise unbroken stream of information might be overwhelming to the reader and writer alike.

Sample Paper

While there is at least some consensus among both conservatives and liberals that campaign finance reform may be needed, media coverage of this issue can be a partisan excuse for attacks on unpopular organizations or politicians. While I did not find factual inaccuracies in the coverage, there was certainly bias because of selective coverage and because of who was actually allowed to speak on this issue.

"When Liberty Is Not So Sweet" appeared in the British magazine the *Economist* in the same week that the U.S. House of Representatives, in the unnamed reporter's words, "buried campaign finance reform" (26). The article characterizes the American Civil Liberties Union as a major opponent of reform; given its purist view, its members are officially, though not unanimously, against any restriction of advertising or other forms of political speech. The writer then extends this counterpopulist purism to other ACLU positions. The ACLU's "rights first" stand, the author argues, was appropriate in more restrictive eras like the 1950s and the 1960s, but is now counter to the desires of the people it claims to protect.

The *Economist* itself is clearly aimed at an international audience. Headquartered in London, it includes prices for many different countries on its cover. Both its title and its articles indicate an emphasis on business and investing, and its ads are predominantly for large investment concerns, business travel, and expensive consumer products (e.g., Rolex watches). Its target audience, then, might be defined as wealthy (or would-be wealthy) adult business people and investors with an interest in international news.

The article itself has a noticeable anti-ACLU bias. The *Economist* does not quote the ACLU or its positions at all; the closest it comes is with a rebelling former ACLU legal director, Burt Neuborne, who now calls the organization "anachronistic." An article by two members of the Chicago Law School attacking the ACLU's "purism" is also quoted approvingly; the article ran in the somewhat conservative magazine the *Atlantic Monthly*. Earlier in the article, there are briefer quotes and citations from the conservative former House speaker Newt Gingrich and from polls by conservative news organizations like the *Wall Street Journal* and Fox News.

The only break from this pattern is one paragraph summarizing the results of a poll commissioned by a First Amendment foundation, the Freedom Forum. Overall, though, there is strong emphasis on perspectives from conservative publications in general and from lawyers opposing the ACLU in particular. No current member or representative of the ACLU is quoted. Nor are any citizens, voters, or campaigning politicians. The resulting bias is conservative and anti-ACLU—though the assumption underlying the article, in contrast with that of some conservative politicians, is that campaign finance reform is a desirable thing.

Liberal coverage is hardly less biased, though. The *Nation* magazine article "Free Speech and Campaign Myth," written by Ellen Miller and E. Joshua Rosenkranz in April 1998, details the opposition of Senator Mitch McConnell to campaign finance reform. McConnell has argued that restrictions on campaign advertising are counter to the First Amendment guarantees of freedom of speech. Miller and Rosenkranz claim that McConnell quotes selectively from Supreme Court decisions to back his views, and that he ignores free speech concerns when they apply to art and political protest: "McConnell's First Amendment applies only to the wealthy special interests who finance campaigns" (22).

The *Nation* is known for its liberal editorial viewpoint, and both the selection of columnists (e.g., Pollitt, Cockburn) and the topics that they cover focus on the progressive, liberal side of American politics. The relatively few ads in the magazine are for liberal political forums in New York City, politically oriented publishers, and progressive companies like Working Assets, a long distance service. Their audience appears to be primarily highly literate and politically active urban liberals.

Unlike many publications, The *Nation* identifies the professional and political affiliations of its writers. Ellen Miller is identified as "executive director of Public Campaign," while E. Joshua Rosenkranz is the "executive director of the Brennan Center for Justice at N.Y.U. law school." This article is written, it seems, from the perspective of two proreform urbanites, both of whom are experienced in law or politics themselves.

Senator McConnell is quoted extensively throughout the article, although his quotes are always parried by the authors, so that they also always get the last word. There are no quotes from voters, organizations opposed to reform, or from anyone else on McConnell's side. There are no other sources quoted in the article, although a couple of Supreme Court decisions are paraphrased.

The continual focus of this article is on Senator McConnell, although by extension the authors are attacking other opponents of campaign reform. In the opening paragraph, there's a comparison of McConnell with a chicken; strutting around the Senate "like the cock of the walk" (22). This personal animus may be justified, but the article abandons any pretense to objectivity. It is noticeably less diverse in its sources than the *Economist*'s article, but it relies more on close legal argumentation than the *Economist*'s freewheeling willingness to bend the Bill of Rights for the sake of practicality.

In the online realm, there are a number of even more avowedly partisan Web sites on virtually any issue. Public Campaign, however, is a nonpartisan Washington, DC-based political organization supporting campaign finance reform. Its web page has a sprawling but easily readable layout, with professional-quality logos and icons for press releases, web links, and programs sponsored by the group. The opening page is highly responsive: It includes a street mailing address for their headquarters, telephone and fax numbers, an e-mail address for "comments and questions," and a separate e-mail address to report problems with the site.

Beginners to this issue can peruse a straightforward list of "20 Things You Can Do." Newcomers can browse an "Organizational Profile" that describes Public Campaign's origins and aims. Bios and e-mail addresses for all the staff members are also provided. For those who are convinced enough there is then a "Join Public Campaign" page with a registration form.

The site does include other points of view via web links, though these links are largely to other proreform groups. The opening page features icons leading to an alphabetized list of campaign finance groups in every state, as well as to a list of national groups like Common Cause. There are a few links to nonpartisan governmental agencies like the Federal Election Commission, as well as to both the Democratic National Committee and the Republican National Committee.

The site is quite current, as the opening page includes links to four different campaign finance related press releases from the last two weeks, the most recent of which was published today. An archive page compiles press releases from as far back as April 1997. The press releases—most of which are attributed to their president, Ellen Miller—are overwhelmingly in favor of campaign finance reform. For example, one news article is titled "New National Survey Shows Robust Support for Clean Money, Public Financing of Elections." The press releases themselves are based on Public Campaign's own studies and analysis, and the few outside quotes tend to come from politicians (usually Democratic) supportive of Public Campaign. For example, the press release for September 23, 1998, "The Color of Money," is supported by quotes from Ellen Miller (director of Public Campaign), John Lewis (a Democratic Congressional representative from Georgia), and Luis Guitierrez (a Democratic Congressional representative from Illinois). No Republicans, campaign funders, or opponents to reform are quoted. These releases are meant to provide a proreform slant on the news, presumably to readers who are already inclined to such ideas.

Perhaps the most unusual feature of the site is its listing of major financial supporters. For a page that is so strongly biased toward campaign finance reform, perhaps they thought it only fitting that they should reveal their own sources of funding.

I did not find, then, any inaccurate reports from these print or online sources; instead, the question worth asking was "Who are they quoting, and who are they not quoting?" Melissa Ehman, a former San Francisco mayoral candidate for the socialist Peace and Freedom party, recalls that she didn't encounter difficulties with accuracy in the local press; it was more what they chose to cover and how they covered it. "A lot of the coverage of the smaller [mayoral] candidates, when there was any, was 'That wacky San Francisco race!' Even CNN used that angle. When they showed third-party people, they'd pick the crazy ones."

This selective coverage also affects people's perceptions of campaign finances, in her view.

People are becoming aware that, say, one candidate with a pile of money can unfairly drown out another. But people don't extrapolate to third-party candidates. Third parties don't get elected because they don't get the money and don't get heard. Without media coverage, you're marginalized.

It should be noted that both the *Economist* and the *Nation* assume the basic necessity for campaign finance reform. The *Nation* points its finger of blame at a conservative senator and his cronies, though, while the *Economist* blames liberal legal advocates at the ACLU. The Public Campaign Web site doesn't print any response from whomever it happens to be currently blaming. But while an awareness of bias in media coverage of this issue is useful, it has to be applied carefully to each situation. After all, a publication's editorial policy doesn't always equate directly with its coverage. As [socialist candidate] Ehman notes, with some surprise, "Conservatives [in the media] were often nicer to me than the supposed liberals."

Works Cited

Ehman, Melissa. Telephone interview. 24 Dec. 1998
Miller, Ellen and Joshua Rosenkranz. "Free Speech and Campaign Myth." *Nation*. 27 Apr. 1998: 22–25
Press Release: New National Survey Shows Robust Support for Clean Money, Public Financing of Elections. Public Campaign. 3 Apr. 2000. 13 Apr. 2000. <http://www.publiccampaign.org/press_releases/pr4_3_00.html>.
"Press Release September 23 1998: The Color of Money." Public Campaign. 23 Sept. 1998. 13 Apr. 2000. <http://www.publiccampaign.org/pr9_23_98.html>.
"Public Campaign: Organizational Profile." Public Campaign. 13 Apr. 2000. 13 Apr. 2000. <http://www.publiccampaign.org/who.html>.
"Public Campaign: Real Campaign Finance Reform." Public Campaign. 13 Apr. 2000. 13 Apr. 2000. <http://www.publiccampaign.org>.
"When Liberty Is Not So Sweet: Campaign Finance Reform Has Been Stifled at Birth by Defenders of Free Speech." *Economist*. 4 Apr. 1998: 26

Focus On: Media Watchdogs

While readers can't always be aware of the bias and misinformation present in what they read, the United States is fortunate to have a number of self-appointed "media watchdogs" who monitor the press for such flaws.

One guardian of journalistic integrity is the *Columbia Journalism Review*. *CJR* is a mix of media critiques, discussions of ethics, and career guidance; its Web site includes a handy guide to the owners of print and broadcast companies. *CJR* has traditionally been wary of pursuing specific media outlets for bad journalism, preferring to track trends and industrywide problems. That has changed recently, though, given the competition from an aggressive newcomer, *Brill's Content*.

Brill's shook up the media by naming names in its pursuit of shoddy journalism. It debuted with a bang in 1998, accusing Kenneth Starr and his office of illegally leaking grand jury testimony to the press. It has repeatedly tagged TV newsmagazines like *60 Minutes* and *Dateline* for misleading reports. Most importantly, it has subjected "soft" journalism—such as teen's and women's magazines, some of which engage in fakery and advertiser bribery that anywhere else would be firing offenses—to the kind of scrutiny that their audiences deserve but have not been accorded. For example, *Brill's* revealed that "reader's letters" at *YM* were cooked up by the magazine staff, who arrogantly and patronizingly assumed that they could know what really mattered to their young readers, regardless of what genuine readers had to say. Soon afterward, *Brill's* exposed *Cosmopolitan*'s tendency, under former editor Bonnie Fuller, to fabricate persons and quotes.

The online world also provides quick and accessible media critiques. The fastest out the gate is Scott Shuger, media critic for the online magazine *Slate* (www.slate.com). Shuger reads the day's major papers (*New York Times*, *Los Angeles Times*, *Washington Post*, *USA Today*, and the *Wall Street Journal*) and files an online summary and analysis of them, sometimes as early as 3:30 that morning—long before most readers have even awakened. *Slate*'s closest rival, the online magazine *Salon* (www.salon.com), also devotes significant space to media reporting; it broke the story that the White House "drug czar" Barry McCaffrey had quietly paid magazines and prime-time TV shows to alter their content to include antidrug messages.

Entire Web sites, in fact, have arisen to scrutinize the media, most notably Powerful Media (www.powerfulmedia.com) and Jim Romensko's MediaNews (www.medianews.com). One site, the Online Journalism Review (www.ojr.org), is entirely devoted to scrutinizing the wildly unregulated world of online reporting.

It's also as important to look at what the media doesn't cover as what it does cover. Project Censored, run by Sonoma State University students since 1976, has become a force in publicizing stories that, though perhaps run by small publications or the alternative press, are pointedly ignored by the mainstream media. Each spring, Project Censored publishes a book covering such stories, and excerpts are often prominently featured in alternative press publications around the country.

Finally, there are the ying and yang of media watchdogs: AIM (Accuracy in Media) on the conservative side, and FAIR (Fairness and Accuracy in Reporting) on the liberal side. Both organizations publish newsletters, maintain extensive Web sites, and organize conferences. In dissecting political coverage for bias they can be quite partisan themselves, but they are none the less valuable for it. Similarly, the conservative Media Resource Center analyzes the liberal media, while the anticapitalist Adbusters lampoons advertising and draws attention to its influence on the media through such events as "Buy Nothing Day."

No matter what their political viewpoint or their method of publishing, though, media watchdogs ask essentially the same set of questions: Are there reputable sources for this story? Is there any conflict of interest in this reporting? What assumptions are being made by this journalist? How does media coverage shape our actions and expectations? Since we all rely in part on the media for our view of the world, these questions concern more than just other journalists: They concern all of us as readers, viewers, and listeners.

Sources

"Accuracy in Media." AIM. 26 Dec. 1999. <http://www.aim.org>.

"Adbusters Culture Jammers Headquarters." Adbusters. 26 Dec. 1999. <http://www.adbusters.org/main/index.html>.

"Columbia Journalism Review." *Columbia Journalism Review.* 26 Dec. 1999.<http://www.cjr.org>.

"Fairness and Accuracy in Reporting." FAIR. 20 Dec. 1999. 23 Dec. 1999. <http://www.fair.org>.

"Http://www.brillscontent.com." *Brill's Content.* 22 Dec. 1999. 24 Dec. 1999. <http://www.brillscontent.com>.

Ledbetter, James. "The Media Critics: The Internet—A Thousand Voices Bloom." *Columbia Journalism Review.* March/April 2000: 46

"Media Resource Center." Media Resource Center. 20 Dec. 1999. 20 Dec. 1999. <http://www.mrc.org>.

"Online Journalism Review Frameset." Online Journalism Review. 22 Dec. 1999. <http://www.ojr.org>.

Philips, Peter and Project Censored. *Censored 2000: The Year's Top 25 Censored Stories.* New York: Seven Stories Press, 2000

"Project Censored: Tracking the News That Didn't Make the News." 9 Apr. 2000. <http://www.projectcensored.org>.

Rosman, Katherine. "The Secret of Her Success." *Brill's Content.* Nov. 1998: 102–111

Roth, Gabriel. "SFBG News: Project Censored 2000." *San Francisco Bay Guardian.* 5 Apr. 2000. 9 Apr. 2000. <http://www.sfbg.com/News/34/27/cen1.html>.

Shuger, Scott. "Slate—Today's Papers." *Slate Magazine.* 14 Apr. 2000. 14 Apr. 2000. <http://www.slate.com>.

Taylor, Rachel. "Signed, Whoever." Jul./ Aug. 1998. *Brill's Content.* Online. America Online. (Accessed 9 Dec. 1998)

Questions to Consider

1. Does the political bias of a group like AIM or FAIR make their allegations of bias by other journalists any less believable? Why or why not?

2. If you were analyzing the day's news from different newspapers, the way that Scott Shuger does, what kinds of differences in coverage would you look for? Why might these differences be important?

3. What forums are within your community for people to voice criticisms about media coverage? How could your media be made more responsive to such concerns?

PEER READING

> **In-Class:** Read and respond to the papers written by your class-
> mates. Review the peer reading instructions you used for paper #1
> and organize your reading groups in the same manner for this paper.

Peer reading worksheet: Paper #2

Writer:

Partner:

Are there any parts that you found confusing or insufficiently explained?
Why?

Who is quoted in the paper? Is there anything else you might you want to
ask them? What other sources or points of view could the writer include?

Does the writer's use or characterization of any of the media sources seem
overly biased? How might they give a fairer description?

Which details in the body of the essay worked especially well? What parts
could use more detail or a more direct example?

Overall, how might the writer improve this paper?

REVISING THE PAPER

> **Assignment:** Revise your rough draft. Then add it to a folder that includes your draft, your peer reading worksheet, and the shorter assignments.

Varying Your Sources

There's no law against going over your sources one at a time as you develop the body of your paper; some "compare and contrast" narratives work well this way. But usually it's a ploddingly dull way to develop your narrative. It can also be misleading: No one source can fully explain any one aspect of your topic.

Try to vary your sources by combining different or even opposing viewpoints within the same paragraph, or at least by combining different types of information (interview, statistics, media accounts, your own recollections, etc.)

In order to prevent your paper from being overwhelmed by lengthy quotes, you can also combine quoted phrases with paraphrases that carry the gist of the rest of the quote. This is especially useful when you're using a lot of information from interviews, because relying solely on direct quotes will soon make the paper belong more to your interviewee than to you!

Focus On: The *Los Angeles Times*/Staples Fiasco

Journalism has a special role in the preservation of democracy. But journalism is also a business, and a big business at that. Journalists work hard to keep financial considerations from affecting their judgment; and yet with waves of media mergers that fold smaller outlets into massive, publicly held conglomerates like AOL-Time Warner, Disney, and Viacom, financial pressures are increasingly affecting what you see, hear, and read. One notorious example of this is the deal struck by the *Los Angeles Times* and the office supply company Staples.

The *Los Angeles Times* is the only nationally prominent daily newspaper in the American West, and is on nearly equal terms with journalistic heavyweights like the *New York Times* and the *Washington Post*. Like those papers, the *Los Angeles Times* kept its editorial and advertising departments separated—advertisers couldn't dictate the content of articles or review articles before publication, and *Times* salespeople couldn't offer a nice write-up in an article in exchange for an ad purchase.

Enter Mark Willes. Hired as a Times Mirror Co. CEO in 1995 from his previous job at General Mills, he arrived determined to move the *Times* like a product—to sell words as efficiently as selling boxes of sugary cereal to kids. He wanted, he said, to "blow up" the wall between the advertising and writing departments; backing him up was newly hired publisher Kathyrn Downing, who also lacked any newspaper experience. In October 1999 the *Times* published a special edition of its Sunday magazine, covering the opening of the Staples Center, a sports arena, and an entertainment complex in Los Angeles. The problem? The *Times* held a financial stake in the Staples Center, a journalistic conflict of interest that it did not acknowledge in its supplement. Worse, the publisher had secretly worked out profit sharing deals with the Staples Center.

When the arrangement was revealed, journalists were appalled; even the previous publisher of the *Times* came out of retirement to denounce his successors. The CEO and the publisher of the *Times* dismissed any criticism, but as the uproar increased, they finally appointed *Times* journalist David Shaw to conduct his own investigation. Shaw concluded that "The *Times'* credibility and integrity—ultimately the only commodities a newspaper has to offer—have been severely compromised at a time when public confidence in the press is already in deep decline." Several months later, anger among the newspaper's staff at their loss of reputation caused publisher Kathryn Downing to be pushed out of her job.

As megacorporations increase the fiscal pressure on the journalists that they hire, such lapses are becoming increasingly common. "The bigger these conglomerates get, the less important their journalism gets and the more vulnerable that journalism becomes to the conglomerate's other interests," explained magazine publisher Steven Brill in an editorial on media mergers.

> These mega-companies, therefore, present a new, sweeping, and unprecedented threat to free expression, independent journalism, and a vibrant, free marketplace of ideas. Their sheer enormity makes it almost routine that they are covering a subject involving one of their own divisions or some competitor of one of their enterprises.

Disney owns ABC, and when Disney chairman Michael Eisner told a reporter: "I would prefer ABC not cover Disney .... I think it's inappropriate for Disney to be covered by Disney," the message was received loud and clear by his underlings. Days later, ABC axed a story on convicted pedophiles working at Disney theme parks. In 2000, ABC sank even lower by featuring the sock puppet from Pets.com commercials in not one but three programs: *Good Morning America, Nightline,* and *Who Wants to Be A Millionaire.* At no point was it mentioned that Disney, ABC's owner, is also part owner of Pets.com. Similar conflicts of interest have also surfaced in programming and reporting by NBC (owned by General Electric, and partnered with Microsoft) and CBS (owned by the massive media conglomerate Viacom).

This weakening ethical standard in publishing also makes newspapers vulnerable to any financial pressure. The *San Jose Mercury News* caved in when, after running a story on the ploys of used car dealerships, the dealerships pulled their advertising from the paper's automotive section. In return for a renewal of their advertising, the paper ran a full-page ad on the benefits of buying from used car dealerships.

The unrestrained chase for profits can even lead to vulnerability from government intervention. In April 2000 the online magazine *Salon* revealed that 26 magazines—including *U.S. News & World Report, Newsweek, Reader's Digest, TV Guide, People, Vibe, Family Circle, Seventeen, Parade,* and *USA Week-*

end—had received payoffs from the White House Office of National Drug Control Policy for running antidrug content. Previously, *Salon* had discovered similar collusion with the producers of such television programs as the *Drew Carey Show, Beverly Hills 90210,* and *ER.*

The problem is so overwhelming that it can be hard to know where to turn. It is possible to find out just who owns what media outlet, and what their other financial interests are. The *Columbia Journalism Review* now maintains an "owner search engine" on their Web site that allows you to type in the name of any media source to find out who owns it. But such vigilance on an everyday basis isn't practical for most consumers. Still, reading and watching independently owned media helps, as does relying on more than just one media source for your news.

Sources

Barringer, Felicity. "Merger Brings New Publisher and Editor in Los Angeles." *New York Times.* 15 Apr. 2000: A9

Brill, Steven. "The Mega Threats." *Brill's Content.* April 2000: 23–27

"CJR—Media Ownership." *Columbia Journalism Review.* Mar. 2000. 10 Apr. 2000. <http://www.cjr.org/owners/index.asp>.

Forbes, Daniel. "The Drug War Gravy Train." *Salon.* 31 Mar. 2000. 10 Apr. 2000. <http://www.salon.com/news/feature/2000/03/31/magazines/print.html>.

———."Salon News: Prime Time Propaganda." *Salon.* 13 Jan. 2000. 10 Apr. 2000. <http://www.salon.com/news/feature/2000/01/31/drugs/>.

Kaufman, Leslie. "The Sock Puppet That Roared: Internet Synergy of Conflict of Interest?" *New York Times.* 27 Mar. 2000: C1

Rosenwein, Rifka. "Why Media Mergers Matter." *Brill's Content.* Dec./Jan. 2000: 93–95

Shaw, David. "Full Disclosure." *Columbia Journalism Review.* Mar./Apr. 2000: 27–33

———."Los Angeles Times Special Report: Crossing The Line." *Los Angeles Times.* 20 Dec. 1999. 10 Apr. 2000. <http://www.latimes.com/news/reports/line/>.

Waxman, Sharon. "Los Angeles' Troubled Times: Management Is up Against the Crumbling Wall Between News and Advertising." *Washington Post.* 9 Nov. 1999: C1

Questions to Consider

1. What media sources do you get most of your news from? Do you know by whom they are owned? If net access is available, it may help to consult the *Columbia Journalism Review* site for this question. (See Sources above.)

2. What media sources are there in your town that you think might not be affected by being part of a large conglomerate—that is, that

are independently owned or nonprofit organizations? How does their news coverage differ from other media sources?

3. Are there any advertisers that may want to sway newspaper coverage of the issue that you're researching? Is there any potential for a conflict of interest in the media; that is, might media companies have a financial stake in your issue?

3

Examining Solutions

FINDING ORGANIZATIONS ASSOCIATED WITH THIS ISSUE

Assignment: Assemble a list of organizations or individuals concerned with your issue. This list doesn't need to be comprehensive, because it's just a starting point for further research. You can begin by consulting librarians, looking in the Yellow Pages, seeing who's mentioned in the articles you collected, and asking these organizations or individuals for further contacts.

Government Sources of Information

One of your best sources for information may be the biggest organization of all—the U.S. government! It's the world's largest publisher, and many of its publications are free or available at little cost. Though their style is rather dry, and they have an unsurprisingly U.S.-centered view of the world, most government publications are crammed with information:

Federal Information: 1-800-688-9889 (http://fic.info.gov). This federal clearinghouse is invaluable in helping to direct your inquiry to the right department or publication.

U.S. Government Printing Office: (202) 512-1800 (http://www.access.gpo.gov /su_docs/sale.html). You can order specific publications from them, or a catalog listing publication titles by topic.

Local Government or Representatives. Staff members for your elected representatives (mayor, senator, representatives) may be able to refer to relevant publications or upcoming public meetings.

Local Government Agency. Check your telephone directory for state, local, or federal agency branches in your area: Some will have useful publications on hand, or can at least refer you to an office that does.

County Courthouse. Here you can examine the proceedings of court cases that relate to your issue; you can also look up public documents (wills, filings, deeds, etc.) of people or organizations that you are researching.

Monthly Catalog of Government Publications. Most libraries carry this catalog in its paper or computerized form, although they may not carry all of the publications it lists. It's also available at http://www.access.gpo.gov/su_ docs/dpos/adpos400.html

Government Publications Index. Available on CD-ROM at some libraries, this covers a greater period than the monthly catalog and allows for faster keyword searching.

Freedom of Information Act. Much beloved by investigative reporters and concerned citizens, the FOIA is a powerful (if slow) tool for serious research. It allows you access to and usually copies of nonclassified documents deemed relevant to your inquiry. Even classified information may be released in censored form, though sometimes all you'll receive is page after page with everything blacked out but "the" and "and." For more information on how to make a FOIA request, see this book's appendix.

Journalist Resources. Since many journalists rely on government documents, they've developed some useful online resources. Try the Poynter Institute for Media Studies (1-888-POYNTER, www.poynter.org), or the group Investigative Reporters and Editors (www.ire.org); both put out a number of guides to using public records.

Finding Organizations

Here are a few ways to get started:

Look at Your Research. Look at the books and articles you've accumulated. Who wrote them? Who's quoted in them? If their hometown, corporate, group, or school affiliation is noted, you may be able to track them down by phone.

See the Phone Directory. You may find businesses or organizations in the Yellow Pages that are related to your field of inquiry. There may also be governmental listings (e.g., Blue Pages) of state and local agencies.

Check the Library. Check the *Encyclopedia of Associations*, which covers private and public groups in all fields and the *Research Centers Directory*, which covers nonprofit and academic research organizations. The *Research Services Directory* lists individual experts in numerous fields. You can also try the *Encyclopedia of Business Information Sources* and the *State and Regional Associations of the United States*. All of these guides, which may be in your library's reference section, provide names, addresses, phone numbers, contacts, and details about these groups. Finally, you can also look online; another guide, the *National Trade and Professional Associations of the United States*, can also be accessed at http://www.d-net.comcolumbia/pip00003/search.htm

Use a Web Search Engine. A web search engine might turn up organizations with a web presence, although it's often difficult to tell how well established or legitimate they are. If they list contacts, phone numbers, or a street address, and have links with recognized groups, then they're more likely to be legitimate.

Ask Online Groups. By asking in a relevant newsgroup or e-mail list, you may be able to quickly find a number of useful organizations. But remember to follow the netiquette and guidelines mentioned in the previous chapter's section on Internet Interviews.

Sample Response

I've found a number of groups that handle campaign finance reform, primarily through web searches and through the *Encyclopedia of Associations*. I discovered the Federal Elections Committee, though, by calling the Federal Information Center.

American Civil Liberties Union (ACLU)
125 Broad St., 18th Floor
NY NY 10004
(213) 549-2585
http://www.aclu.org

The Cato Institute
1000 Massachusetts Ave., NW
Washington DC 20001-5403
(202) 842-0200
http://www.cato.org
jbrito@cato.org

Common Cause
1250 Connecticut Ave., NW, #600
Washington DC 20036
http://www.commoncause.org

Federal Elections Committee (FEC)
999 E St NW
Washington DC 20436
(800) 424-9530
http://www.fec.gov
webmaster@fec.gov

The Heritage Foundation
214 Massachusetts Ave NE
Washington DC 20002-4999
(202) 546-4400
http://www.heritage.org
info@heritage.org

Public Campaign
1320 19th St NW, Suite M-1
Washington DC 20036
(202) 293-0222
http://www.publiccampaign.org
mengle@publiccampaign.org

Focus On: Madelyn Hoffman and Ironbound

Ironbound is a unique neighborhood in Newark, New Jersey. It received a wave of immigrants from Portugal in the 1950s and 1960s, and now has a

Portuguese population of over 30,000. Walk through town, and you'll find the latest Portuguese newspapers, soccer fans watching Portugal's soccer games on satellite TV, and Portuguese fish markets. Blended into this neighborhood's ethnic mix are many Hispanics and African Americans. What they all share in common, though, is that they have modest incomes and are sick of having toxic waste shoveled at them. But unlike many other poor neighborhoods, Ironbound residents had a surprise waiting for would-be polluters: They fought back.

Environmental clashes in Ironbound first began in 1979, when a young teacher named Madelyn Hoffman was shocked to hear that a secret dump of toxic waste had been discovered in a warehouse by her home. As she recalls, "The Newark fire director said that Ironbound was a toxic time bomb ready to explode." Ironbound was already burdened by more than its fair share of toxins. The neighborhood, bordered on three sides by railroad tracks, already had a sewage treatment plant, an incinerator, and a Superfund site. Illicitly dumped trash and industrial wastes were a constant problem. The Superfund site, discovered in 1983, was an old factory for producing Agent Orange; located just 1,000 feet from the local farmer's market, it was declared by the EPA to have one of the highest concentrations of dioxin in the world. As EPA spokesperson Rich Cahill told the *New York Times*: "These people have been through hell—toxic waste, solid waste, all kinds of waste. They felt the shock of being a Superfund site. Guys in moon suits were going into their houses to collect their vacuum cleaner bags."

Hoffman and her colleagues soon formed the Ironbound Committee Against Toxic Wastes. The group prevented further dumping in the neighborhood, and successfully pressed to have the dioxin site cleaned up more quickly. They discovered, though, that it was not to be their last fight. The state of New Jersey approved plans in 1994 for Wheelabrator Technologies to build a sludge processing plant in Ironbound; it would handle solid and hazardous wastes from surrounding municipalities. The Ironbound Committee Against Toxic Waste once again went into action. Now led by resident Arnold Cohen, and with the assistance of Tiwana Steward-Griffin, of the Rutgers University Environmental Law Clinic, residents turned to a 1994 executive order by President Clinton against "environmental racism"—that is, the tendency of cities and manufacturers to dump their wastes and waste processing plants into poor minority neighborhoods. While Clinton's order was directed to federal agencies, and not to state agencies like the ones controlling Ironbound's fate, the committee was able to convince neighbors and state officials that building another incinerator in an already dangerously contaminated neighborhood was wrong. In March 1997 the State Department of Environmental Protection denied Wheelabrator the final permit for their plant.

In recent years Madelyn Hoffman has gone from a concerned citizen to a leading voice in statewide environmentalism. She formed the Grass Roots Environmental Organization, and in 1998 ran as a Green Party candidate for vice president and for governor. She is running in the 2000 election for the House of Representatives. And Ironbound's successful fights are setting an important precedent for other poor neighborhoods; in early 1998 the EPA announced a policy of enforcing "environmental justice" for similar communities. With increasing scrutiny of where dumps are located and on the building of minority-attended schools atop old dumps, even more citizens are now taking their health into their own hands and challenging the dumping of toxins near their homes.

Sources

Bullard, Robert and Beverly Wright (eds.). *Confronting Environmental Racism.* Cambridge, MA: South End Press, 1993

"Candidate List." Women's Voting Guide. 5 Jun. 2000. <http://www.womenvote.org/candlist.html>.

"Center for Health, Environment, and Justice Home." Center for Health, Environment, and Justice. 4 Jan. 2000. <http://www.essential.org/cchw/index.html>.

"The EcoJustice Network." EcoJustice Network. 4 Jan. 2000. <http://www.igc.org/envjustice/>.

Levy, Clifford. "A Portuguese Village in Newark." *New York Times.* 6 Oct. 1995: C1

"Living on Earth Transcript: Ironbound Community Stops Sewage Plant." Living on Earth. 4 Apr. 1997. 4 Jan. 2000) <http://www.loe.org/archives/970411.html>.

Mansnerus, Laura. "NYT Archives Article: Newark's Toxic Tomb." 8 Nov. 1998. New York Times. 5 Jun. 2000. <http://www.nytimes.com>.

Smothers, Ronald. "Ironbound Draws Its Line at the Dump, and Wins." *New York Times.* 29 Mar. 1997: 22

Teciher, Stacy. "Schools Atop Dumps: Environmental Racism?" *Christian Science Monitor.* 4 Nov. 1999: 3

"Vice Presidential Nomination." The Green Party of New Jersey. 4 Jan. 2000. <http://www.gpnj.org/vpnomin.html>.

Weintraub, Irwin. "Fighting Environmental Racism: A Selected Annotated Bibliography." June 1994. University of Idaho. 4 Jan. 2000. <http://egj.uidaho.edu/egj/weint01.html>.

Questions To Consider

1. How did research into other organizations by Ironbound residents help their group?

2. What might have prevented Ironbound's solution from working? What other options might they have had if this solution had failed?

3. What area do you know of that acts as a dumping ground? Does that area have a economic or racial profile that would make Ironbound's approach usable? Why or why not?

LOOKING FOR PUBLICATIONS BY ORGANIZATIONS

Assignment: Using your organization list, look for pamphlets or web pages by these groups, or statements they've made in the press, or call them for information. What is their response to the problem? What kind of solutions do they propose?

(Note: As with the previous assignment, this is only meant to give you a start! Actually contacting these organizations and getting their publications will be a continuing assignment that may take weeks or months.)

Understanding Statistics

While community and interest groups are often happy to give you all kinds of anecdotes and statistics, you have to take these with a grain of salt. After all, they're presenting facts that make their cause look better, so they'll tend to ignore information that works against them.

Statistics are powerful tools in their efforts; it's hard to argue with people who have the numbers on their side. But numbers are not what they always seem to be. Many of the rules and examples that follow are from a superb book by John Allen Paulos, *A Mathematician Reads the Newspaper* (New York: Anchor Books, 1995). Two older but equally useful texts are the weighty *Use and Abuse of Statistics* by W. J. Reichmann (New York: Penguin Books, 1973), and Darrell Huff's entertaining *How to Lie With Statistics* (New York: W. W. Norton, 1954).

Unrepresentative Sampling—Polls may be swayed by who does or doesn't choose to respond. Examples:

1. If Fortune magazine polls its readers on the presidential race, will the results mirror the general population? (Not when its readers are primarily white male business executives.)

2. A college's survey says the average graduate earns $40,000 a year. (But successful ones are more likely to respond than bankrupt failures).

3. A 900-number poll. (Are people who call 900 numbers representative of the entire public?)

Incomplete Sampling—Polls can have a shockingly low response rate: as little as 20 percent, according to an investigative piece in the *New York Times* (Van Natta Jr., Don. "Polling's 'Dirty Little Secret': No Response." 21 Nov. 1999: 4–1). Many polls simply discard "no-answer" responses, heedless of the fact that those who do choose to answer will not represent the general population.

Median versus Average—Averages are the sum divided by the number of sources, and so will be affected by any unusually high or low aberrations; the median is that point at which half of the respondents are lower and half are higher, thus giving a better representation of how most respondents are. Example: A politician claims the average tax rate is 40 percent; that may be true, but a relatively few superrich pull the curve up. The median tax rate—what half the population pays less than, and half more than—might be closer to 20 percent.

Incidence versus National Totals—If someone wants to downplay a problem, they give the incidence rate: "1 in 100,000 are affected." Doesn't sound likely to happen to you, does it? But to play up a problem, state the raw number of national occurrences: in this case, "nearly 3,000 people." That's a lot of people taken all together—enough to fill a scary public service ad, a documentary, or a class-action lawsuit.

Restating a Question—Polls are notorious for the extent to which their phrasing can affect an answer. Example: When asked if the poor deserve more financial assistance, most people say "Yes." When asked if the poor deserve more welfare or food stamps, most people say "No." Although the questions are not identical, both sides will now claim: "Most people agree with us!"

"Don't Know"—Adding a "Don't Know" option to a poll can produce dramatically different results. Without this option, many respondents feel obliged to give an opinion to a pollster, even if they know nothing about an issue. The resulting poll can show a population that appears much more opinionated than it actually is.

Numbers Out of Context—An overly narrow or broad sampling can be unrepresentative for a population. Example: Vietnam MIAs (Missing in Action) seem high (2,000) until seen in the context of World War II MIAs (80,000) and Korean War MIAs (8,000).

Numbers in a Changing Context—A change in numbers may not reflect a change in the participants; rather, the pool of participants may have changed. Example: Average SAT scores have declined over the last 2 decades. Are we becoming less educated? Not necessarily; it used to be that only the most prepared students went to college. More students from a wider array of backgrounds take the SAT now, including those with lower scores who were generally absent from the earlier exams.

Anchoring—After first hearing a number or explanation, people tend to judge subsequent numbers or events in those terms, no matter how arbitrary or false the initial information may have been. This psychological tendency becomes especially troublesome when false initial data gets reinforced through repetition (see below). Example: Mention the number 2 million to one group of people and then 100 million to another; then ask them to estimate the population of Argentina. The latter group's estimates will be far higher.

Repeat It Enough Times and It's True—Avoid numbers that seemingly everyone quotes as "true," even though there isn't a shred of direct evidence for it. Often these numbers are false or have been misinterpreted from the original source. Your only defense is to insist on actual research to back up these claims.

Uneven Media Coverage—"If it bleeds, it leads" is the old journalist's maxim. If someone cites how many media stories have been written about something as evidence—"You hear about it on TV all the time!"—then they're on shaky ground. Media coverage often has little direct relation to severity. Examples:

1. In one 2-year period, even the staid *New York Times* ran .02 page-one cancer stories per 1,000 deaths, and 138 page-one airplane crash stories per 1,000 deaths (Paulos 81).

2. Legal drugs kill far more people every year than illegal drugs; which gets more coverage?

False Causality—Two phenomena may commonly occur around each other, but they don't necessarily cause each other to happen. Example: People who drink a certain brand of expensive bottled water tend to be healthier than the general public, but the people who buy expensive bottled water also tend to be in the middle- to upper-income groups and thus have better health care; the water itself isn't making the difference.

Sampling Error—When a survey gauges an event or trend by "sampling" a smaller group—for example, polling 1,000 people to gauge the attitude of the nation—then a certain amount of error is inevitable. There will be some discrepancy between the group and the actual population as a whole. Error is decreased by larger samples, a sample that clearly represents a cross section of the population, by clearly worded questions, and by higher response rates. Polling and other sampling techniques should always indicate their margin of error. Although we typically quote specific numbers because it's more convenient, a statistician gives an accurate range of possible figures. That's why, for example, two election candidates with ratings of 41 percent and 43 percent, in a poll with a 3 percent margin of error, are in a "statistical dead heat." The first candidate's range extends as high as 44 percent and the second's is as low as 40 percent; without further polling, no winner can be accurately predicted. Their "lead" may be meaningless.

False Precision—The margin of error also tells the magnitude of the figure that's worth quoting. There's no point in saying that politician A has 41.3 percent of the vote when the real range is anywhere from 38 percent to 44 percent. And when you're adding up lots of different polling results, your "roundest" or least-exact one determines your range of error. If one poll respondent reports incomes to the cent and another reports incomes to the dollar, you can only accurately cite figures to the dollar. A common example of this false precision is in food labeling. There are almost certainly not exactly 250 calories in the candy bar that you're eating. There are probably 230 to 270 calories in there, depending on variations in each candy bar's manufacture.

Understanding Graphs and Charts

Graphs and other visual aids are user-friendly ways of presenting statistical data, because you don't need to interpret raw numbers to get their gist. They're a good means of presenting complex data to a lay reader.

They're also typical ways of giving information to a casual reader, which is why more accessible newspapers like *USA Today* rely so heavily on them. You're getting third-hand information in a newspaper graph: First the raw numbers are created by a researcher, then they are condensed and simplified for the press release that the article quotes from, and finally they are reinterpreted and further simplified by a graphics department. What finally emerges as a graph can be distorted or downright misleading. Here's what to watch out for:

Changing the Axis Proportion—By making an axis more or less precise (e.g., changing it from $1 million per inch to $10 million per inch) what was once a slight rise turns into a dramatically steep slope, and vice versa.

Changing the Zero Line—Graphs that shorten their vertical axis by starting at a number higher than zero give the false impression of a greater magnitude of change. This is one of the most common flaws in newspaper graphs.

Misleading Proportion—Doubling the proportions of a figure quadruples its volume. Example: Car maker A sells twice as many cars as maker B. Representing this with a car drawing twice the height and length of the other drawing is misleading, since maker A's car drawing is now really four times the volume of the other.

Connotative Graphics—The use of artwork or symbols can add a biased connotation to otherwise strictly factual data. Examples: (a) a merger chart that represents a conglomerate as a devouring octopus; (b) Cartoon graphics that incorporate a rising graph of company profits into a picture of a smiling worker.

Linear Extrapolation—The assumption that a trend will continue in a linear fashion. This error is sometimes made in the "projected" portion of a graph. Not all phenomena increase or decrease at the same rate indefinitely: there may eventually be diminishing returns or a sudden arc upward or downward. Examples:

1. Giving your dog an extra pound of meat a day may increase his weight by 1/5 pound. But put 100 pounds of meat in his bowl, and he probably won't gain 20 pounds in one day!

2. AIDS. Epidemiologists often note that viral infections increase slowly and regularly for years before reaching a "critical mass" of carriers, at which point they explode upward.

Changing the Basis of Comparison—Let's say that you want to alarm the public about government spending. You unfurl a map that shows that spending on widgets equals the tax revenue from every state from Nevada to Ohio, not including Texas and Illinois. With all these states shaded in, the map will look ominous indeed. Now let's say you want to calm down the public about widget spending. You unfurl a map that shows just two states shaded in: New York and California. The entire rest of the country is unshaded. Doesn't look so threatening now, does it?

What's happened here is that one basis of comparison—state income, which hardly correlates with size (tiny Rhode Island, for example, outproduces massive North Dakota)—is being jammed into a map format whose normal basis of comparison is size. Always keep an eye on what the real basis of comparison is, because maps and other visual representation—describing an amount of money by how high a pile of dollar bills it would make, for example—can often obscure the relevant basis for comparing or understanding data.

Sample Response

Among campaign finance reform efforts, Common Cause makes the most noise in the media. But its Web site, while quick to report the outrageous spending by politicians and their cronies, is nebulous on specific solutions.

Instead, it works as a watchdog and as a state-by-state advocate for bills seeking greater candidate accountability and greater controls on "soft money," or the unregulated contributions that corporations and special interest groups make to political parties. Common Cause provides e-mail addresses for various senators so that you can write them about your support for the latest version of such reform; there are also calls for letter writing campaigns to the Federal Elections Commission (FEC), in protest of their choice of a new chairman, and to CBS to pressure it to follow up on a proposal to grant free air time to candidates ("Common Cause: Take Action").

The weakness to Common Cause's approach is in the resistance of Congress to passing such laws; neither side is interested in cutting off their donors, and so they persist in passing such bills in only one chamber of Congress. You can send all the e-mails you want to your senator, but it still isn't in their personal interest to change such laws. And even if such a bill were passed, it would be challenged by such free-speech advocates as the American Civil Liberties Union (ACLU).

Public Campaign is more specific in its goals. It created a "Model Legislation for Clean Money Campaign Reform." It addresses the concerns that would have dogged the bills previously supported by Public Campaign, usually by alterations made in response to the ACLU, thus lessening the chance that it would encounter that group's opposition ("Clean Money Campaign Reform").

In short, the bill provides that:

1. Candidates using government funds cannot also use private or personal funds.
2. After raising enough seed money in $5 amounts from individuals, candidates qualify for government Clean Money funding.
3. If their opponent refuses to follow the rules for Clean Money and persists in raising "dirty" money from private sources, then the Clean Money candidate can receive matching funds to stay competitive ("Clean Money Campaign Reform").

The total cost for the system is estimated at $1.3 billion per 2-year election cycle ("Just the FAQs"). The advantage of this proposal is that it does not force reform on candidates, leaving their free speech unabridged. The question, though, is whether candidates would use Clean Money if they didn't have to, and whether Congress would fund this program. Though $650 million a year is chump change compared with the larger expenditures Congress approves, it's still enough money that an opportunistic senator might score points by cutting it from the budget.

The ACLU remains opposed to limits on spending because it sees them as a limit on free speech ("Support Constitutional Campaign Finance Reform"). While the ACLU offers no solution to campaign finance, it makes clear that it doesn't like limits on fund raising, different mail or broadcast rates for Clean Money candidates, required record keeping of small contributions (e.g., $20), the ability of the Federal Elections Commission to contest campaigns while an election is still in progress, and any ban or restriction on

Political Action Committees (PACs)—that is, the industry and labor groups that contribute much of the soft money in elections ("February 20, 1997 Letter … ").

The ACLU's stand has the advantage of constitutional purity: *if* one defines money as equivalent to speech, then these objections insure that speech would be unhindered. But that's a big if. The ACLU's stand also leaves us where we started: in a system of "might is right," where the candidate with the most money usually wins.

The Web sites for both the conservative Cato Institute and the Heritage Foundation include a number of annotated papers on campaign finance. Cato Institute author Bradley Smith argues that the separation of "soft" and "hard" money is in fact working quite well, and has the advantage of not infringing on the First Amendment. In fact, he claims the existing limits on hard money ($1,000 by individuals to a candidate, $5,000 to a PAC) hurt because they force politicians to campaign longer and discourage those who lack the stamina to chase down such "small" amounts. Smith also attacks federal financing as too supportive of "extremist" candidates of the ultraleft and ultraright, thus "forcing citizens to pay for others to express opposing opinions" ("Campaign Finance Reform"). Smith goes on to argue that "Contrary to the assumption that large contributions are undemocratic is the reality that most challenges to the status quo and most working-class political movements have been financed by wealthy donors" ("Campaign Finance Regulation").

The Cato Institute's arguments presume that unrestricted campaign funds will flow to the "best" candidate rather than to the candidate who grants favors to wealthy donors—though in the view of the wealthy, perhaps that's exactly who the best candidate is. The complaint about the public funding of "opposing" views misapprehends the nature of elections. Voters are liable to change their minds at any point—otherwise, why campaign or debate at all? Anyone's stance is liable to be opposing, at least in retrospect. We can only know that a view opposes ours after our vote is cast; up until then we may change our mind. Finally, Smith's contention that the wealthy are the best friends of working-class movements is hard to believe. But like the ACLU, Smith's approach has the advantage of simplicity and of not clashing with the Constitution.

A similar argument is raised through the Heritage Foundation by Lamar Alexander. In his 1996 run for president, he claims, donation limits forced him to attend fundraisers daily: "As a result, I became acquainted with a great many good Americans capable of giving $1,000 (who probably represent a cross section of about one percent of all the people in the country)." His implication is that had he been able to get this fundraising out of the way with a few unlimited donations, he'd have had more time to mingle with working people. Furthermore, limits favor incumbents who already have donors at hand, and wealthy individuals who can ignore limits by simply using their personal fortune ("Off With the Limits").

Alexander's argument has the advantage of sounding reasonable, as constantly attending fundraisers does sound like a drain on candidates. But will a well-connected incumbent's advantage of a donor list evaporate with a lifting of limits? Now, instead of being $1 million or $2 million ahead of a challenger, they can be $10 million or $20 million ahead. The stakes will be raised on both sides, but the uneven ratio may remain the same.

As for the contention that time away from the wealthy at fundraisers will be spent with working-class people instead, well, it's a little hard to believe. It's a nice thought, and it may be true for Mr. Alexander, but I've yet to see a politician who wouldn't rather spend their free time with their well-educated and well-fed peers.

Works Cited

Alexander, Lamar. "Off With the Limits: What I Learned About Money and Politics When I Ran for President." Heritage Foundation. 26 May 1996. 13 Apr. 2000. <http://www.heritage.org/library/categories/govern/lect568.html>.

"Clean Money Campaign Reform." Public Campaign. 13 Apr. 2000.<http://www.publiccampaign.org/cleanmoney.html>.

"Common Cause: Take Action." Common Cause. 19 Apr. 2000) <http://www.commoncause.org/get_involved/action.htm>.

Gora, Joel. "February 20, 1997 Letter to Senator McConnell on the Bipartisan Campaign Finance Reform Act of 1997." American Civil Liberties Union. 20 Feb. 1997. 13 Apr. 2000. <http://www.aclu.org/congress/ls022097a.html>.

"Just the FAQs." Public Campaign. 17 Apr. 2000. <http://www.publiccampaign.org/DA.html>.

Smith, Bradley. "Campaign Finance Reform: Soft Money and the Presidential System." Cato Institute. 14 May 1997. 13 Apr. 2000. <http://www.cato.org/testimony/ct-bs051497.html>.

———. "Campaign Finance Regulation." Cato Institute. 13 Sept. 1995. 13 Apr. 2000. <http://www.cato.org/pubs/pas/pa238.html>.

"Support Constitutional Campaign Finance Reform." American Civil Liberties Union. 13 Apr. 2000. <http://www.aclu.org/congress/campaignfinance.html>.

Focus On: Rescue MUNI

While San Francisco's MUNI public transit system has the most celebrated vehicles in the world, such as cable cars and the antique streetcar line that runs along Market Street, by the late 1990s the buses and light rail that actually carry most city residents were in deep trouble. Breakdowns and employee absenteeism were common, and riders were increasingly fleeing a system that couldn't stick to any recognizable schedule.

Underfunded public transit and public frustration became an explosive mixture. One mayor lost an election in part due to this anger, and a monthly bicycle rally turned into a near riot. City politicians continued to insist that service was improving, would improve at any moment, or simply couldn't be helped. "MUNI riders have to get real," Mayor Willie Brown bluntly told reporters when asked about the possibility of the buses ever meeting their published schedules. This was easy for him to say—he wasn't riding the bus to work.

Two passengers did get real about bus schedules. Ken Neimi and George Musser both rode MUNI every day to work, and both were bothered that nobody was addressing the daily problems of riders. The only model that fit was the Straphangers Campaign, a grassroots riders' group that started in New York City in 1979. Two decades later, it was still raising a fuss with provocative ads and by using the courts to get better service for riders. Out of desperation, Musser and Neimi formed their own grassroots group, Rescue MUNI, in September 1996. They adopted as their logo a city bus with a bandage wrapped around it. Though the task was a far cry from Musser's day job as the editor of an astronomy magazine, the two took it to heart. Offering membership for $10—a fee they waived for anyone who couldn't afford it—they soon gathered enough funds and frustrated commuters to start their own informal survey of MUNI's service.

In the first two weeks of February 1997, over 100 volunteers took note of how long they had to wait for various bus and train lines to show up. When Musser and Neimi compiled the results and released a report the following month, rider frustration couldn't be ignored anymore. It was all over the media; according to the survey, 25 percent of all buses and trains ran late. As Rescue MUNI's report put it: "This means that a commuter who takes MUNI to and from work can expect to be delayed *every other day*. Riders who transfer once a day can expect to be delayed *every day*." The report also pointed out which three lines were the worst offenders, with late runs 55, 43, and 42 percent of the time, respectively. These lines, perhaps not coincidentally, ran through low-income and minority neighborhoods.

The report matched some of MUNI's own internal data, and it was presented in an impressive manner. The methodology (how the survey was conducted), results, and suggestions for improvement were all explained. A short press release summarizing the findings accompanied the report, allowing the media to quickly report the survey's results.

Although MUNI service still has a long way to go, few people now dispute Rescue MUNI's basic findings; in fact, reforms like bus timetables and improved on-time performance were pushed through from the resulting public pressure. Rescue MUNI now conducts the survey annually, and they successfully sponsored a transit reform initiative (Proposition E) that passed by a wide margin in the November 1999 city elections. The group that started out of the frustration of two bus riders now has the ear of City Hall and the media alike.

Sources

Bowman, Catherine. "Bus Riders Union Won't Stay Seated." *San Francisco Chronicle*. 31 Mar. 1997: A1

Delgado, Ray. "MUNI's Report Card: Not Improving." *San Francisco Examiner*. 8 Apr. 1998: A1

Epstein, Edward. "MUNI Manager Announces New, Precise Timetables." *San Francisco Chronicle*. 2 September 1999: A23

"Fix the MUNI." Z San Francisco. 6 Jan. 2000. <http://www.zpub.com/fixmuni/>.

Gledhill, Lynda. "MUNI Barely Gets Passing Grade From Passenger Group: Small Upgrade From Rating Bestowed Earlier This Year." *San Francisco Chronicle.* 29 Oct. 1998: C2

Kennedy, Randy. "Agency Relents on Subway Ad." *New York Times.* 18 Mar. 2000: A12

Nolte, Carl. "Consistently Late Buses, Streetcars Earn MUNI a Poor Rating." *San Francisco Chronicle.* 20 Mar. 1997: A17

"Rescue MUNI." Rescue MUNI. 6 Jan. 2000. <http://www.rescuemuni.org>.

"Straphangers Campaign." Straphangers Campaign. 6 Jan. 2000 <http://www.straphangers.org>.

Sward, Susan. "Measure Designed to Improve MUNI Rolls to Victory: Rider Frustration Led to Initiative." *San Francisco Chronicle.* 3 Nov. 1999: A23

"Tri-State Transportation Campaign Home Page." Tri-State Transportation Campaign. 6 Jan. 2000. <http://www.tstc.org>.

Questions to Consider

1. What factors might affect the accuracy of Rescue MUNI's figures?

2. How might the point of view of Rescue MUNI and its volunteers be biased?

3. What are the advantages to making an informal, volunteer survey like Rescue MUNI's?

ANALYZING HOW AN ISSUE AFFECTS OTHER COMMUNITIES

Assignment: Search for articles detailing this problem as it has affected other communities, even in other countries. What solutions have other communities tried for similar problems? Might these solutions work in your community? Why or why not?

Finding Scholarly Articles on Your Subject

There are a number of ways for you to track down articles on your subject; these include periodical indexes, journal indexes, computer indexes, and specialized indexes. General sources like encyclopedias and periodicals will help give you a grasp of the basics of your topic, but soon you'll need the kind of specific detail found through periodical indexes. To get even harder data—that is, to find articles that are aimed at fellow professionals within the field, rather than at an inexperienced public audience—you'll need to look at the specialized indexes for your field.

CD-ROM indexes and online indexes can provide a more efficient way of searching, though each computer resource is different in its level of specialization. Some are aimed at general use, while others are intended for professional-level research. Don't be intimidated by these, though. Articles from popular periodicals make a fine starting point for you and your readers; and as your knowledge progresses, you'll find the specialized journals both easier to understand and more useful.

Periodical Indexes

The Magazine Index. Begun in 1976 and available in CD-ROM, online, and on microfilm. This index catalogues 400 magazines. While it's useful for general research, it does emphasize popular magazines. You may not find the specialized information required to sustain deeper research.

National Newspaper Index. lists articles by subject from five prominent newspapers: the *New York Times, Christian Science Monitor, Washington Post, Wall Street Journal,* and *Los Angeles Times.*

New York Times Index. (Started 1913; available in print, CD-ROM, and online). As the premier national newspaper, the *New York Times* should be one of your first stops. The index lists articles alphabetically by subject. Every issue of the *New York Times,* beginning with the first issue in 1851, is available on microfilm; more recent articles are also on CD-ROM and online. This is especially useful for social issues, politics, and arts reporting.

Newspaper Abstracts. With citations beginning in the late 1980s, this computerized index and summary covers about 30 national and international newspapers.

Reader's Guide to Periodical Literature. (Available in print, CD-ROM, and online). This index covers hundreds of general and special-interest magazines, including nearly all the ones that you'd find at a typical newsstand. It's ideal for current events coverage, especially for public reactions at the time of past events. From 1802 to 1906 this was titled *Poole's Index to Periodical Literature.*

Journal Indexes

These five indexes, available in print and CD-ROM, are produced by the publisher of the *Reader's Guide to Periodical Literature*, so they're similarly organized:

Humanities Index. Started in 1974, this index covers nearly 300 periodicals in archeology, area studies, arts, classics, folklore, languages, literature, philosophy, and religion.

Social Science Index. Started in 1974 and updated quarterly, this index covers about 300 periodicals in anthropology, economic, environmental science, geography, law, medicine, political science, psychology, and sociology.

General Science Index. Started in 1978, this covers over 100 journals in astronomy, atmospheric science, biology, botany, chemistry, environmental science, genetics, mathematics, medicine, microbiology, nutrition, oceanography, physics, psychology, and zoology.

Education Index. (Founded 1929.) Covers over 300 journals in education and the arts.

Business Periodical Index. (Founded 1958.) Covers journals in business, economics, finance, and regulation.

Computer Indexes

Your library may have some of these indexes; they're often easier and more efficient than paper indexes. They're updated several times a year, but typically only cover articles from the last decade or less.

ABI/Inform. Indexes journals in business, economics, health care, and management, and also provides the full text of about a third of these articles.

ERIC. Indexes education-related journals; it is also a clearinghouse for the texts of these articles.

InfoTrac. This is a metaindex covering the *Academic Index* (scholarly journals), *General Periodicals Index* (popular magazines and business periodicals), *Government Publications Index*, and the *National Newspaper Index*.

Medline. Indexes periodicals in medicine, nursing, and pharmacology.

MLA Bibliography. Indexes journals in folklore, languages, linguistics, and literature.

PAIS (Public Affairs Information Service). Indexes consumer news, economics, government, and politics.

Psychlit. Indexes psychology journals.

Sociofile. Indexes journals in anthropology, health, psychology, and sociology.

Online Indexes

Commercial online indexes are often more powerful and current than printed indexes or CD-ROM. You may either download their information to disc, print it out, or order a copy by mail. They charge for their time, however, with prices ranging from inexpensive public use to very expensive professional services. Your school library may have reduced rates or even provide free services for students, though.

Dialog: a service covering hundreds of databases, including periodicals, statistics, and full-text articles. (www.dialog.com)

First Search: a search engine that covers indexes and full-text articles for periodicals and newspapers. (www.ref.oclas.org/html/fs_pswd.htm)

Info Trac Search Bank: encompasses and updates their CD-ROM index resources.

Lexis: a search service and database covering full texts of legal cases, filings, and statutes on the federal and state level. (www.lexis.nexis.com)

Nexis: provides summaries and full texts from over 8,700 periodicals and newspapers. (www.lexis.nexis.com)

Other Sources Inside the Library

Special Collections. Libraries often have unique collections by subject or author that are shelved separately from the main library stacks. Ask the staff if there are special collections relating to your subject.

UnCover. This is a keyword-driven database and article-delivery service covering nearly 1700 journals (www.carl.org/uncover/).

Metacrawler. Includes a number of WWW search engines (www.metacrawler.com).

EBSCOhost. Features Academic Search (full text of over 1,000 journals), ERIC (index and abstracts in education research), and CINAHL (index and abstracts in health care). A password is needed to access this site, though your school may have automatic access (www.epnet.com/ehost/login.html).

WEBSPIRS. Silver Platter's Electronic Reference Library includes PsychINFO, MEDLINE EXPRESS, and ERIC. A password is needed to access this site, though your school may have automatic access (http://webspirs.silverplatter.com/cgi-bin/er18.cgi).

AskERIC. Has ERIC materials from 1991 to the present. A password is needed to access this site, though your school may have automatic access (http://edrs.com/cgi-bin/askERIC).

Stat-USA/Internet. Has business and economic information produced by the federal government. A password is needed to access this site, though your school may have automatic access (www.stat-usa.gov).

FedWorld Information Network. Run by the National Technical Information Service, and assembles and links a variety of government Web sites (www.fedworld.gov).

Looking Outside Your Library

Government Publications. Check your library's reference desk for the *Monthly Catalog* published by the U.S. Government Printing Office (GPO). It lists prices and ordering information for all government publications.

Interlibrary Loans. Even if your library doesn't have a crucial source, it may have an interlibrary loan agreement with a library that does. Ask your librarian how to arrange for a book transfer.

Special Collections. Other libraries may have a special collection or archive on your subject. Your library may be familiar with these collections, and you can also consult the reference guide *Directory of Special Libraries and Information Centers*.

Public Broadcasting. Contact your PBS station to see whether they've broadcast any documentaries on your topic. You may be able to order a copy or a transcript.

Bookstores. While it takes libraries time to order and process new books, bookstores generally have new books available immediately upon publication. The drawback, of course, is that you'll have to buy the book! Try checking these trade catalogs in your library or bookstore: *Books in Print* or *Subject Guide to Books in Print*.

Pamphlets. To find what pamphlets are available in your library or through other agencies, check the *Vertical File Index: A Subject and Title Index to Selected Pamphlet Material*. To find what organizations may have published such material, see *The Encyclopedia of Associations*, which covers private and public groups in all fields; also try the *Research Centers Directory*, which covers nonprofit and academic research organizations. Both guides provide names, addresses, phone numbers, contacts, and details about their publications.

Using Your Own Statistics and Charts

Are library sources on your topic few and far between? Is the data you're finding simply unconvincing to you? If you're prepared to invest some extra time in this research, an informal survey can be useful for impressionistic and personal data—especially when you don't have the time or resources to undertake a large enough survey to get reliable statistics.

First, specify your target group; what type of people will be most useful to speak with? Decide on what types of questions you'll use: open-ended, direct (yes/no), multiple choice, or rated (e.g., on a scale of 1 to 5).

You may survey by phone, mail, or in person at a relevant location. Since it is an informal survey, the number of respondents is not crucial—though more is better, since this lowers the chances of your data getting skewed by an exception or two.

Type your survey questions for legibility, and try to keep them to take 5 to 10 minutes to answer at the most. Prepare for refusals from respondents; some surveys, particularly mailed ones, can have a low response rate, so make many more copies than the replies you expect to receive.

Avoid biased questions, with loaded or prejudged words. Your question should not assume too much knowledge on the part of your respondents; if they're not familiar with the issue, they're either not useful respondents, or they need to be debriefed on the issue fairly before you ask them any questions about it.

Just because you make a survey doesn't mean that you have to use the results, because not every question will provide a clear or useful one. You may end up citing the results of only one or two of your questions. Be prepared to get results that you don't expect, or to get none at all. It could mean that (a) your questions were poorly designed; (b) your group sample isn't a representative cross section; or finally (c) there is some factor you haven't considered that you now need to add into your work. That's why you have a tentative hypothesis—it can be changed at any time by new research results.

Sample Response

The "Law Library" web page of the U.S. House of Representatives has links to the constitutions and campaign finance laws of various states and countries; their inclusion gives lawmakers an awareness of how others arrange their election process. Maine's new election laws are of particular interest, as are the measures taken by our neighbor, British Columbia.

In 1995, British Columbia's Election Act created a new system of candidate nomination, advertising, and financing. Candidates may be nominated by collecting 25 signatures and making a deposit of $100 (about U.S. $75) ("Guide to the Election Act"). This takes enough effort to prevent flippant candidacies, but is in reach of someone willing to stake a little money and spend an afternoon collecting signatures.

Candidates can then buy advertising at the lowest commercial rate on TV and radio, and in print. They cannot spend more than $50,000 on their campaign, however. (The limit can be raised for larger voting districts.) Similarly, political parties are limited in their budgets, with a ceiling of $1.25 per registered voter per electoral district ("Guide to the Election Act"). A "third-party" advertiser (e.g., interest groups, corporations, unions) first has to register with the province's Chief Electoral Officer, and is then restrained to a $5,000 budget ("Media Obligations").

For candidates, political parties, and third parties alike, the identity of contributors of more than $250 has to be disclosed publicly. Anonymous contributions are limited to $50; political parties can accept a total of up to $10,000 in anonymous donations, while individual candidates are limited to $3,000 ("Guide to the Election Act").

British Columbia's system has some clear advantages over ours. It does not restrict speech, just the spending of large quantities of money to broadcast speech. This forces candidates to use debates, interviews, and in-person appearances to convey their views to the public, rather than relying on the bludgeoning but impersonal power of TV advertising. And while third parties and major political parties can gather some funds to get their message across to voters, they can't overwhelm other points of view by sheer force of money.

Of course, such fiscal limitations would come under fire in the United States as a restriction of free speech, even though it is the repetitive paid broadcasting of speech, and not the expression of any belief, that is actually being restricted. A more serious problem is that the law's fiscal limits are arbitrary: There's nothing magic about the $1.25 or $10,000. What's more, there's no indication of indexing to account for inflation. I suspect that a few years from now there will be a debate over the adjustment of this figure to a higher level. With this adjustment comes the possibility of a grab by hungry politicians for a much higher figure.

In Maine, one such system already is in place, but only on a voluntary basis. The state's Clean Election Act provides full financing for candidates who collect a sufficient number of $5 donations. Candidates collect 50 (House) or 150 (Senate) $5 checks before a March 16 deadline. This screens out truly marginal or gag candidates, while not presenting too much of an obstacle to poor or newcomer candidates. Once they have advanced to the general election, candidates can then spend state funds up to $12,000 in House races and $40,000 for the Senate. In return, they are not allowed to take any outside contributions. (Goldberg A9).

In the 2000 election, 115 of the state's 374 registered candidates took this clean money option (A1). The advantages are obvious, and similar to those of the British Columbia plan: a leveled playing field for candidates who are poor or not political insiders, and a loosening of the choke hold that corporate and labor special interests have on political candidates. But the Clean Election Act's continued survival is due to the very fact that makes it vulnerable to failure: It is voluntary. If candidates don't want to be "clean," they can go and raise obscene amounts in the old-fashioned way. This voluntary aspect means that the state can't be sued by a candidate for restricting free speech, but it also means that politicians could just ignore the clean option en masse—or that those who do choose clean money might find themselves overpowered by a less regulated "dirty" opponent.

The British Columbian plan strikes me as a good start. But in adapting it to this country, I would find a less arbitrary way of determining the money limits, as well as a way of indexing them so that they wouldn't be vulnerable to renegotiation every few years. And, as in the case of Maine, I think a voluntary public funding plan may be the only constitutional way to enact such reforms at the state level; this would avoid legal challenges, but we would also need constant public pressure on politicians to get them to accept Clean Money and its restrictions.

Works Cited

Goldberg, Carey. "Mainers Try a Donation-Free Campaign." *New York Times.* 1 Apr. 2000: A1

"Guide to the Election Act." Elections British Columbia. 1 Jun. 1999. 19 Apr. 2000. <http://www.elections.bc.ca/guidebooks/p855_toc.html>.

"Guide to Election Communications." Elections British Columbia. 1 June 1999. 19 Apr. 2000. <http://www.elections.bc.ca/guidebooks/p870_toc.html>.

"Media Obligations Under the New Election Act." Elections British Columbia. 1 Jun. 1999. 19 Apr. 2000. <http://www.elections.bc.ca/guidebook/p862_toc.html>.

U.S. House of Representatives. "Internet Law Library; Election, Qualification, Removal, and Lobbying of Public Officials." Pritchard Law Webs. 31 Mar. 2000. 19 Apr. 2000. <http://www.priweb.com/internetlawlib/149.htm>.

Focus On: Grameen Microloans

How can looking at other communities inspire a solution? In Chicago, community businesses and entrepreneurs have joined "lending circles" in which they secure each other's small business loans. The circle is run through Chicago's Women's Self-Employment project, which in a 3-year period lent to over 60 low-income women—all without a single default. These loans have helped build jewelry classes, clothiers, and security companies. All five women in each circle are responsible for a member's loan, and no more than two members at a time can take out a loan. This helps spread the burden of financing through the whole group, and makes use of peer pressure as a sort of "social collateral," as *Forbes* magazine has dubbed it.

The notion started in Bangladesh, where the Grameen Bank pioneered the concept of microloans, and it's spread from Third World countries to American cities. The microloans to these lending circles specifically help "credit risks" in low-income groups prove that they can help each other to prosperity. In Bangladesh alone, over a thousand Grameen branches have helped two million primarily female customers, and have financed the building of 325,000 homes.

Our country places a great emphasis on the myth of personal initiative, that is, the hardy individual who starts a business from scratch. But through mutual support these entrepreneurs help each other build businesses together that none of them could have built alone. Considering how many other community enterprises rely on mutual responsibility, Grameen's vision may be a much more realistic one for the beginning entrepreneur.

Even so, a banking concept from Bangladesh may have struck foreigners as being not terribly relevant to their own countries. But Grameen Bank founder Muhammad Yunus has continued working to spread his ideas to other countries by forming the nonprofit Grameen Trust. He can now rightfully claim that "these millions of small people with their millions of small pursuits can add up to create the biggest development wonder."

Sources

Auwal, Mohammed A. "Promoting Microcapitalism in the Service of the Poor: The Grameen Model and Its Cross-Cultural Adaptation." *The Journal of Business Communication*, Jan. 1996: 27

Bornstein, David. "The Barefoot Bank With Cheek." *Atlantic Monthly*. Dec. 1995: 40

Brill, Betsy. "A Little Credit, A Huge Success." *San Francisco Examiner*. 2 May 1999: A1

Counts, Alex. *Give Us Credit: How Muhammad Yunus's Micro Lending Revolution Is Empowering Women From Bangladesh to Chicago*. New York: Random House, 1996

"Grameen Foundation USA." Grameen Foundation. 28 Jul. 1999. 29 Dec. 1999. <http://www.grameenfoundation.org>.

Khandker, Shahidur. *Fighting Poverty With Microcredit: Experience in Bangladesh.* New York: Oxford University Press, 1998

MacFarquhar, Emily. "A Banking Lesson From Bangladesh." *U.S. News and World Report.* 3 Apr. 1995: 41

"The Official Grameen Bank Website." Grameen Communications. 20 Jul 1999. 29 Dec. 1999. <http://www.grameen.com>.

Ratcliffe, Robin and Elizabeth Thompson. "Microfinance Resources." *Whole Earth.* Spring 1998: 96

Skousen, Mark. "The For-Profit Antipoverty Agency." *Forbes.* 15 Nov. 1999: 138

Todd, Helen. *Women at the Center: Grameen Bank Borrowers After One Decade.* Boulder, CO: Westview Press, 1996.

———. "The Grameen Bank: A Small Experiment Begun in Bangladesh Has Turned Into a Major New Concept in Eradicating Poverty." *Scientific American.* November 1999: 114–119

Yunus, Mohammed and Alan Jolis. *Banker to the Poor: Micro-Lending and the Battle Against World Poverty.* New York: PublicAffairs Books, 1999

Questions to Consider

1. What makes microloans so successful? What keeps people from failing to pay back their loans to other members of these lending circles?

2. In order to adapt this solution from Bangladesh to America, what changes might have to be made?

3. Do you think microloans would work in any of the communities that you belong to? Why or why not?

INTERVIEWING AN OFFICIAL OR ACTIVIST ABOUT SOLUTIONS

Assignment: Interview at least one official or activist about the various solutions that you've compiled. What are their responses or reactions to these ideas? Do they think these solutions will work? Why or why not? How do they respond to criticism of the solutions that they favor?

Spin Control

The best way to get specific answers in an interview is to ask specific questions. So far, your interviews have centered on asking people about the general outlines of a problem, and for general ideas on how to go about solving it. Once you start asking them about specific solutions, though, you'll often get surprisingly well-thought-out answers. After all, at some point they've probably had to think carefully about whether or not to try this solution, and so chances are they have a well-informed opinion about it.

If you have the time, you could even interview two or more people with substantially different perspectives on the subject. For example, you might ask people who have different political views, social status, etc. Another useful contrast would be between someone who'd have to implement a solution and someone who would be affected by it.

But don't let someone's point of view completely shape the conversation. Ask questions that an opponent or a skeptic might ask. You don't have to be confrontational about it—there's no need to hit someone with "But isn't this idea just a waste of time and money?" Instead, ask the question hypothetically and attribute it to an actual or imaginary opponent: "What would you say to someone who didn't think this could work because of .... " etc. Interviewers on TV often use this more gentle approach.

Even if you try to keep the conversation focused on specific details and inclusive of other points of view, your subjects may keep pulling it back to their own advantage. This is known in the political world as "spin control." Here are a few forms of spin to be alert for:

Euphemism—The use of neutral-sounding words (e.g., "downsizing" for mass firings) instead of negative-sounding ones; or the use of grandiose titles for minor efforts ("Strategic Planning Task Force" for a committee).

Sloganeering—A phrase may be so vague that it has no real meaning or substantial detail, and yet its repeated use will make it sound like a grand theme. Examples: "A thousand points of light," and "A bridge to the twenty-first century." When you run into one of these, keep asking "What exactly does that mean? What exactly will happen?"

Non Sequitur—A Latin phrase meaning "It does not follow." Someone stumped by a difficult question may give a long answer about another subject entirely; they're hoping that you'll get so caught up in this new issue that you'll forget about the original question.

Exclusion—The easiest way for someone to "win" over an opponent is to never even acknowledge their existence. If you frame an argument entirely in your own terms and leave out other points of view, then of course you'll win—in your mind, at least, if no one else's.

Finding People to Interview

Interview sources can include authors of the works or articles you've read, someone mentioned in your readings, or simply an acquaintance or some one you've looked up. It's much more than merely talking to acquaintances—though they can help too! Finally, and most importantly, always ask for further leads. Even if you hit an apparent dead end with someone, they may know someone else who can help you.

Consult the section earlier in this chapter on Finding Organizations, because many of those methods work for finding individuals. Here are a few additional ways to get started:

Ask Acquaintances. Even if you don't know someone with experience in an issue, one of your friends or instructors may. If you can say that a friend or acquaintance referred you, it may also be easier to get your foot in the door of a potential interviewee than if you are just calling cold .

Academic Experts. College departments at your own school or at other schools may have instructors familiar with your issue. The department secretary or department head is often the best person to call first; they will know about the individual specialties of each faculty member, and this may narrow your search more rapidly, especially if you're dealing with a large university and a diverse faculty. Even if the person you subsequently contact doesn't have the time or expertise to discuss the issue with you, they can probably provide a person to contact or a few starting points in your research.

Bulletin Boards/Ads. You can post a notice online on Usenet or on a campus bulletin board explaining what you're researching and asking to hear from others with experience in that field. Remember to include your name, number, or e-mail address, and the best hours to contact you. Be aware, though, that sources who respond to ads may be less reliable than ones you've discovered on your own; they're coming to you, and that may include people unqualified to talk honestly or accurately about the subject.

Advocacy Organizations. Check the Yellow Pages, or the *Encyclopedia of Associations* at the reference desk of your local or public library. Both will list nonprofit and business organizations, addresses, contact names and numbers. One of these organizations may be able to direct you to individuals worth interviewing. Be aware that while some groups are intended to be nonpartisan public services, others will be highly biased or even have specific financial and political self-interests at stake in the positions that they espouse.

Sample Response

Common Cause is a citizen's lobby financed solely by the individual contributions of its 250,000 members. It has no party affiliation and does not back specific candidates ("Common Cause: Take Action"). Although its Web site and most of its press releases emanate from the national level, it also maintains state-level offices.

Jim Knox is the executive director of California Common Cause, and he sees their primary goal as "open, honest, and accountable government. To achieve that, we think it's important to limit contributions, limit spending, and clarify funding sources in election finances." At the state level, this has been achieved primarily through supporting proreform legislation, voter initiatives, and serving as a watchdog for bad political behavior.

Knox points out that federal campaign finance reform—which relies on Congress and the Supreme Court—differs from state-level reform, which is driven by citizens. "My experience has been that there's virtually no chance of the [state] legislature passing meaningful campaign finance reform. All the campaign reforms in California, back to Prop 9 in 1974, have been through state initiatives." Nonetheless, these initiatives have to be carefully worded. The reform language in winning propositions in 1988 and 1996 as undercut by state court decisions that struck down the overall propositions.

One such state-level reform is Public Campaign's "Clean Money Model Legislation." Knox was generally supportive but also skeptical of it.

> We supported it in Maine and Arizona, but frankly it's a bit unrealistic in California. It's too easy to qualify for funding, and the price will be phenomenal. We supported partial public financing, but I have doubts whether the public is ready for full financing. Opponents will tap into public distaste for giving money to politicians.

He nonetheless feels full financing is a worthwhile eventual goal, and that even partial financing will help clean up elections and make third-party candidates more viable.

While the laws adopted by British Columbia are fairly comprehensive, Knox notes that they are of limited use to the United States. The key, as is often the case with campaign finance reform, is the Supreme Court's *Buckley* ruling, which equated political spending at some level with free speech.

Canada is not constrained by *Buckley*, whereas we've historically tried to address campaign finance reform within the framework of *Buckley*. Our political assessment is that it's probably not a good idea to challenge *Buckley* head on, because we might lose ground in the current Supreme Court.

It should be noted that, after my interview with Jim Knox, the Court did in fact rule favorably on just such a challenge—that is, it "reaffirmed that limits can be placed on the amount of money individuals contribute to political candidates" (Richey 1). It may turn out that the Canadian system is a more viable model for the United States than previously thought.

Knox acknowledges that there may also be a "kernel of truth" to Lamar Alexander's contention that unlimited contributions would free him up to spend more time with the citizenry. But as Knox points out, the smaller the contributions, the broader the base of support a candidate needs—an argument that also points to more contact between candidates and voters.

Knox acknowledges that it's not easy to strike a balance between free speech and fair elections. "It's always difficult. But the public interest is not served when candidates can drown out the speech of others. The level of spending involved has a chilling effect on others, and it restricts access to public office." The few federal reforms in place perform a vital function; and he points to the partial public funding of presidential elections as one of the movement's success stories. "How else could you have unknown candidates from Georgia or Arkansas winning out over a well-known incumbent?" But without a scandal on the scale of Watergate—when this last round of reforms occurred—it seems unlikely to Knox that federal reforms will be pursued much further. "We got close in 1996," he says, "but it takes a lot of public pressure for Congress to do what it is naturally inclined not to do."

Works Cited

"Common Cause: Take Action." Common Cause. 19 Apr. 2000. <http://www.commoncause.org/get_involved/action.htm>.
Knox, Jim. Phone interview. 23 Dec. 1998
Richey, Warren. "Court Affirms Campaign Finance Limits." *Christian Science Monitor.* 25 Jan. 2000: 1

Focus On: Yellow Bikes

Pioneered by cyclists in Portland, Oregon, "Yellow Bikes" are old, donated bikes, scavenged from residents, the police, and thrift stores. They are fixed up, painted bright yellow from top to bottom, and left on city streets for anyone to ride whenever they need them. When you're done, you simply leave it for the next passerby to use. Attracted by the prospect of less noise, less air pollution, and more parking, cycling activists in a wide range of American cities have followed Portland's lead: Berkeley, California, Madison, Wisconsin, St. Paul, Minnesota, Austin, Texas, Spokane, Washington, Bellingham, Washington, Olympia, Washington, and Princeton, New Jersey, to name just a few.

The free bike movement was inspired by a similar "White Bike" program in 1960s Amsterdam, Holland. Unfortunately, most of these bikes were soon stolen or thrown into city canals. The same fate met early efforts in the United States, despite attempts to make the bikes as ugly and conspicuous as possible. The 50 bikes of Spokane's "Purple Bike" program soon wound up stolen or in the Spokane River. All of St. Paul's Yellow Bikes were stolen within two years. After a much-lauded launch in 1994, Portland's 800 bikes were gone or mangled within a year or two; finally, its founder disconnected his phone and left the state.

Yellow Bikes provide an excellent example of how difficult it can be to tell whether or not a solution "works." Beneath the apparent initial success or failure of an idea can lurk a future reversal of fortune. Sometimes an idea just needs more time to develop, or perhaps a few modifications to turn a "loser" into a brilliant success. The St. Paul Yellow Bike program now uses a "library card"-style system; users can show up at designated "hubs" to borrow a bike for free for the day, or even for long-term "checkouts."

In Amsterdam and Copenhagen, new attempts at free biking in the 1990s met with failure yet again. Rather than give up, proponents tinkered with the idea further. In Amsterdam, a "Depo System" premiered in 1997, consisting of shelters constructed about a quarter of a mile apart throughout the city, each with space for about 20 bikes. For a $3 deposit, riders use a touch screen terminal to select another shelter as their destination. When riders reach their destination shelter, the bike is automatically locked back up and their deposit returned. A "smart card" is also in the works. A similar system is used in the city center of Copenhagen, providing 1,800 bikes to tourists and residents alike. Advertising in the shelters and on the bikes helps cover program expenses.

Cities in the United States are turning to Europe once again for Yellow Bike inspiration. In addition to the borrowing card system in St. Paul, shelter- and deposit-based designs are being proposed to revive the foundering Yellow Bike programs in other cities. A typically American twist has also turned up in Berkeley—Yellow Bikes entirely supported by advertising. In March 2000, the online startup Gmoney.com had scattered 200 Yellow Bikes around the U.C. Berkeley campus. The bikes are plastered with Gmoney.com stickers, so the company gets an eco-friendly means of advertising while the town gets a bit of relief from traffic.

Yellow Bikes may become a common sight in cities, and the stolen bikes of early years just written off to experience. Even if it "fails" again, some might argue, if people are riding their stolen bikes instead of driving cars then were the Yellow Bikes such a complete failure?

Sources

"Bellingham's Yellow Bike Free Community Bikes Program." Mt. Baker Bike Club. <http://www.nas.com/bikeclub/yelbike.html> (Accessed 2 Jan. 2000)

"Copenhagen Free City Cycle." Cycle Import of Scandanavia. 2 Jan. 2000). <http://www.cios.com>.

Holtz, Jane. *Asphalt Nation: How the Automobile Took Over America, and How We Can Take It Back*. Berkeley: University of California Press, 1998

Keating, Joe. "Free Wheels." *Bicycling*. May 1995: 30. EBSCO. Online. 2 Mar. 1998.

Marech, Rona. "Web Site's Bike-Share Program." *San Francisco Chronicle*. 17 Mar. 2000: A24

Richtel, Matt. "Dutch Make Bikes Smarter Than Thieves." *New York Times*. 5 Nov. 1998: E3

"Santa Cruz Yellow Bike Project." Santa Cruz Yellow Bike Project. 2 Jan. 2000. <http://www.cruzio.com/~yelobike/>.

"Take This Bike, Please." *New York Times Magazine*. 18 Dec. 1994: 17

"Where Trust Rides a Yellow Bike." *New York Times*, 9 Dec. 1994: A16

"Yellow Bike Coalition of St. Paul & Minneapolis." Yellow Bike Coalition of St. Paul & Minneapolis. 2 Jan. 2000. <http://www.Yellowbikes.org>.

"Yellow Bike Project." Cunningham & Cunningham, Inc. 2 Jan. 2000. <http://c2.com/ybp/>.

Questions to Consider

1. Would Yellow Bikes work in a community that you belong to? Why or why not?

2. Assume that your community tried a Yellow Bike pilot program. How would you decide whether or not it was a success, that is, whether or not it should keep getting support?

3. What other appliances, vehicles, or resources within your community could be shared in this way? What difficulties would a sharing plan have to deal with?

PAPER:
DESCRIBE THE POSSIBLE SOLUTIONS TO YOUR ISSUE

Assignment: Outline possible solutions to the community problem you've been researching, including proposals that you may or may not agree with. How have others responded to these ideas? Have they tried them before? What have other communities tried? What were the results? How has the media responded to these problems and solutions?

Sorting Out Conflicting Claims

Knowledge does not exist in a neat, unified form. It is messy. It gets pushed and pulled between different people's opinions, and what qualifies as "accurate knowledge" or "progress in this field" depends on whom you ask.

Take this textbook, for example. I wrote it because I was dissatisfied with the other textbooks available to me as a writing instructor. There is no one way to teach composition, and many instructors can't even agree on which aspects of writing are worth teaching! So you are not looking for The Facts about your topic: There aren't any. There are, however, many conclusions and observations made by individuals. You'll have to sift through their various—and often conflicting—testimonies in order to tentatively reason out your own beliefs.

That means that the interviews and sources you gather may disagree with each other. So whom do you believe? When trying to decide whether a claim is credible, consider the following:

- Is the claimant an expert in this field? What are their qualifications?
- How much evidence do they provide to back up their claims?
- Do other recognized experts or relevant respondents support them?
- Do your own experiences back up their claims?
- Do many people believe this claim?

That said, not every supposed expert has good advice, and there are beliefs that many people agree with—even claiming that they are backed up by their own experiences—that later prove to be unwarranted. At this point, you don't have to reach a conclusion about whether or not a person's claim is right or wrong. You can admit that it stumps you, too, and simply describe their point of view as accurately as possible so that readers can draw their own conclusions. Or perhaps you can agree with some claims, but not with others that they make. You don't need to line up experts into yes/no columns and agree or disagree wholeheartedly. Your agreement may be partial, and in any case it may change over time.

Concluding A Paper

You may find the most challenging part of this essay to be its conclusion. A typical mistake is simply restating your introduction; you may even hear teachers advising this. It's bad advice. Don't waste your reader's time by repeating yourself. Every line you write should add something to the reader's understanding. Here are a few approaches that will make your conclusions count:

Looking Ahead: Extend your observations about the past and present into the future. Based on what you've described, what may or may not happen?

Further Information: Where can a reader interested in your subject learn more? What sources have you touched upon that are worth looking into further?

Call for Action: What can concerned readers do? Are there groups they could form or contact? What might they achieve over the long term?

Finish Your Introduction: Open your essay with a question or unfinished anecdote, leaving the reader in suspense until you answer the question or finish the story in the conclusion.

Raise New Questions: The best writing often raises even more questions than those it set out to answer. What new questions does your research raise?

Summarize: A rewording or condensed version of the basic points of your piece is to be used only when your essay is so complicated that the reader needs a summary.

Endings Worth Avoiding:

1. If possible, don't simply restate your thesis and findings.

2. Avoid beginning with *in conclusion, therefore,* or *thus.* It's hot air: your reader already knows you're ending here, because they can see it on the page!

3. While you do want new and useful ideas in your conclusion, don't throw in completely new information that isn't clearly connected or explained by your paper.

Sample Paper

Campaign finance reform may not attract the media attention it deserves, but there are certainly many groups working behind the scenes on both sides. As I looked over reform efforts, Common Cause was the first to catch my eye, probably because it makes the most noise in the media. It is a citizen's lobby financed solely by the individual contributions of its 250,000 members. It has no party affiliation and does not back specific candidates.

Its Web site shows its work as a watchdog and as a state-by-state advocate for various bills seeking greater candidate accountability and greater controls on "soft money," or the largely unregulated contributions that corporations and special interest groups can make directly to political parties. At the state level, this has been achieved primarily through supporting proreform legislation and voter initiatives, and serving as a watchdog for bad political behavior. Its Web site provides e-mail addresses for various senators so that you can write to them about your support for the latest version of such reform ("Common Cause: Take Action").

Passing reform—any reform at all—would slow the wave of money crashing into political campaigns. But the weakness to this approach lies in the resistance of Congress to passing such laws; neither side is interested in cutting off their donors, and so they persist in passing such bills in only one chamber of Congress. You can send all the e-mails you want to your senator, but it still isn't in their personal interest to change such laws. And even if such a bill were passed, it would be challenged by such free-speech advocates as the American Civil Liberties Union (ACLU).

But Jim Knox, the executive director of California Common Cause, points out that federal reform—which relies on Congress and the Supreme Court—differs from state-level reform, which is driven by citizens. "My experience has been that there's virtually no chance of the [state] legislature passing meaningful campaign finance reform. All the campaign reforms in California, back to Prop 9 in 1974, have been through state initiatives." These initiatives have to be carefully worded; winning propositions in 1988 and 1996 were later struck down in court.

Perhaps with this in mind, the proreform group Public Campaign painstakingly worded its "Model Legislation for Clean Money Campaign Reform," thus lessening the chance that it would encounter the ACLU's opposition. The bill provides that:

1. Candidates using government funds cannot also use private or personal funds.
2. After raising enough seed money in $5 amounts from individuals, candidates qualify for government Clean Money funding.
3. If their opponent persists in raising "dirty" money from private sources, then the Clean Money candidate can receive matching funds to stay competitive ("Clean Money Campaign Reform"). The total cost for the system is estimated at $1.3 billion per 2-year election cycle ("Just the FAQs").

The advantage of this proposal is that it does not force reform on a candidate. The question is whether candidates would use Clean Money if they didn't have to, and whether Congress will fund it. Though $650 million a year is chump change compared with other expenditures, it's enough money that a senator might score points by cutting it from the budget. Some states might also object to it; as Jim Knox notes: "We supported it in Maine and Arizona, but frankly it's a bit unrealistic in California. It's too easy to qualify for funding, and the price will be phenomenal."

The ACLU acts as a gatekeeper among reformers in this debate: Anything more aggressive than Public Campaign's model is likely to run into ACLU opposition. The ACLU remains opposed to limits on spending because it sees them as a limit on free speech ("Support Constitutional Campaign Finance Reform"). While the ACLU offers no solution to campaign finance, it makes clear it *doesn't* like limits on fund raising, different mail or broadcast rates for Clean Money candidates, required record keeping of small contributions (e.g., $20), the ability of the Federal Elections Committee to contest campaigns while an election is still in progress, and any ban or restriction on Political Action Committees (PACs). ("February 20, 1997 Letter ... ")

The ACLU's stand has the advantage of constitutional purity: if one defines money as equivalent to speech, these objections insure that speech would be unhindered. That's a big if. The ACLU's stand also leaves us where we started: in a system of "might is right," where the candidate with the most money usually wins.

This view is seconded by the Web sites for the conservative Cato Institute and the Heritage Foundation, both of which include papers on campaign finance. Many of the Cato Institute's papers are by Bradley Smith. He argues that the separation of "soft" and "hard" money is working well, and has the advantage of not infringing on the First Amendment. In fact, he claims the existing limits on hard money ($1,000 by individuals to a candidate, $5,000 to a PAC) hurt because they force politicians to campaign longer and discourage those who lack the stamina to chase "small" amounts. Smith also attacks federal financing as supportive of "extremist" candidates, thus "forcing citizens to pay for others to express opposing opinions" ("Campaign Finance Reform"). Smith goes on elsewhere to argue that "Contrary to the assumption that large contributions are undemocratic is the reality that most challenges to the status quo and most working-class political movements have been financed by wealthy donors." ("Campaign Finance Regulation")

The Cato Institute's arguments presume that unrestricted campaign funds flow to the "best" candidates, rather than to candidates who grants favors to wealthy donors—though in the view of wealthy, perhaps that's exactly who the best candidate is. The complaint about the public funding of opposing views misapprehends the nature of elections. Voters are liable to change their minds at any point—otherwise, why campaign or debate at all? Anyone's stance is liable to be opposing, at least in retrospect, and we can only know that a view opposes ours after our vote is cast. Finally, Smith's contention that the wealthy are the best friends of working-class movements is hard to believe. But like the ACLU, Smith's approach has the advantage of a laissez-faire simplicity and of not clashing with the Constitution.

A similar argument is raised through the Heritage Foundation by Lamar Alexander. In his 1996 run for president, he claims, donation limits forced him to attend fundraisers daily: "As a result, I became acquainted with a great many good Americans capable of giving $1,000 (who probably represent a cross section of about one percent of all the people in the country)" ("Off With the Limits"). His implication is that had he been able to get this fundraising out of the way with a few unlimited donations, he'd have had more time to mingle with working people. Furthermore, limits favor incumbents who already have donors at hand, and wealthy individuals who can ignore limits by simply using their personal fortune.

Alexander's argument seems reasonable, as attending fundraisers does sound like a drain on candidates. Even Common Cause's Jim Knox admits that there may be a "kernel of truth" to Lamar Alexander's contention that unlimited contributions would free him up to spend more time with the citizenry. But as Knox points out, the smaller the contributions, the broader the base of support a candidate needs—an argument that also points to more contact between candidates and voters.

Furthermore, will a well-connected incumbent's advantage of a donor list evaporate with a lifting of limits? Now, instead of being $1 million or $2 million ahead of a challenger, they can be $10 million or $20 million ahead. The stakes will be raised on both sides, but the uneven ratio remains the same. And as for the contention that time away from the wealthy at a fundraisers will be spent with working-class people instead—it's a nice thought, but I've yet to see a politician who wouldn't rather spend their free time with their well-educated and well-fed peers.

We are not the only country to grapple with these issues. In 1995, British Columbia's Election Act created a system of nomination, advertising, and financing. Candidates there may be nominated by collecting 25 signatures and making a deposit of $100 (about U.S. $75) ("Guide to the Election Act"). This prevents flippant candidacies, but is still within the reach of someone willing to stake a little money and spend an afternoon out with a clipboard to collect the necessary signatures.

To advertise their positions, candidates can buy advertising at the lowest commercial rate on TV and radio, and in print. They cannot spend more than $50,000 on their campaign, however. (The limit can be raised for larger voting districts.) Parties are limited in their budgets, with a ceiling of $1.25 per registered voter per electoral district ("Guide to the Election Act"). A "third-party" advertiser (e.g., interest groups, corporations, unions) has to register with the province's Chief Electoral Officer, and is then restrained to a $5,000 budget ("Media Obligations").

For candidates, political parties, and third parties alike, the identity of contributors of more than $250 has to be disclosed publicly. Anonymous contributions are limited to $50; political parties can accept a total of up to $10,000 in anonymous donations, while individual candidates are limited to $3,000 ("Guide to the Election Act").

British Columbia's system does have advantages. It does not restrict speech, just the spending of large quantities of money to broadcast speech. This forces candidates to use debates, interviews, and in-person appearances to convey their views to the public, rather than the bludgeoning power of TV ads. While parties can gather some funds to get their message across, they can't overwhelm others.

The law's fiscal limits are admittedly arbitrary: There's nothing magic about the $1.25 or $10,000. What's more, there's no indication of indexing to account for inflation. I suspect that a few years from now there will be a debate over the adjustment of this figure to a higher level. With this adjustment comes the possibility of a grab by hungry politicians for a much higher figure.

In Maine, one such system already is in place, but only on a voluntary basis. The state's Clean Election Act provides full financing for candidates who collect a sufficient number of $5 donations. Candidates collect 50 (House) or 150 (Senate) $5 checks before a March 16 deadline. This screens out truly marginal or gag candidates, while not presenting too much of an obstacle to poor or new candidates. Once they have advanced to the general election, candidates then can spend state funds up to $12,000 in House races and $40,000 for the Senate. In return, they are not allowed to take any outside contributions (Goldberg A1).

In the 2000 election, 115 of the state's 374 registered candidates took this clean money option (A1). The advantages are obvious, and similar to those of the British Columbia plan: a leveled playing field for candidates who are poor or not political insiders, and a loosening of the choke hold that corporate and labor special interests have on political candidates. But the Clean Election Act's continued survival is due to the very fact that makes it vulnerable to failure: It is voluntary. If candidates don't want to be "clean," they can go and raise obscene amounts in the old-fashioned way. This voluntary aspect means that the state can't be sued by a candidate for restricting free speech, but it also means that politicians could just ignore the clean option en masse—or that those who do choose clean money might find themselves overpowered by a less-regulated "dirty" opponent.

The British Columbian plan strikes me as a good start. But in adapting it to this country, I would find a less arbitrary way of determining the money limits, as well as a way of indexing them so that they wouldn't be vulnerable to renegotiation every few years. And, as in the case of Maine, I think a voluntary public funding plan may be the only constitutional way to enact such reforms at the state level; this would avoid legal challenges, but we would also need constant public pressure on politicians to get them to accept Clean Money and its restrictions.

The more serious problem facing such models in our country is that fiscal limitations would come under fire as a restriction of free speech, because the Supreme Court's *Buckley* ruling equates political spending at some level with free speech. As Common Cause's Jim Knox notes:

> Canada is not constrained by *Buckley*, whereas we've historically tried to address campaign finance reform within the framework of *Buckley*. Our political assessment is that it's probably not a good idea to challenge *Buckley* head on, because we might lose ground in the current Supreme Court.

It should be noted that, after my interview with Jim Knox, the Court did in fact rule favorably on just such a challenge—that is, it "reaffirmed that limits can be placed on the amount of money individuals contribute to political candidates" (Richey 1). It may turn out that the Canadian system is a more viable model for the United States than previously thought.

Even within our own borders there is cause for hope. Knox points to the partial public funding of presidential elections as one of the movement's success stories. But without a scandal on the scale of Watergate—when this last round of reforms occurred—it seems unlikely that federal reforms will be pursued further. "We got close in 1996," he says, "but it takes a lot of public pressure for Congress to do what it is naturally inclined not to do."

Works Cited

Alexander, Lamar. "Off With the Limits: What I Learned About Money and Politics When I Ran for President." Heritage Foundation. 26 May 1996. 13 Apr. 2000. <http://www.heritage.org/library/categories/govern/lect568.html>.

"Clean Money Campaign Reform." Public Campaign. 13 Apr. 2000. <http://www.publiccampaign.org/cleanmoney.html>.

"Common Cause: Take Action." Common Cause. 19 Apr. 2000. <http://www.commoncause.org/get_involved/action.htm>.

Goldberg, Carey. "Mainers Try a Donation-Free Campaign." *New York Times.* 1 Apr. 2000: A1

Gora, Joel. "February 20, 1997 Letter to Senator McConnell on the Bipartisan Campaign Finance Reform Act of 1997." American Civil Liberties Union. 20 Feb. 1997. 13 Apr. 2000. <http://www.aclu.org/congress/ls022097a.html>.

"Guide to the Election Act." Elections British Columbia. 1 Jun. 1999. 19 Apr. 2000. <http://www.elections.bc.ca/guidebooks/p855_toc.html>.

"Just the FAQs." Public Campaign. 17 Apr. 2000. <http://www.publiccampaign.org/DA.html>.

Knox, Jim. Phone interview. 23 Dec. 1998

"Media Obligations Under the New Election Act." Elections British Columbia. 1 Jun. 1999. 19 Apr. 2000. <http://www.elections.bc.ca/guidebook/p862_toc.html>.

Richey, Warren. "Court Affirms Campaign Finance Limits." *Christian Science Monitor.* 25 Jan. 2000: 1

Smith, Bradley. "Campaign Finance Reform: Soft Money and the Presidential System." Cato Institute. 14 May 1997. 13 Apr. 2000. <http://www.cato.org/testimony/ct-bs051497.html>.

———. "Campaign Finance Regulation." Cato Institute. 13 Sept. 1995. 13 Apr. 2000. <http://www.cato.org/pubs/pas/pa238.html>.

"Support Constitutional Campaign Finance Reform." American Civil Liberties Union. 13 Apr. 2000. <http://www.aclu.org/congress/ campaignfinance.html>.

Focus On: Astroturf Lobbying

Have you ever belonged to Citizens for State Power, a group that opposes the federal deregulation of electricity? How about the Advancement of Sound Science Coalition, which would limit restrictions on pesticide use? Or CARE (Concerned Alaskans for Resources and Environment), which advocates more clear-cutting rights? Or maybe Californians Against Utility Company Abuse, which helped stymie the use of electric cars? Perhaps the Citizens for Medicare, which opposes government regulation of prices for prescription drugs for the elderly? And what about People for the West!, which is fighting for inexpensive mining rights?

No? You may rest assured that very few other citizens have joined them either. These groups were funded almost exclusively by utilities, chemical companies, oil companies, and mining companies, and had very few actual individual citizens involved with their efforts. Nicknamed "astroturf," these groups are examples of a common lobbying tactic by moneyed interests: adopting a grassroots appearance to hide lobbying that is in fact almost solely financed by unpopular businesses or investors. Under the guise of "concerned citizens," these groups use public relations firms to bombard the media with issue ads and politicians with voter letters. Because citizen's groups don't need to disclose their funding, they can serve as a front for special interests.

When these ploys are uncovered, though, they can backfire. Software giant Microsoft was pushed to admit in 1998 that it planned a campaign of carefully manufactured newspaper editorials and letters to the editor by concerned citizens, even though these letters were in fact created by writers hired by Microsoft. The company had planned to cite this "public" support when defending itself against charges of unfair monopolistic practices. Not that they were particularly shamed by these disclosures—for the company was caught again in late 1999, when it was revealed that newspaper ads opposing the antitrust trial of Microsoft, signed by hundreds of professors and run at great cost in the *New York Times* and *Washington Post*, were in fact secretly paid for by Microsoft through a front organization.

A similar strategy backfired for tobacco companies in 1995, when it was revealed that United States Tobacco and R. J. Reynolds Tobacco hired the Winston Salem-based PR firm Walt Klein & Associates Inc. to produce thousands of "original looking" letters to politicians from concerned voters. Types of paper and fonts were varied on each letter to make them look more genuine. Despite being unmasked in this attempt, astroturf groups remain a favorite ploy of tobacco companies.

Similarly, the pharmaceutical industry has repeatedly used astroturf groups to maintain a profitable grip on high-priced drugs for the elderly. The most recent example came in late 1999, when the Pharmaceutical Research and Manufacturers Association fronted a group calling itself the Coalition for Better Medicare, and funded a $30 million anti–price control advertising campaign. One senior activist group, the National Council of Senior Citizens, labeled it "a systematic campaign of lies," and NCSC director Steve Protulis excoriated the coalition as "a phony group fully funded by the drug industry's trade association."

Still, the line between astroturf and a genuine citizen's group is not always clear; for example, some groups can receive quite a bit of outside financing but still have many genuinely concerned citizens volunteering their efforts. There are some signs, however, that a "citizen's group" may be nothing more than a shell covering lobbying by special interests:

- Slick, professional looking ads, Web sites, and other promotional materials.
- Frequent ad placements in major media outlets, e.g., large ads in national newspapers (*USA Today, New York Times*, etc.) and magazines.
- Little effort to solicit donations from potential members. (Real citizen's groups are often starved for money, and say so in no uncertain terms.)
- Their materials don't mention any actual community meetings or conferences for concerned citizens to get together.

- The use of prewritten letters to politicians, where all you have to do is fill in you name and send it.

While actual citizen's groups also use some of these tactics, their presence should alert you to the possibility of astroturf.

Free speech guarantees that moneyed interests have just as much right to express their opinions as private citizens; their use of misleading names, while not ethical, is also a form of free speech. But such efforts should be known for exactly what they are: a form of deception.

Sources

"Astroturf: Phony Grassroots Marketing." Canadian Broadcasting Corporation. 4 Jan. 2000. <http://opera.cbc.ca/grass.html>.

Brinkley, Joel. " 'Unbiased' Ads For Microsoft Came at a Price." *New York Times.* 18 September 1999: A1

Downey, John. "Grass Roots?" Triad Business News. 29 Sept. 1995. 4 Jan. 2000. <http://www.triadbusiness.com/1995/grass.html>.

Ewen, Stuart. *PR! A Social History of Spin.* New York: Basic Books, 1996

Goldstein, Kenneth. *Interest Groups, Lobbying, and Participation in America.* New York: Cambridge University Press, 1999

Hammond, Keith. "Astroturf Troopers." *Mother Jones.* 4 Dec. 1997. 4 Jan. 2000. <http://www.motherjones.com/news_wire/grightwing.html>.

McWilliams, Brian. "Microsoft Plans Sneak PR Campaign." PC World Online. 13 Apr. 1998. 4 Jan. 2000. <http://www.pcworld.com/news/daily/data/0498/980413164654.html>.

Overby, Peter. "Medicare." *All Things Considered.* National Public Radio. KALW, San Francisco. 3 Aug. 1999

Sanchez, Samantha. "How the West Is Won: Astroturf Lobbying and the 'Wise Use' Movement." *The New Prospect.* Mar./Apr. 1996. Altnews. 30 Nov. 1998) <http://www.altnews.com.au/twscairns/west.htm>.

"Seniors Picket Drug Association." National Council of Senior Citizens. 5 Apr. 2000). <http://www.ncscinc.org/press/prpharma.htm>.

Silverstein, Ken. "APCO: Astroturf Makers." Multinational Monitor. Mar. 1996. 4 Jan. 2000. <http://www.essential.org/monitor/hyper/mm0396.09.html>.

Stauber, John and Shledon Rampton. *Toxic Sludge Is Good for You: Lies, Damn Lies, and the Public Relations Industry.* New York: Common Courage Press, 1995

Questions to Consider

1. What ads have you seen on TV or in print that looked like they might have been astroturf lobbying? Why?
2. Would anyone involved in your issue have a reason to use astroturf lobbying? Why or why not?

3. Are there any ads or citizen's groups that you've encountered in your research that might be astroturf lobbying? What makes you think that they are or aren't?

PEER READING

> **In-Class:** Read and respond to the papers written by your class-mates. Review the peer reading instructions you used for paper #1 and organize your reading groups in the same manner for this paper.

Peer Reading Worksheet for Paper #3

Writer:

Partner:

Are there any parts that you found confusing or insufficiently explained? Why?

Who is quoted in the paper? Is there anything else you might you want to ask them? What other sources or points of view could the writer include?

Does the writer's characterization of any of the solutions seem overly bi-ased? How might they give a less partisan description?

Did the essay's conclusion add to your understanding of the paper? Would removing it change your understanding? Could this conclusion be im-proved?

Overall, how might the writer improve this paper?

REVISING THE PAPER

Assignment: Revise and print out a new version of the paper. Then add it to a folder that includes your first draft, your peer reading worksheet, and the shorter assignments.

Inclusive language

As you revise your draft, remember not to limit yourself to whatever points of view you happen to agree with; the purpose of this paper is to describe as many solutions as you can in as fair a manner as possible. Here are some other deliberate or inadvertent exclusions to watch out for:

Sexist Language—Using "he" to describe a generic person is a historical artifact in our language, because in the 19th century the British Parliament declared it the "universal gender." Although we don't have a neuter word to replace it, using "he" today implies the exclusion of women. Use "they" instead; it's a usage that the New Oxford English dictionary now accepts. (Be aware, though, that some more traditionally minded readers won't accept this.) Your other option, although it's clumsy, is always to say "he or she," "his or her," etc. Similarly, don't bother describing someone as a "spokesman" or "workman"—"spokesperson" or "worker" will do just fine.

Have You Tried to Contact Everyone Involved?—It may be impossible to contact every person, or even a few people, involved in the issue that you're researching, but do try to contact people from at least more than one side of the issue. Even if they don't respond (see below), it's important that you attempt to be balanced.

"No Comment"—Were your calls to a person or agency not returned or cut short? It's not as bad as you might think. If you mention in your paper that you tried contacting these people, it helps assure the reader that your quotes and sources aren't deliberately biased—that you did, in fact, try to contact everyone involved.

Often you can turn the lack of response on its head and make an issue of it. Why is this person or agency not communicating with the public? What does this say about the state of affairs in the community? What does it say about the need for communication?

Old Research—Look through your old notes and interviews for material that might be reusable. Just because it's old research doesn't mean that it should be excluded; some of the information that you uncovered in researching your previous papers may actually fit better into this paper.

"Facts" That Refute You and Others—Imagine that one of your sources produces a fact or statistic that appears to completely refute your beliefs or the beliefs of others that you quote in your paper. Does this effectively end the argument? Absolutely not. Include the fact in your paper, note where you got it from, and what their interest in providing this fact might be. Then examine it as closely as you can, using the statistics or spin hints from previous assignments. Just how reliable is this "fact"? How might it apply or not apply to this situation? Are there similar facts from other independent sources that back it up?

The mark of a good experiment is that is verifiable—it can be repeated or backed up by other independent sources. Treat crucial facts from your sources with the same caution.

Focus On: Modern Slavery

When we think of slavery today, we usually think of the past: of the geno-cidal enslavement of native populations in the Caribbean and South America by the Spanish, and the slavery of African Americans that lasted for centuries in North America. Such horrors can only be revisited today through history books, slave narratives, and visits to such historical sites as the Underground Railroad and the bloody battlegrounds of the Civil War. Slavery has become a part of our past, and abolition a faint memory.

Or has it? Amazingly, slavery continues to flourish in such countries as Sudan, where it is encouraged by the chaotic lawlessness of a 3-de-cades-long civil war; and in Mauritania, where it continues to be tacitly ac-cepted as part of a long-standing tradition of slave ownership in the country, and is supported by deliberate misreadings of the Koran in much the same way that Americans once justified slavery through selective use of the Bible. It should be noted, too, that secret and smaller-scale slavery rings have also been discovered in such countries as the United States and Israel. In Sudan and Mauritania, though, slavery operates openly, with the acceptance of many governmental and religious authorities.

Like their predecessors in the 19th century, concerned citizens world-wide have once again formed abolitionist groups to crusade against slavery. The most prominent of these groups is Christian Solidarity International, but many nondenominational abolitionist groups like the Boston-based American Anti-Slavery Group have also joined the fray.

Some of these groups have revived one of the oldest tactics of abolition: simply buying slaves out of their slavery. Fundraising drives have been held from Switzerland to California to finance these "buybacks." Students, ap-palled by tales of children and adolescents their own age being forced into slavery, have joined in this mission. In 1999, in the California town of Sunnyvale, for example, more than a dozen high school students made a 50-mile march to publicize and raise money for the cause. Thousands of slaves have been freed through such efforts.

Who could disagree with such a noble cause? A lot of people, as it turns out: UNICEF calls these slave buybacks "intolerable," and most human rights groups have also distanced themselves from this tactic. Why? Be-cause in buying back slaves, abolitionists are inadvertently perpetuating the slave economy by giving slave owners a financial incentive to continue enslaving others. Buybacks subsidize the slave trade. In fact, many freed Sudanese slaves are recaptured and reenslaved so that their owners can sell them yet again.

Slave buybacks are a classic example of how a noble cause can generate equally noble opposition. It may seem sometimes as if nobody could possi-bly oppose some of the solutions that you've researched on your issue, and that nobody could possibly take a contrary position. Who can support slav-ery? Who wants more drunk driving fatalities, or birth defects, or deaths from cancer? Who is in favor of more crime and suicide? But opposition to a solution does not mean opposition to recognizing the existence of a problem; it simply means that someone may believe that there is a better way to deal with the problem, and that they believe that other proposed solutions may actually be counterproductive.

A noble or a well-intentioned solution is not always a good solution. An idea should not be judged simply by its intent, but also by its results.

Works Cited

"The American Anti-Slavery Group." The American Anti-Slavery Group. 19 Jan. 2000. <http://www.anti-slavery.org>.

Christian Solidarity International (CSI). Christian Solidarity International. 19 Jan. 2000. <http://www.csi-int.ch>.

Cotton, Samuel. *Silent Terror: A Journey Into Contemporary African Slavery*. New York: Writers & Readers, 1999

Finnegan, William. "A Slave in New York." *New Yorker*. 24 Jan. 2000: 50–61

"Modern Day Slavery Flourishes in Sudan." *San Francisco Chronicle*. 3 May 1999: A22

"Sunnyvale Students Hike for Freedom: Plight of Slaves Inspires Fund-Raiser." *San Francisco Chronicle*. 22 May 1999: A18

Questions to Consider

1. Could slave buybacks be adapted to work against slavery, rather than perpetuating it? How? What other approaches could abolitionists take?

2. What other solutions to social problems strike you as being well intentioned but possibly counterproductive? Why?

3. Could any of the solutions that you have examined in your own issue have little effect, or even backfire and worsen the problem in some way? How?

4

Working Toward Solutions

LISTING OUT THE PROS AND CONS OF VARIOUS SOLUTIONS

> **Assignment:** List out all the pros and cons that you can think of for the solutions you described in your previous paper. Ask others for any additions to the list. This list does not need to be in the form of an essay response; rather, it is for your own reference as you construct arguments for later assignments.

Inductive and Deductive Logic

This textbook is based on inductive logic: taking small observations and building them into a larger premise. By starting with fragments of evidence, you eventually construct a tentative premise, or a hypothesis.

Of course, this fails to take account of the messiness of an actual research project. Some data won't quite be accounted for by your theory, or may actively contradict you. You may not be able to find a satisfactory theory, or your theory may change after you reevaluate your data. You'll have to acknowledge all these contradictory impulses in your research and writing. Your path may loop back to the very beginning and start all over again! This is not a bad thing, nor should it be avoided or hidden in your papers. The friction that you're encountering is called *learning*.

Inductive logic is preferred for pure science, because it's never too sure of itself. This tentative sort of belief doesn't sway people: it sounds weak and indecisive. There is another form of logic, though, known as deduction. This is when you start with a general premise (a thesis) and apply it to specific examples. The general premise is assumed to be correct, and the specific examples reinforce it. This is the mode of logic preferred in politics, religion, and applied science. You sound more confident, and it's easier to take action: Your thesis means you "know" what should happen. Deduction also has its dangers: Your general premise may be untrue, thus tainting your perspective on all the evidence. And the false confidence that deductive logic encourages may have terrible consequences.

To form a belief, it is best to use inductive logic. But to persuade others to take action on your belief, deductive logic is your most effective tool. Once you've carefully considered your beliefs inductively, there are a number of deductive ways to persuade someone deductively:

Arguing From Positive Evidence—This is the simplest form of argument; if an experience bears out a claim, then that claim is true. Example: If marijuana relieves symptoms of glaucoma, then it is medicinal. Marijuana relieves the symptoms of glaucoma; therefore marijuana is medicinal.

Drawback: The opening statement in this kind of argument may be based on a false causality. For example, what if *any* treatment's placebo effect helped glaucoma? In this case, marijuana would not necessarily be the real cause of medicinal effects. A more blatant example: If the sun rises this morning, then I rule the world. The sun rose this morning. Therefore, I rule the world.

Arguing From Negative Evidence—If experience does not bear out a claim, then that claim is not true. Example: If drug use does not drop after increased jail times, then harder sentencing is not a deterrent. Drug use did not drop after harder sentencing. Therefore, harder sentencing is not a deterrent.

Drawback: false causality (see above).

Process of Elimination—By eliminating all other possible solutions, only one is left that makes sense. Example: We can't stop the supply of drugs coming in; we can't eliminate the profit motive behind dealing them; therefore we must focus on reducing the demand for drugs.

Drawback: By excluding some solutions, you may create the impression that one alternative is the only alternative. Example: The statement above doesn't mention buyer penalties, crop destruction, or legalization. A more blatant example: Our fridge is empty; we have no can opener; therefore, we must resort to cannibalism. (Why not just order pizza?)

Reducing to Absurdity—If taking an opponent's argument to its logical extreme creates an absurdity, then your argument may appear to be the only reasonable alternative. This is a version of the process of elimination. Example: If marijuana is legalized for glaucoma, what's to stop it being prescribed for stress? What's to stop cocaine, heroin, or LSD from being prescribed for psychological ailments? Anyone could claim sufficient symptoms to use any drug legally; therefore, we must continue a ban on all illicit drugs.

Drawbacks:

1. What you consider absurd may seem reasonable to someone else. Example: Some people may think that prescribing marijuana for stress really is a good idea.
2. You may exaggerate out of the realm of possibility. Example: Would anyone really consider heroin to be as benign a treatment as marijuana?

Making Logical Explanations

Logic involves taking observations and connecting them to a theory that explains their presence. Simply noting that there is a correlation between two things—that one condition appears to precede, parallel, or succeed another—is not an explanation. It is merely an observation, and its implications are not self-evident. You must explain why they might have this connection.

You must not only point out the possible range of explanations for the correlation, you must then note which is the most likely explanation. Which fits the most with what is already known in this field? Does it also account for other observations that you've made?

Sometimes there is no explanation because the correlation is just a coincidence. Or the two things may be correlated by a shared factor that isn't causal. To pick up a previous example, let's say that you notice that people who drink a certain brand of bottled water are healthier than people who don't. This may turn out to have more to do with most drinkers of bottled water having higher incomes—and thus better health care—than with any curative property in the water itself.

Be careful not to confuse cause and effect; that is, don't be too quick to attribute cause and effect to either side of a correlation. Public guardians constantly argue over whether certain songs and images cause a violent society, or whether a violent society causes violent songs and images. Sometimes cause and effect are so entangled that it becomes impossible to know which came first: It's the classic "which came first, the chicken or the egg?" dilemma. Be ready to acknowledge whether a correlation is unclear in this way.

Finally, often no one explanation can cover all correlations. Sometimes even two seemingly contradictory explanations can be accepted at the same time. For example, do antilock brakes on cars prevent accidents by reducing skidding, or do they cause more accidents by instilling a false sense of security and sloppier driving? These two theories, while apparently contradictory, may both be right at the same time.

This exact sort of dilemma underlies modern physics: Some tests "prove" that matter operates as a particle, while other tests "prove" that it operates as a wave. Both—until some theory can account for the discrepancy in testing or logic—have been provisionally accepted as "true." Logical explanation is not always an all-or-nothing proposition.

Sample Response

The "Model Legislation for Clean Money Campaign Reform," developed by Public Campaign and published on their Web site, strikes me as the best solution to the issue of election financing. The advantages and disadvantages of this approach are:

Advantages

- It eliminates the need for candidates to grant favors or extra time to wealthy campaign contributors. This can also allow them to spend more time with common citizens and to develop their positions on various issues.

- Because it does not actually restrict spending—candidates are not forced to use clean money—it would pass muster under the current Supreme Court rulings that essentially equate campaign spending with free speech.
- It is unlikely to be challenged by the ACLU or other civil liberties organizations.
- Similar programs have been successfully implemented in some states.
- Matching funds would prevent candidates from buying an election.
- It may increase the election chances for those coming from traditionally underrepresented and underfinanced communities.
- It would open up elections to third parties with popular support (i.e., $5 donations) but who currently lack the machine politics muscle of established political parties.
- The minimal requirements for financing would discourage the uncontrolled financing of frivolous or truly marginal parties.
- As more recipients of electoral aid are elected, there will be more defenders of such financing in the legislature.

Disadvantages

- If the Supreme Court decided someday that campaign money and ads were not equivalent to free speech, then Public Campaign's model might not be aggressive enough to take advantage of this change.
- As it is dependent on government financing, it is vulnerable to budget cuts by the legislature, particularly in the early years, when the government would still be filled with incumbents used to the old "dirty" money system.
- Corporations and special interest groups may lobby against it, as it diminishes the current efficacy of their contributions.
- Free market or laissez-faire proponents of "might makes right" may resent government interference with "stronger" (i.e., better-financed) candidates.
- The number of $5 contributions needed to qualify (and the $5 figure itself) are arbitrary. Furthermore, a legislature may alter these qualifications so as to effectively shut out smaller third parties.
- Those seeking minimal government spending may decry it as a boondoggle, especially if an unusual or controversial candidate or party ends up qualifying for financing.
- If a very wealthy or well-backed candidate decides to pour massive amounts of money into a campaign, the matching funds for other candidates could prove expensive to the government.

Focus On: Vita Needle Company

With Americans living longer and more productive lives, employers need to start rethinking their attitudes to older employees. Even as the number of elderly Americans rises, the average age of retirement has declined, due in part to compulsory retirement and incentives for early retirement—measures that often pave the way for replacement by younger, less-experienced, and lower-paid workers. At the same time, pensions and elderly care costs are rising rapidly as our population ages; our most experienced workers are becoming our most expensive dependents.

Some countries have already begun to seek ways of reintegrating older workers into the labor force; in the Netherlands, for example, retired workers can go to agencies like 65+, which places them in largely part-time jobs working at reception desks and acting as museum docents. But in the United States, with a business culture that demands both rising profits and technological change, bosses and employees have become used to framing the fate of older workers as an either/or question: "Either they get early retirement, or they leave at the minimum age for retirement." As with many community problems, this either/or thinking leaves out other options. The Vita Needle Company, in Needham, Massachusetts, has broken through such limiting attitudes.

Founded in 1932 by Oscar Nutter, who was already 68 years old, Vita Needle has never shied from keeping its more experienced workers. The average age of its workers is 72, and Nutter himself continued running the company right up until his death at the age of 96. Vita's factory, built in a converted ballroom, includes an "eighties bench," where a team of octogenarians work a metal press. As bencher Marion Archibald explains: "I didn't want to just sit at home and watch the dust collect." That sentiment is seconded by others in the factory, like 79-year-old machinist Bill Ferson: "Retirement isn't good for anybody."

Mason Hartman, the current president, and the great-grandson of the founder, knows that businesses shy away from older workers out of a fear of their health problems and aversion to change. But, as Hartman points out, older workers have advantages: They are experienced, have strong work habits, and have had to learn new technologies many times before. They often have more free time and fewer family commitments than younger workers, and their health costs are picked up by Medicare. When other businesses in the area downsized older workers, Hartman eagerly snapped them up for Vita. Now these former bank clerks, waitresses, and bakers have all embarked on a new career.

These older workers don't feel alienated from the Vita workplace, because it's aged right along with them. Although plans at computerization are now afoot, the most common office equipment is still the typewriter and the clipboard; fax machines and copiers are nowhere to be found. Equipment may be old but still useful, and so it isn't shown the door. Neither are old workers; Vita has never laid off a worker or asked one to retire in its 65-year history. By staying loyal and constant to its workers, Vita has earned the same in return. As Hartman explains, "Our equipment and approach have stayed relatively constant. Our workforce is very loyal, very dependable and highly motivated."

This constancy inside the factory doesn't mean that the company is hesitant about reinventing its products for a changing marketplace. Its tubes and needles, some handmachined to the thinness of a human hair, are used by diabetics and heart surgeons alike, as well as by computer chip manufacturers and car makers. This combination of employee loyalty and innovation has led Vita's sales to double in the last 5 years—proof that an openness to a variety of solutions for community business practices can pay off.

Sources

DeVries, Charlotte. "Progress Does Not Need to Be Complete Destruction of the Past." Northfield News Online (Northfield MN). Updated 30 Jan. 1998. Http://www.northfield.org/ news/backissues/980130/opin/progress.html (Accessed 10 Jan. 2000)

Flaherty, Julie. "A Company Where Retirement Is a Dirty Word." *New York Times*. 28 Dec. 1997, Business: 1

Marcus, Jon. "Associated Press Story: Time Stands Still at Vita Needle Company." Thomas Register on the Internet. 30 Dec. 1997. 25 Nov. 1998. <http://www.vitaneedle.thomasregister.com/olc/vitaneedle/ap14.htm>.

Simons, Marlise. "Retired, Rehired: Dutch Fill Crucial Work Force Gap." *New York Times*. 23 April 2000: A6

Statistical Abstracts of the United States: 1997. U.S. Bureau of the Census. Washington DC: GPO, 1998

"Vita Needle Company Home Page." Vita Needle Company. 7 Jan. 2000. <http://www.vitaneedle.com>.

Questions to Consider

1. What are the potential advantages to Vita's approach to technology?

2. What are the potential disadvantages to their approach to technology?

3. What businesses in your own community run or could run with the help of older workers? What measures might help encourage companies to hire older workers?

ARGUING FOR A SOLUTION

Assignment: Consider the solutions that you described in your previous paper. Construct a brief argument for what you think is the best solution(s). Assume that your audience will be indifferent or in favor of some other approach.

Logical Fallacies

In our previous assignment we saw how all forms of deductive argument have weaknesses that can undermine their credibility. While those weaknesses are so inherent that it's difficult to avoid them entirely, there are some types of false argumentation—known as logical fallacies—that have no place in any logical argument.

Some of these have already been discussed in this textbook (e.g., false causality, repetition, and non sequitur). Most of the fallacies added below are appeals to illogical forms of evidence. If you find any of these errors in your own work, root them out. If you find them in the sources you've been using, then it should cast at least some doubt on the accuracy of your source.

Personal Attack—Also known as an ad hominem argument, an attack on a person rather than their ideas. Example: "Who cares what you think? You're just a … [fill in the blank]."

Appealing to Ignorance—Implying something must be true because it is not proved false. Example: "We have nothing to disprove that the U.S. government is an elaborate alien conspiracy."

Appealing to Pity—Arguing for special treatment for sentimental or piteous reasons. An understandable argument, but not a strictly logical one.

Playing to the Crowd—Appealing to the desires or emotions of a mass of people, often through unifying terms like "we" or by flattering people on how clever and righteous "we" all are. Example: Any political campaign speech.

Mass Appeal—Asserting that something is true simply because many people believe it is true, regardless of their authority or intelligence. You may as well say "A million idiots can't be wrong!"

Appeal to Tradition—Asserting that something is right because it is old or "that's how it's always been."

Appeal to Novelty—Asserting that something is better because it's newer. Progress or innovation does not mean the same thing as "improvement."

Appeal to Wealth—Using money as a criterion of personal value so that those with more money are more likely to be right. Example: "If you're so smart, why aren't you rich?"

Irrelevant Authority—An appeal on matters outside one's field of expertise. For example: asking celebrities about issues that do not relate to their work.

From Hypothesis to Thesis

The Hypothesis.   A hypothesis is a theory that tries to account for the evidence that you have collected. By this time, after examining an issue and the solutions proposed for it, you've probably developed at least some theory of what the causes of this issue are, and what the best solution(s) might be. But your hypothesis should be tested at each stage of your investigation into an issue. You need to ask yourself: With what I know now, do I still believe this hypothesis to be true? Why?

Coming to an apparent dead end or a contrary finding does not mean that your hypothesis is wrong. It may simply mean that your methods or assumptions were faulty. Nonetheless, you should question the validity of your hypothesis when confronted with what appears to be compelling evidence to the contrary. If you have evidence that does not support your theory, you may move in several directions with it:

1. Investigate your evidence for flaws or a differing context that may explain why it only appears to contradict your hypothesis
2. If you cannot find any such explanation, admit it in your paper. Do not simply leave out inconvenient evidence. You may be unwilling to alter your hypothesis at this point, but you should at least acknowledge the unresolved issues facing it
3. Alter your hypothesis to account for the new evidence.

The Thesis.   Now that you're writing a persuasive argument, you'll be pressing that hypothesis into service as a thesis. It is no longer being presented to the public as just a theory; it is now a proposition, a claim that you believe to be true, and one that you'll be setting out to prove through a collection of evidence.

While you may begin with a simple explanation, the point of an essay is to give an increasingly nuanced exploration of the strengths, weaknesses, and examples of this theory in practice. A thesis is weak when it has simply been restated with phrases such as "Once again we see" and "As I said before," or if it is presented without any dissenting perspectives; these are signs that there hasn't been real development between the introduction and the conclusion. Nor should you feel the need to be all pro or all con. If you're split over an issue, don't pretend to know the answer—admit it and explain exactly why you can't decide. These knotty problems are often the beginnings of a more interesting discussion.

Finally, remember that a piece of evidence that seems self-evident to you may not to someone else. Take each piece of evidence that you present and ask of it: "So what?" If you can still give a further explanation of why that piece of evidence is important, then do so. Then look at your longer explanation, and ask of it: "So what?" Repeat this process until you've exhausted its usefulness.

Sample Response

It's hard for any ordinary citizen to feel that our elections aren't at least slightly rigged—and maybe very rigged—against the little guy. And so, naturally enough, there have been many movements to reform campaign finance. But nearly all fail, either by running up against the self-interest of politicians or by colliding with the First Amendment guarantee of free speech. While only citizen pressure can shake politicians out of their inertia, the latter problem can be avoided with a model legislation developed by the reform group Public Campaign.

Its "Model Legislation for Clean Money Campaign Reform" gives candidates the option of running a government-funded Clean Money campaign. While the proposal is a comprehensive one, the basics are simple:

- After raising enough seed money in $5 amounts from individuals, candidates qualify for government Clean Money funding.
- Clean Money candidates cannot also use private or personal funds.
- If an opponent raises "dirty" money from private sources, the Clean Money candidate can receive matching funds ("Clean Money Campaign Reform: Draft Legislation").

Because candidates are not forced to use Clean Money, it would pass muster under the current Supreme Court rulings that essentially equate campaign spending with free speech. For this same reason, it wouldn't be challenged by the American Civil Liberties Union or other civil liberties organizations.

The benefits would be dramatic and immediate. This system would eliminate the need for candidates to grant favors or extra time to wealthy campaign contributors. This can also allow candidates to spend more time with common citizens and to develop their positions on various issues. Can you imagine an election where, instead of hosting $200 a plate fundraising dinners, candidates actually have time to meet with their constituents, and have time to do more than just smile and shake your hand?

Wealthy candidates could no longer simply "buy" an election by steamrollering over opponents. People without a fat roll of cash on hand—people like you and me—would no longer be scared off from serving the country. Imagine a ballot that, for once, actually looked like the population outside: Instead of middle-aged wealthy white men, there would also be women, minorities, the young, the poor.

It's not pure political fantasy; this system works, and versions of it are already in use in Vermont and Maine. And although it does cost some money—a nationwide total of about $1.3 billion per 2-year election cycle, by Public Campaign's estimate—the government spends more than that on a single B-2 bomber ("Just the FAQs"). It works out to less than $3 a year for every American—the price of a couple of coffees.

Is democracy worth $3 a year to you?

Works Cited

"Clean Money Campaign Reform." Public Campaign. 13 Apr. 2000. <http://www.publiccampaign.org/cleanmoney.html>.
"Just the FAQs." Public Campaign. 17 Apr. 2000. <http://www.publiccampaign.org/DA.html>.

Focus On: Richard Seed

Someone looking for an example of false authority could do little better than Dr. Richard Seed. On January 6, 1998, the world was shocked by a report on the National Public Radio show *All Things Considered:* A Harvard Ph.D., Dr. Richard Seed, was proposing the opening of a human cloning clinic in Chicago. He predicted that after a few early and expensive clones for upward of $1 million each, prices would drop and a market for 200,000 clones a year would develop. He opined that the godlike assumption of the powers of creation were not only ethical but inevitable: "You can't stop science."

There were a few problems with Seed's latest plan, to put it mildly. He had no medical degree (his doctorate was in physics), no money, no institutional affiliation, and no particular experience in cloning. While the NPR report noted some of these hurdles, hundreds of papers and TV shows leapt upon Seed and his plan. Here was a kooky Dr. Frankenstein straight out of central casting, and "a Harvard Ph.D." at that. Seed was swept up in a whirlwind of public statements and television appearances, culminating in being the star attraction on ABC's *Nightline.* On the show, he only half-jokingly offered to clone host Ted Koppel. The more informed statements of actual biologists and bioethicists were largely lost in all the sensational reporting, as were Seed's rather slim qualifications. As Arthur Caplan, a University of Pennsylvania bioethicist, complained: "Seed was legitimated by the very people who should have been scrutinizing him."

Both of Seed's brothers are surgeons. His older brother, John, dismissed him and his plan as "bombastic and boastful." But his younger brother, Randolph, was more widely quoted with this claim: "He's perfectly capable [of cloning humans] if he gets some financing." But Randolph was not exactly a disinterested party, nor was this Seed's first attempt at an ambitious get-rich-quick scheme. He and Randolph had already attempted an unsuccessful fertility clinic in Chicago in the early 1980s. A few years later, Richard was approaching Chicago bankers with a $35 million plan to corner the world fish meal market. "He said, 'I'm the world's smartest man,'" one investment banker recalled. "In Richard's case what made it unusual was that he wasn't kidding." The plan had no takers. Seed's latest plan was possibly spurred on by an even more pressing need to get rich quick: a bank had recently foreclosed his mortgage and evicted him from his home.

Thanks to the lightweight reporting on Seed, religious and political leaders worldwide issued condemnations of him and his plan. House majority leader Dick Armey thundered, "Human cloning should remain the province of the mad scientists of science fiction." Two hastily written bills to ban human cloning were immediately presented to Congress, although they were eventually voted down.

In the fall of 1998, Seed announced the proposed lucky recipient of his first attempt at cloning: himself. The following year saw the formation of a company, Clonaid, but otherwise little progress toward his goal. There were some gaffes, though: At one British press conference, he revealed that he might not consider cloning gay people, since they had a "genetic defect." In a late 1999 television appearance he ridiculed his interviewer's "limited brain" for daring to bring up ethical concerns with human cloning.

Perhaps Seed will prove the experts wrong, and have Richard Seed and Ted Koppel clones toddling around by the time you read this. But another result is predicted by Cornell University animal science professor Robert Foote: "This bizarre proposal of Doctor Seed's is getting a lot of press and will create a feeling in society and subsequent regulations which will hurt good research."

Sources

"Bioethics for Beginners." University of Pennsylvania Center for Bioethics. 12 Jan. 2000. <http://www.med.upenn.edu/~bioethic/outreach/bioforbegin/index1.html>.
"Fears of a Clone." *Observer* (London), 11 Jan. 1998: 23
Holden, Constance. "Random Samples." *Science*. 25 Jun. 1999: 2083
"Human Cloning Plans." *All Things Considered*. National Public Radio. 6 Jan. 1998.
Johnson, Dirk. "From Hubris and Hysteria, A Global Furor Over Cloning" *New York Times*, 24 Jan. 1998: A1
Kolata, Gina. "Proposal for Human Cloning Provokes Dismay and Disbelief." *New York Times*, 8 Jan. 1998: A22
_____ *Clone: The Road to Dolly, and The Road Ahead*. New York: William Morrow, 1999
"New Scientist Planet Science/Cloning Report." New Scientist. 12 Jan. 2000. <http://www.newscientist.com/nsplus/insight/clone/clone/clone.html>.
"Richard Seed." *Hard Talk*. BBC America. 16 Dec. 1999
Taylor, Chris. "Seed Seeing Double." *Time* Magazine Daily. 7 Sept. 1998. *Time*. 26 Nov. 1998. <http://www.time.com/daily/>.
Weiss, Rick. "Senate Blocks GOP Drive to Quickly Ban Human Cloning." *Washington Post*, 12 Feb. 1998: A12

Questions to Consider

1. What logical fallacies might Seed be accused of using?

2. What fallacies might Seed's detractors be accused of using?

3. If you were Seed, how might you rephrase his cloning proposal to make it more persuasive?

WRITING A COUNTERARGUMENT

> **Assignment:** Put yourself in someone else's shoes for this assignment, and using your list of advantages and disadvantages, write a counterargument in response to your own editorial.
>
> Keep in mind that you need to come up with an effective and realistic argument for an opponent to have. Coming up with a counterargument that no one would actually make doesn't help develop your argument. For example, writing a "pro–drunk driving" counterargument would be a bit silly. The counterarguments for that sort of topic would be ones over the best way to address this problem. While some issues do indeed have fundamental pro/con disagreement over the existence of the problem itself, others may simply involve a debate over whether there are more effective or efficient solutions than the one you proposed.

Fallacious Questioning

Even if your evidence and your logic are impeccable, an argument can still be undermined by its very premise, that is, the question or thesis that you start out with. A fallacious thesis is usually caused by some preconceived notion or assumption that taints the range of possible answers to your questions. Here are a few varieties of fallacious questioning to watch out for:

Leading Question—Phrasing a question so that someone cannot agree or disagree without committing to an underlying assumption. Example: "Have you stopped taking drugs yet?" The question assumes that you took drugs in the first place; it makes it impossible to answer "Yes" or "No" without agreeing to a unproved claim.

Simplistic Questioning—Irrationally demanding a simple answer to a complex question. Examples: (a) arbitrarily asking that a question be answered in one sentence; (b) Demanding a yes or no response to a situation of considerable ambiguity. (See "bifurcation" below.)

Bifurcation (aka "false dichotomy")—Essentially a form of simplistic questioning. Bifurcation is phrasing a question in an either/or format of only two alternatives, when in fact many alternatives are possible. Examples:

1. "Are you for us or against us?" (Maybe I don't care either way. Maybe I only support your cause in certain circumstances.)

2. "Are we going to jail all burglars for life or are we going to accept a rising rate of theft and mayhem?" (There are different sentences and rehabilitations that might work to lower crime, and they are not being mentioned in this question.)

Circular Reasoning—Assuming in your question or opening statement the truth of the very point you are trying to prove. In doing this, you never actually prove the truth of that initial assumption. This takes two forms:

1. A is true because B is true. And B is true because A is true.
2. A is true, because B is true. And B is true because C is true. And C is true because A is true.

Examples:

1. Aliens exist because it says so in this book, which I know is true because aliens wrote it.
2. Pop music is evil because it incites people to violence. We know people commit violence because crime rates are rising. And crime rates are rising because pop music is evil.

Shifting Definition—Using a word in one sense at the beginning of your argument, and then quietly changing its meaning part way through the argument in order to falsely maintain your conclusion. Example: All crime should be punished harder. But my driving with an expired license isn't exactly a crime, right? So I'm all for fighting crime, but let me off the hook. (You've shifted the definition of "crime" so as to conveniently exclude yourself.)

Avoiding Libel

Libel in the United States is defined as the publishing of a mistruth or false quotation that deliberately seeks to inflict emotional, physical, or fiscal harm upon another person or group. As determined by the 1964 *Sullivan v. New York Times* case, writers must show "actual malice" by publishing with "reckless disregard" a statement that they know to be false.

Certain people and organizations use the threat of entanglement in a libel suit as a way to scare off opponents even when the allegations being made are true. But if you can prove the truth of your claims, your case is in the clear. (Your lawyer's fees won't be, however!)

Because the scrutiny and publicity of a court case only makes a truly guilty party look even worse, libel suits are relatively rare in this country. But before you make serious and potentially damaging allegations in public (and this includes online discussion), make sure that you have one or more trustworthy sources behind your allegations.

Sample Response

Public Campaign's reforms seem like a fine idea in theory. Unfortunately, the real world just doesn't bear out such ideas.

First of all, what exactly is wrong with a well-financed candidate? In an age where politicians can't meet with the hundreds of thousands, or even millions, of voters that they may be serving, TV and radio ads are the only effective way to get their views across to the public. Those ads take money; to choke this off is to choke the candidate's ability to communicate with voters.

What if a very wealthy or well-backed candidate decides to pour massive amounts of money into a campaign? Will the voters be willing to put up with the sight of a government throwing millions upon millions of dollars to match the funds of the Steve Forbeses and Ross Perots of future elections? With election costs rising every year, matching funds for other candidates could prove increasingly expensive to the government. Will Congress really have the patience to keep pouring over a billion dollars into funding Clean Money each election cycle?

Corporate and union PACs—the biggest contributors to electoral campaigns—will also fight this measure, and with good reason. While it's easy to label these groups as "special interests" and "fat cats," that doesn't take away from the fact that they represent the interests of many people. If a business contributes money to a politician, it's not merely on behalf of the owner, it's also in the interest of the firm's employees. When we talk about big political contributors, we're not talking about just 10, 20, or even 1,000 people—we're talking about millions of workers and their families.

Even for those who would support campaign finance reform, this is not a good piece of legislation. The $5 contributions are entirely arbitrary. Why not $10? Why not $20? Why not $100?

In the end, Clean Money is simply another expensive boondoggle. It rewards candidates who would otherwise be too marginal or outside the mainstream to ever get serious backing in the real world—all in the name of opposing so-called special interests that, in reality, actually represent the interests of most American voters.

Focus On: Helen Steel

While Americans enjoy freedom of speech, outspoken citizens in other countries aren't always so lucky. In England, where libel laws are more easily invoked, two penniless activists found themselves at the center of the longest trial in English history.

At the center of the controversy was a six-page leaflet titled "What's Wrong with McDonald's? Everything They Don't Want You to Know." The leaflet was distributed from 1985 to 1990 by a tiny group of ecoactivists, London Greenpeace, who are unaffiliated with Greenpeace International. Passed out to customers as they came and left McDonald's restaurants, the leaflets accused the fast-food giant of cruelty to animals, exploitation of children, deforestation, carcinogenic food, union bashing, and bearing responsibility for poverty in dozens of countries.

McDonald's sued for libel. Informed that defending themselves under Britain's libel laws was nearly hopeless, three of the five defendants immediately apologized. But two—Helen Steel and Dave Morris, both unemployed—refused to back down. The lawyers that they consulted didn't offer them much hope, though.

They said that it's very costly to fight a libel action. As Steel recalled in an interview with Enviroweb:

There's no legal aid for libel and … if, as in our situation, you didn't have any money and you had no legal experience the very difficult battle of defending a libel action would be made almost impossible. Effectively you would be banging your head against a brick wall…. But at the end of the day we didn't have much choice. There was no way I was going to apologise for something that just didn't deserve an apology.

When the case came to trial in 1994, it emerged that McDonald's had been spying on the group with plants from two different detective agencies. At some London Greenpeace meetings, the corporate spies had actually outnumbered the real members. Undeterred, McDonald's pressed on, spending over $10 million in legal fees. Steel and Morris, lacking money for lawyers but refusing to give up, learned how to defend themselves; they spent mornings on the subway going over briefs. Over 60,000 pages of documents and 130 witnesses were produced, and the trial stretched into the longest in English history.

McDonald's was reduced to claiming that cola was nutritious because water was a nutrient, that growing chickens in tiny cages was humane, and that Steel and Morris had posed a real danger to their $32 billion company. The result was a public relations disaster. The judge found that McDonald's was accurately accused of exploiting children, cruelty to animals, antiunion and low-wage policies, and marketing unhealthful products as "nutritious food." He also ruled that claims of deforestation, impoverishment, and cancerous products were libelous, and ruled for the company, awarding them a mere £60,000. Meanwhile, hundreds of thousands of curious trial watchers read the leaflet online, and activists started similar campaigns in dozens of countries. British TV ran recreations of the trial, and CBS's *Sixty Minutes* ran a segment sympathetic to Morris and Steel.

Unlike the United States, Britain's libel laws have continued to be surprisingly resistant to modernization. As recently as April 2000, a British court ruled that an Internet service provider was liable for critical comments posted about a rather unloved public figure, the physicist Laurence Godfrey. Nonetheless, the same basic precautions of verification and research that would prevent an accusation of libel in the United States would also generally work in the United Kingdom.

And what of the "McLibel" defendants? They're appealing the ruling, after which they're hauling the British government into the European Court of Human Rights, in order to overturn the country's oppressive libel laws. And Helen Steel, an unemployed bartender, turned her fame and court experience into a new career—as a student in law school.

Sources

Bogus, Carl. "Ronald McDonald Is a Bully." *Nation.* 24 Nov. 1997: 31

"Helen Steel Interview." Enviroweb. 7 Jan. 2000. <http://www.enviroweb.org/mcspotlight-na/people/interviews/helen.html>.

Lyall, Sarah. "Britain's Big 'McLibel' Trial (It's McEndless, Too)." *New York Times.* 29 Nov. 1996: A4

————."British Internet Provider to Pay Physicist Who Says E-Bulletin Board Libeled Him." *New York Times*. 1 Apr. 2000: A5
"McDonald's-Corporate." McDonald's. 26 Dec. 1999. <http://www.mcdonalds.com/corporate/>.
"McLibel." Narr. Morley Safer. *Sixty Minutes*. CBS. 28 Dec. 1997
"McLibel Listserve Home File." Animal Rights Resource Site. 26 Feb. 1998. 27 Nov. 1998. <http://arrs.envirolink.org/maiLists/mclibel/>.
"McSpotlight." McInformation Network. 2 Dec. 1999. 26 Dec. 1999. <http://www.mcspotlight.org>.
"Media—Britain: McDonald's Libel Case Reopens Debate About Censorship." Interpress Service. 6 Jan. 2000. <http://www.oneworld.org/ips2/jan99/08_07_009.html>.
Petley, Julian. "An Unsavoury Business." *Index on Censorship*. Sept. 1998: 64
Vidal, John. *McLibel: Burger Culture on Trial*. New York: The New Press, 1997

Questions to Consider

1. Whether or not you agree with their position, imagine that you are a lawyer for McDonald's. How would you argue in favor of their position?

2. Bearing in mind that they did win the case, are you convinced by the arguments for McDonald's? Why or why not?

3. How might the defendants have prevented a libel suit?

WRITING A REBUTTAL

Assignment: Write a rebuttal to the previous assignment's counter-argument. Take each of "their" points one at a time and respond to them.

When writing this assignment, you might also try your hand at including some of the web page elements that are explained in this section. For example, where would you use the paragraph and boldface tags?

Web Page Basics

What Your Browser Sees. When your browser goes to a web page, it receives instructions encoded into the page about how it should look, what text should be in italics or boldface, where each paragraph starts, what links go where, and what multimedia effects to include. These instructions, which are invisible to the casual user, are called *tags*. They are written in HTML (Hypertext Markup Language) and are always placed within < > brackets so that browsers know not to display them as part of the actual text.

These tags often come in pairs, with the first telling the browser where to start an action and the other featuring a backslash to tell it where to stop. For example, <STRONG> and </STRONG> indicate where to start and end boldfaced text. Other tags, like the tag to start new paragraphs, don't need a closing tag.

Here's how an actual paragraph might use these tags:

Although <STRONG>Abbey Road </STRONG> was the last album recorded by the Beatles, it wasn't the last one released by them; delays in production caused <STRONG>Let It Be </STRONG> to reach the record stores last.

Unlike other Beatles albums, which were produced by George Martin, <STRONG> Let It Be </STRONG> was produced by Phil Spector, famed as the inventor of the "Wall of Sound" approach to pop music.

And here's how that combination of tags and text will look on a browser:

Although **Abbey Road** was the last album recorded by the Beatles, it wasn't the last one released by them; delays in production caused **Let It Be** to reach the record stores last.

Unlike other Beatles albums, which were produced by George Martin, **Let It Be** was produced by Phil Spector, famed as the inventor of the "Wall of Sound" approach to pop music.

Getting up And Running. All documents written in HTML need the same few tags to get them up and running ...

```
<HTML><HEAD><TITLE></TITLE></HEAD><BODY>
```

And they all need the same two tags to end the document: </BODY></HTML>

No matter what else you add to a web page, you must have these tags in this order. So let's look at a simple example that prints merely one sentence:

```
<HTML><HEAD><TITLE>A Simple Web Page</TITLE></HEAD>
<BODY><P> The freedom of the press is limited to those who
own one. </BODY></HTML>
```

When read by a web browser, a title in the browser window reading **A Simple Web Page** will appear, and only one sentence will appear within your browser's screen:

```
The freedom of the press is limited to those who own one.
```

Of course, this is only the simplest form of a web page. There are many HTML tags that add form and functional to your page, although people rely on these tags the most:

Tags   *Purpose*

```
<BODY> </BODY>          Body demarcates the visible document
where text and images will be.
```

```
<BR>                    Break puts in a line break, much in the
same way that <P> does.
```

```
<CENTER></CENTER>       Center places text or an image in the
center of the page.
```

```
<EM> </EM>              Emphasis puts text in italics.
```

```
<H1> </H1>              Header puts a section title in head-
line type. The higher the number (<H2>, <H3> ... ), the
smaller the font.
```

```
<HEAD> </HEAD>          Head provides document information to
your browser. The title tag needs to be within this Head
section.
```

```
<HR>                    Horizontal Rule puts a separating line
across your page.
```

```
<HTML> </HTML>          HTML tells a browser that this is a hy-
pertext document for the WWW.
```

```
<P>                     Paragraph starts a new paragraph
```

```
<STRONG> </STRONG>      Strong puts text into boldface.
```

```
<TITLE> </TITLE>    Title identifies your document; it's
displayed at the top of a browser screen.
```

Creating Web Documents

There are, of course, a dizzying array of programs out there for creating flashy web pages. But even the simplest computer can do the job, because an HTML document can be created on any word processor. Just add in the tags and you're set!

When you save your finished document, save it as a "text-only" (txt) file. Most word processors offer these formatting options after you choose their "Save As" command. This will remove the formatting (bold face, font size, etc.) from your document, but don't worry—your tags are now there to tell the browser where and how to display these details.

When you save your document, give it a brief descriptive name (write a note to yourself, in case you forget what the name means) and add the html suffix, as in this file name:

```
welfarepaper.html
```

Or, if you're on a system like DOS that only accepts a three-letter suffix, you'd call it:

```
welfarepaper.htm
```

How Do I Get it on The Web?   If your instructor or school is creating a web page for the whole class, it might be as simple as saving your HTML documents on a disc and handing it in to them. If you want your own Web site, it gets a little more complicated. You'll need to find an Internet service provider: either a commercial service like America Online, or perhaps a student account at your school. Ask that provider if they offer personal web pages or "FTP storage." If they do, then it's just a matter of uploading the HTML documents to this part of your account. Since software varies between providers, it's best to ask them individually how to upload these documents. You'll also need to create an "index" page and links between different parts of your site; this book's next assignment has more information on how to do that.

And now you have a web page! If you want to update it, or change your index to add new links and documents, all you have to do is upload or hand in a new version of the HTML document.

Sample Response

Opposition to Public Campaign's model of campaign finance reform, Clean Money, tends to come in three forms: that it's unusually restrictive, that it costs too much, and that there's nothing "dirty" about the current system of finance.

Clean Money is not restrictive: In fact, it leaves candidates free to finance their campaigns with their own or contributors' money. Yes, it does ban so-called soft money, but that's only used for party-building activities, and therefore doesn't impact any individual candidate's campaign. Clean Money merely provides incentives, not penalties, for candidates to campaign under its guidelines. It is designed to provide funds at a level sufficient for candidates to run ads and make public appearances, only now they won't have to resort to tacit favors for wealthy contributors.

That said, Clean Money does cap its funding. If a very wealthy candidate decides to pour an enormous sum of money into a race, then at some point the opponent's Clean Money matching funds would stop. This helps prevent the system from being bankrupted by one or two exceptionally expensive races, freeing it to fund the vast number of races that do not have such candidates. Fortunately, voters often know when someone's blatantly trying to buy out a race; campaigns by multimillionaires and billionaires like Ross Perot, Michael Huffington, Steve Forbes, and Al Checci have all gone down to defeat in the past.

The fact is, Clean Money is a bargain. The $5 contributions used to qualify for Clean Money can help offset some of the cost. Most of the money for this system will come through indirect savings, though. When senators approve bombers and cargo planes that the Pentagon never asked for, or approve highways that no one particularly wanted—will it surprise any of us if arms conglomerates and construction unions have been filling their campaign chests? With politicians no longer in the back pocket of powerful labor and industry Political Action Committees (PACs), a lot of pork will vanish from the federal budget.

Some will argue that these PACs represent "you and me," the workers of America. But can a donation from a union PAC truly represent the wide range of beliefs among its members? While a union might accurately express its members' beliefs on issues directly related to working conditions, it's arrogant to think that it could represent them for the wide range of social, foreign, and domestic issues that a political candidate has to deal with.

Business PACs have even less claim to mainstream legitimacy. The large companies behind big-business PACs are publicly held and traded, which means that their fiscal duty is to Wall Street, that is, to their shareholders, not to their workers. Business PACs represent the interest of high-ranking executives and their major stockholders, and that's hardly a cross section of American society.

Clean Money allows individual citizens to express their support of a candidate through a $5 donation—enough money to prevent a frivolous vote, but not so much that you couldn't pull it from your wallet for a campaign volunteer on Main Street. We've lived for years with politicians whose moneygrubbing has kept them from mingling with and understanding the concerns of common citizens. No democracy can function without fair elections involving all the people, and Clean Money restores that fairness to our country.

Focus On: Supermarket PTA Announcements

No matter how well thought out your ideas are, they'll have little use if they can't reach other members of your community. While college research papers are expected to meet certain formats and requirements of the college community, other communities may rely on very different media—radio, television, web pages, bulletin boards, community meetings, and so on—that require your ideas and proposals to be written or delivered differently.

This was just the problem facing the Henry Cooper Comprehensive School, in the English city of Hull. The school serves Orchard Estates, one of Hull's poorest neighborhoods, and it suffers from one of the worst truancy rates in England. The Parent Teacher Association (PTA) at the school is a badly needed link between the school and the community's families. Not only does it keep parents informed about their children's progress in school, it also helps teachers stay aware of any challenges that their students are facing at home. PTA meetings are vital for giving community members a chance to inform each other about school programs and community projects that can help improve the future of Orchard Park's children.

Although the school worked hard to prepare refreshments and announcements for these meetings, few parents showed up. The traditional manner of announcing meetings—giving students a notice to take home—was simply not working. The students who were absent the most often, and most in need of help, were also the least likely to have delivered these notices in the first place.

If notices in the newspaper were rarely read, and school bulletin boards were useless to parents who never visited, there was one other innovative approach: announcements in the supermarket. The school approached local Tesco and Kwik Save markets and helped them to draw up 30-second announcements for school meetings, each broadcast once an hour. As school head teacher David Bird explains:

Letters sent home by pupil post don't always reach the parents. We know that a lot of the parents will be in the local supermarkets at some point of the day, so this is one of the most effective ways to contact them.

The school's innovative thinking paid off. Seventy percent of the parents targeted by these announcements showed up at the next PTA meeting. Although that still leaves many parents to reach, the success of these announcements has encouraged the school to use the system to also broadcast exam dates. As the Henry Cooper Comprehensive School discovered, getting the right words together is only half the battle of community writing: You also have to get the word out.

Sources

Rowe, Mark. "Spuds 8p Off—PTA Meeting 8 pm." *The Independent* (London). 8 Feb. 1998: 13

"Sir Henry Cooper Index Page." Sir Henry Cooper School. 24 July 1997. <http://www.rmplc.co.uk/eduweb/sites/pearson/index.html>.

Thornton, Karen. "Lateral Thinker; Straight Talker." *Times Educational Supplement*. London Times. 18 Sept. 1998: 20

Questions to Consider

1. Why did the supermarket PTA announcements succeed where others did not?

2. What would be the best way to reach members of your own community? Why?

3. Head teacher David Bird has been lauded as a "lateral thinker"—that is, one who approaches a problem from a new perspective—for his way of solving these types of problems at the Sir Henry Cooper School. If you wanted to get a different perspective on your issue, or to stand outside of it and look in, how would you go about doing that?

PAPER:
EXPLAIN AND DEFEND A SOLUTION

Assignment: Explain and defend a solution or set of solutions to your issue. Explain its advantages and disadvantages, and address objections that others may have. How can readers get involved with the solutions that you've proposed? Explain to them how and why they should help, where they can go to offer assistance, and basic steps that they can take to avoid compounding this community problem. If you wish, you can write this as a web document.

Providing Enough Evidence

There is a difference between a claim and evidence; simply saying that something is true doesn't make it so. It must be shown to be true first. And not all evidence, no matter how truthful it may appear, is going to be relevant to your topic. Some of the evidence that is relevant may not even support you! Evidence doesn't simply "prove" your point—it is the whole mass of details, some of which are contradictory, that relate to your subject.

Most importantly, evidence isn't simply "the facts." Shoveling facts upon a reader is no substitute for an actual argument. The implication of these facts may seem obvious to you, but you can't assume that about your reader. Facts are mute: They cannot speak for themselves. You must interpret them for the reader. So when you present a fact—whether it be an expert's quote, a statistic, or an eyewitness account—you should explain why this fact is important and why its source should be believed.

A claim backed by a single fact, no matter how impressively explained, is often not sufficient to carry an argument. You need to sustain a discussion by offering other examples that show a pattern of evidence. If you rely too much on any one example or source, and that example later turns out to be untrue or misinterpreted, it will topple your entire argument. Try, if possible, to show both a depth of examples (e.g., several sources in one community) and a breadth of examples (e.g., from across several different communities). This will prevent your examples from coming off as too shallow or as mere "me too" statements.

Creating a Web Site

When a Web site is created, it starts with a central document called the "index." This is a bit like a book's cover and table of contents; that is, it explains the purpose of the site and lists its contents. Imagine the index as a hub, and all your sites, documents, and images radiating out like spokes on a wheel; or, if you prefer, consider your index as the spider at the center of a web of connected points. So if you're going to create your own Web site, rather than just a document for inclusion in other people's sites, then you'll need to create an index page.

Let's see how one index page might look:

```
<HTML>

<HEAD>

    <TITLE>Paul's Web Page at Dominican College</TITLE>

</HEAD><BODY>

    <H1>Welcome to English 2</H1>

    <IMG SRC="quillpen.gif">

    <P>The following are handouts and helpful materials
for our fall semester course:

        <P><A HREF="assn1.html">Assignment #1</A>, due
on August 29th

        <P><A HREF="aasn2.html">Assignment #2</A>, due
on Sept 1st

        <P><A HREF="assn3.html">Assignment #3</A>, due
Sept 3rd

        <P><A  HREF="http://www.metacrawler.com">
Metacrawler  Search Engine</A>, one of the most useful ways
to explore the web.

    <P><A HREF="mlaguide.html">Guide  to  MLA-style  research
papers</A>

        <P><STRONG>Created by:</STRONG> Paul Collins, paulc@
examplepage.com    <BR>    This    Page's    URL:
http://www.examplepage.com/ paulc/index.com

        <STRONG>Last update:</STRONG> August 1, 2000

    </BODY></HTML>
```

Adding Links to Your Page.   The <A> tag allows your reader to navigate links to different parts of your document, your site, or across the web to another site altogether. This is the basic form of a link:

```
<A HREF="site or document name">put your highlighted text
here</A>
```

This is how it might work if you wanted to send someone to another document within your web site:

```
If your firm is looking for a widget maker, my <A HREF =
"resume.html"> qualifications </A> should be of interest
to you.
```

A reader clicking on the highlighted "qualifications" would then be sent to your résumé page. They can also click on links to other people's sites; in this case, they could jump to another site by clicking on the words "San Francisco SPCA":

```
Dogs  and  cats  are  available  for  adoption  at  the<A
HREF="www.sfspca.org"> San Francisco SPCA</A>, which was
one of the first shelters to stop euthanizing these "un-
wanted" pets.
```

Here are some other examples of what you can do with links:

Sending someone to a newsgroup
```
Plans for light rail are often debated in the <A HREF=
"news:ba.transportation"> Bay  Area  transportation</A>
newsgroup.
```

Sending mail
```
Please  <A  HREF="mailto:jdoe@nyu.edu">send  me  comments
</A> about this web site!
```

Web Multimedia. While graphics, sound, and video are not essential components of most research papers, they certainly can enhance them. Since the Internet's capabilities for using multimedia changes frequently, consult your library or bookstore for how-to books on making web pages. Don't bother initially with expensive volumes loaded with software and the latest bells and whistles. You'll get more use out of a simple, no-nonsense guide aimed at beginners. You can always move on to the glossier titles later!

Or you can do what many professional web designers do: When you find an attractive site on the web, select a command in your browser menu that says *Show Source, View HTML,* or something similarly phrased. It will then display the HTML used on that page, which you can then save or print out for future reference. While the content of the page may be copyrighted, the HTML code framing it is not; there's no reason you can't use it as a template for your own page.

Sample Response

It's hard for any ordinary citizen to feel that our elections aren't at least slightly rigged—and maybe very rigged—against the little guy. PACs (Political Action Committees) increasingly dominate the financing of our elections. These PACs represent industry, unions, and special interests, everyone, that is, except individual citizens. Politicians and would-be politicians spend their time before the election chasing wealthy donors, and after the election paying them back in the form of pork barrel politics. In the meantime, their primary form of contact with common citizens is a deluge of TV and radio sound bite ads, too short to thoroughly explain their beliefs but just long enough for a meaningless comment or a bit of mudslinging at an opponent.

The result of this is that there have been many movements to reform campaign finance. But nearly all fail, either by running up against the self-interest of politicians, or by colliding with the First Amendment guarantee of free speech. While only citizen pressure can shake politicians out of their inertia, the latter problem can be avoided with a model legislation developed by the reform group Public Campaign.

Its "Model Legislation for Clean Money Campaign Reform" gives candidates the option of running a government-funded Clean Money campaign. While the proposal is a comprehensive one, the basics are simple:

- After raising enough seed money in $5 amounts from individuals, candidates qualify for government Clean Money funding.
- Clean Money candidates cannot also use private or personal funds.
- If an opponent raises "dirty" money from private sources, the Clean Money candidate can receive matching funds ("Clean Money Campaign Reform").

Because candidates are not forced to use Clean Money, it would pass muster under the current Supreme Court rulings that essentially equate campaign spending with free speech. For this same reason, it wouldn't be challenged by the American Civil Liberties Union or other civil liberties organizations.

Clean Money is not restrictive: In fact, it leaves candidates free to finance their campaigns with their own or contributors' money. It does ban so-called soft money, but that's only used for party-building activities, and doesn't impact any individual candidate's campaign. Clean Money merely provides incentives, not penalties, for candidates to campaign under its guidelines. It is designed to provide funds at a level sufficient for candidates to run ads and make public appearances in the way that they currently do, only now they won't have to resort to tacit favors for wealthy contributors.

The benefits would be dramatic and immediate. This system would eliminate the need for candidates to grant favors or extra time to fat-cat campaign contributors. This can also allow them to spend more time with common citizens and to develop their positions on various issues. Can you imagine an election where, instead of hosting $200 a plate fundraising dinners, candidates actually have time to meet with their constituents, and have time to do more than just smile and shake your hand?

Wealthy candidates could no longer simply "buy" an election by steamrollering over opponents. People without a fat roll of cash on hand—people like you and me—would no longer be scared off from serving the country. Imagine a ballot that, for once, actually looked like the population outside: Instead of middle-aged wealthy white men, there would also be women, minorities, the young, the poor.

It's not pure political fantasy. This system works, and versions of it are already in use in Vermont and Maine. And although it does cost some money—a nationwide total of about $1.3 billion per 2-year election cycle, by Public Campaign's estimate—the government spends more than that on a single B-2 bomber ("Just The FAQs"). It works out to about $3 a year for every American.

Clean Money is a bargain in more ways than one. Clean Money allows individual citizens to express their support of a candidate through a $5 donation—enough money to prevent a frivolous vote, but not so much that you couldn't pull it from your wallet for a campaign volunteer out on Main Street. These contributions can help offset some of the cost of Clean Money. Most of the money for this system will come through indirect savings, though. When senators approve bombers and cargo planes that the Pentagon never asked for, or fund highways that no one particularly wanted—will it surprise any of us if businesses and unions have been filling their campaign chests? With politicians no longer in the back pocket of powerful labor and industry PACs, a lot of pork will vanish from the federal budget.

What's more, Clean Money keeps costs under control by capping its funding. If a very wealthy candidate decides to pour an enormous sum of money into a race, then at some point the opponent's Clean Money matching funds would stop. This helps prevent the system from being bankrupted by one or two exceptionally expensive races, freeing it to fund the many races that do not have such candidates.

Of course, not everyone will be happy with this legislation. Politicians may not like it, because incumbents—with their longstanding contacts with various PACs and wealthy donors—will no longer have an unfair advantage in fundraising over the new, equally funded opponents that they'll be facing. Now incumbents will have to win elections by virtue of their abilities and ideas, and not simply because they have a fat bankroll to wave around.

Industry, unions, and pressure groups probably won't like it, either. They may even argue that PACs represent "you and me," the workers of America. But can a donation from a union PAC truly represent the wide range of beliefs among its members? While a union might accurately express its members' beliefs on issues directly related to working conditions, it's arrogant to think that it could represent them for the wide range of social, foreign, and domestic issues that a political candidate has to deal with. Business PACs have even less claim to mainstream legitimacy. The large companies behind big-business PACs are publicly held and traded, which means that their fiscal duty is to Wall Street, that is, to their shareholders, not to their workers. Business PACs represent the interest of executives and their major stockholders, and that's hardly a cross section of American society.

Maine and Vermont voters recognized this and have already passed Clean Money laws. That still leaves a long way to go. If you want Clean Money in your state or federal elections, contact Public Campaign directly by calling (202) 293-0222, or by checking out its Web site at publiccampaign.org. We've all lived for years with politicians whose moneygrubbing has kept them from mingling with and understanding the concerns of common citizens. No democracy can function without fair elections involving all the people, and your support of Clean Money will restore that fairness to our country.

Works Cited

"Clean Money Campaign Reform." Public Campaign. 13 Apr. 2000. <http://www.publiccampaign.org/cleanmoney.html>.

"Just the FAQs." Public Campaign. 17 Apr. 2000. <http://www.publiccampaign.org/DA.html>.
"Public Campaign: Real Campaign Finance Reform." 28 Apr. 2000. Public Campaign. 29 Apr. 2000. <http://www.publiccampaign.org>.

Focus On: Ariel Gore

If the media doesn't provide you access to make yourself heard, why not start your *own* media? That's the spirit behind "zines," handmade magazines with small circulations that have begun to make an impact on mass culture. Anyone with a pen and access to a copier can start one, and there are no rules about how to do it from there.

Zines have a long history, ranging from 1940s science fiction and movie fanzines to the underground comic revolution of the 1960s and 1970s. One such early zine in New York, *Punk*, actually lent its name to an entire musical culture. But the modern renaissance of zines and web-based "e-zines" began in the late 1980s and early 1990s, with the spread of neighborhood copy shops, inexpensive computing, and the Internet. While there are many pop culture zines, there's also a more serious side, with general interest zines like *Clamor*, social issue zines like pro-fat *Fat!So?*, such women's zines as *Bitch*, and the labor zines *Temp Slave* and *McJob*.

One of the most successful and pioneering zine efforts is *Hip Mama*, a feminist parenting zine started in 1993 by Ariel Gore. Gore, who was at one time a single teen mother on welfare, was tired of not seeing any media for the needs of mothers like herself. After entering college in her late 20s, she started *Hip Mama* as a senior project, but it grew very quickly from there. To her, being a hip mama is not a pose; it's a matter of knowing your rights as a mother and as a parent, and of raising your child in a safe and sane manner that hews more to the actual needs of your family than to any media image of parenting. "Most people with really little kids don't really look that cool, so it's not necessarily that kind of hipness that I really care about," she explains. Her magazine covered everything from postpartum depression to dealing with divorce and restraining orders, to knowing what to ask for in the delivery room, to simply plugging the books and music that helped keep her sane in the face of the pressures of single motherhood.

The response to Gore's honest and grassroots effort was tremendous, and she found herself publishing her magazine regularly and debating Newt Gingrich on CNN and writing columns for magazines like *Ms*. This all culminated in two books: *The Hip Mama Survival Guide*, a guide to pregnancy, childbirth, and infancy; and *The Mother Trip : Hip Mama's Guide to Staying Sane in the Chaos of Motherhood*, a more personal reflection focusing on the challenges of raising children once they're out of infancy. She also leads two popular Web sites, Hipmama.com and girlMom.com. "People come to Hip Mama looking for perspectives not offered elsewhere," explains girlMom editor Bee Lavender. "We cover it all, from organic baby food to sexuality to chronic illness."

So what do you need to start a zine? Articles, and perhaps some illustrations. A catchy or unusual name helps. There's no standard editing process for zines; some are one-person shows, some are written by the publisher's friends, while still others will accept submissions from anyone. A computer or word processor helps for creating text and layout, but even here there's room for low-tech efforts—plenty of zines are written by hand and laid out by cutting and pasting the articles and drawings onto page-sized sheets.

You'll need access to a copier, of course, though some of the glossier zines hire a print shop to print and bind their work. As for your circulation, some zines are in the single digits, while others reach hundreds of readers. You'll find that copy shops, cafés, music stores, newsstands, and specialty comic stores are among the most likely to stock it.

You are now a publisher!

Sources

Angel, Jen. *The Zine Yearbook Vol. III.* Bowling Green, OH: Become the Media, 1999

Black, Francesca and Hillary Carlip. *Zine Scene: The Do It Yourself Guide to Zines.* Los Angeles: Girl Press, 1998

"Factsheet 5 Web Edition." *Factsheet 5.* 2 Jan. 2000. <http://www.factsheet5.com>.

Friedman, Seth (ed.) *The Factsheet 5 Zine Reader.* New York: Crown Publishing, 1997

Gore, Ariel. *The Hip Mama Survival Guide.* New York: Hyperion, 1998

———."If It's All You Can Do to Get Out of Bed in the Morning, Just Get Out of Bed."

Girl-Mom. 2 Jun. 2000. <http://www.girlmom.com/pinkhair.html>

———.*The Mother Trip : Hip Mama's Guide to Staying Sane in the Chaos of Motherhood.* Seattle, WA: Seal Press, 2000

———."The Mother Trip 2000." Hip Mama. 2 Jun. 2000. <http://www.hipmama.com>

Green, Karen and Tristan Taormino (eds.) *A Girl's Guide to Taking Over the World: Writings from the Girl Zine Revolution.* New York: St Martin's Press, 1997

Kalmar, Veronika. *Start Your Own Zine.* New York: Hyperion, 1997

Lukas, Paul. "Fan's Notes." *Money.* Dec 1999: 281

Robbins, Trina. *From Girls to Grrlz: A History of Women's Comics From Teens to Zines.* San Francisco: Chronicle Books, 1999

Rowe, Chip (ed.) *The Book of Zines.* New York: Owl Books, 1997

———."Zine, Zines, and E-zines: Cover Page." 2 Jan. 2000. <http://www.zinebook.com>.

Wickre, Karen. "Web Zines: An Immediacy Beyond Paper." *New York Times.* 5 Mar. 1998: D10

Questions to Consider

1. How would you expect the content of zines to differ from professionally produced magazines? Why? What need are they filling?

2. What kind of stories in your community get ignored by mainstream magazines or newspapers? Why?

3. If you were to produce a zine about an interest or concern of yours, what would it be about? What specific articles would you include?

PEER READING

In-Class: Read and respond to the papers written by your classmates. Review the peer reading instructions you used for paper #1
and organize your reading groups in the same manner for this paper.

Peer Reading Worksheet for Paper #4

Writer:

Partner:

Are there any parts that you found confusing or insufficiently explained?
Why?

Who is quoted in the paper? Is there anything else you might you want to
ask them? What other sources or points of view could the writer include?

Does the writer's description of their solution seem realistic to you, or is it biased? Do they give a fair description of the competing solutions that they
oppose?

Did the writer provide enough evidence or examples to show why their solution is needed? What would make their essay more convincing to you?

Overall, how might the writer improve this paper?

REVISING THE PAPER

Assignment: Revise and print out a new version of the paper. Then add it to a folder that includes your first draft, your peer reading worksheet, and the shorter assignments.

Revising for Your Own Biases

We've spent a lot of time looking at bias and assumptions in other people's writing. Now check your writing to make sure that you're aware of your own biases and assumptions:

The Truth Is Not Obvious: Stating flatly that something is true does not make it so. Do phrases like *obviously, everyone knows,* and *of course* show up in your paper? These phrases are often shortcuts for people who are unwilling to explain their assumptions about an issue. Chop these phrases out and rewrite that part of your paper so that reasons and research make your point of view obvious to the reader.

The Sky May Not Be Falling: Don't be too quick to turn a few instances of a problem into a blanket statement about your community, country, or the world. Give solid evidence that these parts represent a larger whole in some way. Are these examples a symptom of a bigger problem in your community, or might they be isolated incidents?

Common Sense: This is often neither common nor sensible. It was once so-called common sense that humans would never fly and that the earth was flat. Common sense is a social tradition, not a reason, so don't use it to back up any of your claims.

"People Say": Apply the bias detection from chapter 2 to your own paper. Are you relying on people with the same point of view or background? Do you have sources that are vague or have an unmentioned stake in the issue that may bias their comments?

"God Says": If your religious beliefs define a problem (e.g., it's considered wrong by your religion, and therefore you see it as a problem), be prepared to give a detailed explanation of exactly who holds this view and why. Your congregation leader or a religious scholar at your school may be able to give you some historical perspective on the reasons behind this position, as well as on any debate there may be between believers. If a sacred text is involved, be prepared to quote and cite it; your standards of evidence should be just as high here as for any other kind of source. Also, you should give space to other or opposing perspectives from those dissenting within or outside your religion.

"I Say": Maybe everyone you've read or interviewed disagrees with you about the nature of a problem. Maybe they don't even see a problem. This can be a difficult position, but don't ignore their point of view. You may put your experiences at the center of your writing, but also explain to your readers why you think others may not share your perspective. Use a different line of questioning in your interviews, and try to get some views from other communities, age groups, and socioeconomic backgrounds.

Focus On: Patrick Moore

After you've gathered evidence and prepared an argument, what if you start agreeing with another side, or they start agreeing with you? How do you shift from an adversarial relationship to a working relationship with them? This difficult question has faced many activists, often accompanied by the risk of being labeled a traitor to a cause. Political figures from Michael Collins to Malcolm X have lost their lives for speaking out against divisive and destructive actions by their former allies; they are now seen as heroes for their willingness to negotiate. Others are harder to figure out. When the alcohol industry trade group Beer Wholesalers Institute hires MADD (Mothers Against Drunk Driving) founder Cindi Lamb for an ad campaign, are we to believe that she is a sellout, or simply a realist who has decided that working from the inside is more effective than head-on opposition?

It is precisely this question that has dogged Patrick Moore, a cofounder of Greenpeace Canada. Moore was born into a Canadian family of loggers; his father was once president of the Truck Loggers Association. But after Patrick finished his PhD in ecology at the University of British Columbia in 1972, he became a cofounder of Greenpeace Canada, and spent years at the front lines of environmental struggles in the American West. But by the 1980s he felt the movement had become overly politicized and too quick to criticize industry in a knee-jerk fashion. In the early years, he recalls, "We tried to avoid the hair-shirt mentality that tends to creep in with self-righteousness, dogmatism and that sort of thing."

Moore wasn't prepared to demonize opponents; his whole family was in logging, and they certainly didn't look like demons to him. Nor did they seem deaf to reason or devoid of any good ideas. Moore felt it was unrealistic to expect all logging to stop—were people to simply stop using paper and building homes? He left Greenpeace, and by the late 1980s he found himself working increasingly with the wood products industry to develop what he views as environmentally sound procedures for logging.

As he explained to *New Scientist* magazine:

> When industry and government agree that the environment needs to be taken into account in policy making, and when there are ministries and vice-presidents of the environment, it seems to me it would be a good idea to work with them. When a majority of people decide to agree with you, it is time to stop hitting them over the head.

Moore now consults for logging companies, and is a frequent guest speaker at industry conferences. He often agrees with industry practices, and uses scientific arguments to overturn conventional environmental activist wisdom; he supports, for example, some forms of clear-cutting. This unwillingness to toe the line, and especially his hobnobbing with "the enemy," has made Moore deeply mistrusted by many activists. One Canadian environmental group, the Forest Action Network, posted a "Patrick Moore Is a Big Fat Liar" web page, complete with anti-Moore T-shirts and quotes denigrating the man that they now see as an environmental Judas. Moore, in turn, has sued them for libel.

Moore claims that it is only by meeting with the industry on its own ground that one can influence them. So is Moore a realist building bridges between environmentalism and industry, or a shill for moneyed interests? It's hard to say. But his repudiation of confrontational tactics may show that while argumentation is a means to an end, it is important that the end is not lost sight of. You are not arguing to defeat or humiliate an opponent; you are arguing to improve the human condition. There is a time for head-on opposition and protest, but as an end in itself protest can be more destructive than the ills it means to redress. To recognize the essential humanity of those you disagree with, to be willing to listen to them, and to work toward acceptable compromise is not always how activists are made ... but it is often how they succeed.

Sources

Bond, Michael. "Dr. Truth." *New Scientist.* 25 Dec. 1999/1 Jan. 2000: 74–77
Daifallah, Adam. Home page. "Patrick Moore: Environmental Extremist ... " 9 Jan. 2000. <http://qlink.queensu.ca/~8ad5/column28.htm>.
"Greenpeace Cofounder Discusses Environmentalism ... " University of California at Berkeley Department of Agricultural and Natural Resources. 20 Apr. 2000. <http://dandr.ucop.edu/news/July–Dec1999/moore.html>.
Moore, Patrick. "GreenSpirit." Green Spirit. 9 Jan. 2000. <http://www.greenspirit.com>.
"Patrick Moore Is a Big Fat Liar." Forest Action Network. 9 Jan. 2000. <http://www.fanweb.org/patrick-moore/lies.html>.

Questions to Consider

1. Who do you think has compromised a little too much on an issue recently? Why do you think they did this? Might there have been good reasons for them to do this?

2. Are there any activists or groups that strike you as being unwilling to negotiate or compromise? Do you think it helps keep their mission credible, or is this more likely to backfire on them? Why?

3. If an opponent partly agreed with your argument on the issue you're researching, what would you do next? What would you be willing to lose? Would you meet halfway on some suggestions? Which ones would you insist on having implemented?

5

The Term Paper

THE FINAL PAPER

The Topic: Using your previous work, create a paper that includes the following:

1. Describe a community that you belong to.
2. Describe the manifestations of a problem in this community.
3. Outline possible or existing solutions. What are their advantages and disadvantages?
4. Explain and defend the best solution or combination of solutions.
5. Provide information on what basic steps concerned readers can take, what organizations they can contact, or what sources they can read for more information.

Feel free to include interviews, survey results, lists, quotes, descriptions of similar problems in other communities, or responses by concerned groups or individuals. You or your professor may also wish to create this paper in the form of a web document.

Combining Your Work

Now that you've completed several stages of research, description, and persuasion, this is your time to bring it all together. Although the final paper is the longest paper covered thus far, it shouldn't be too daunting: it's essentially a revised summary of all the work that you've already completed.

Most students approach this by revising their previous papers, chopping out redundant material, and then pasting them together in the order that they wrote them. But if you think your final paper might work better by organizing the raw material of your previous papers in some different order, you're free to do so. There may also be new material that wasn't available for your first or second paper, but didn't really fit into the third or fourth; the final paper lets you include the full results of such research.

156

As you gather your old papers, look over any comments that your instructor or your classmates may have made. These should help guide your revisions. After all, if your instructors are collecting your old monthly papers along with the final paper, they'll be aware of whether you worked to revise and improve these writings.

Revising Your Web Page

If you are creating your paper as a web page, remember that even the best-written web document can be rendered unreadable or unusable by a small error. Here are the most common ones for which to keep an eye out:

Keep it simple. It's tempting to throw in lots of graphics and features on a web page, but these can annoy your readers and open up more chances for errors on your part. Remember that you can always revise your page and upload it again. Start with a simple document, make sure it works properly, and then add no more than one new feature with each update. That way, if something goes wrong, you'll immediately know where the problem is.

Remember your closing tags. This is the most common HTML mistake. If you forget a </STRONG> tag, for example, the rest of your page will be in bold-face.

Use sound and images sparingly. Unlike text, sound and images eat up lots of download time and can quickly wear out a reader's patience. Avoid needless clutter and frustration.

Include your name and e-mail address. These are typically listed at the bottom of a page, and they let readers know who wrote it and how they can contact you with ideas or suggestions.

Note the last update. The last date of revision is also usually listed at the bottom of a page. This lets readers know how timely the text is, and whether or not it has changed since they last visited.

Include your web address. Once your paper's on the web, it's good to include the web address at the bottom of your page, along with your address and update information. That way, even if someone downloads your page and forgets how they found it, they have your address to guide them back again.

Look at it on different browsers. Don't assume that your web page design will look the same on different browser programs. Simple web pages won't suffer from such variations, but ones making more specific use of fonts and background colors might.

Proofread your page. Your page doesn't have to be on the Internet for you to read it on a browser. Just open a browser program on a computer (whether or not it's connected to a modem) and open your HTML documents from within the program. Check for missing closing tags or links that don't show up. And once your web page is online, check it again to make sure that your links actually work.

Use the <TITLE> tag. You have to use it, of course. But many people simply write "World Wide Web" or something inane in this tag. Your readers know they're on the web! Use your title to give them an idea of what this site or this particular document is about.

Sample Final Paper

I don't often think of voters as forming a community, but the group of people who actually do vote is small, and it becomes smaller with each election. The Committee for the Study of the American Electorate found that nationwide turnout in the 1998 primaries was a mere 17 percent of eligible voters; in 10 states turnout sank to record lows, despite the use of such innovations as "Motor Voter" registration. As committee director Curtis Gans noted, "The problem we have is not procedural but motivational" ("Voter Turnout Drops" A18). Even with registration gimmicks, there's an underlying apathy among Americans. My suspicion is that this apathy stems in part from the vast sums of money involved in campaigning. As a voter, I'm increasingly perturbed by the effect this money has on our democracy.

Enormous amounts of money are required for a modern political campaign, and with each election spending records are broken. Much of the money in these campaigns comes from interest groups that then expect that this money will buy them extra pull with their elected officials. Jane Public with her $20 contribution won't get the time of day from anyone, but captains of industry with bulging wallets can expect to plead their case to a senator or a representative. As San Francisco neighborhood activist Ted Loewenberg notes, "We basically leave government to the highest bidder. When we see the communications industry invited to write their own deregulation legislation, the system is corrupted and completely broken." He points out that this corrupting influence seeps down to the local level: "You can't run for city supervisor now without a quarter of a million dollars handy."

As a result, it's hard for any ordinary citizen to feel that our elections aren't at least slightly rigged—and maybe very rigged—against the little guy. PACs (Political Action Committees) increasingly dominate the financing of our elections. These PACs represent industry, unions, and special interests, everyone, that is, except individual citizens. Politicians and would-be politicians spend their time before the election chasing wealthy donors, and after the election paying them back in the form of pork barrel politics. In the meantime, their primary form of contact with common citizens is a deluge of TV and radio sound bite ads, too short to thoroughly explain their beliefs but just long enough for a meaningless message or a bit of mudslinging at an opponent.

Even when a candidate won't take money from such people, all is not necessarily well. In the 1998 and 2000 elections, I was dismayed by the huge amounts of money spent by multimillionaire candidates like Steve Forbes, Al Checci, and Darrell Issa; each seemed determined to buy his way into government. Checci and Issa, running in California, both spent millions of their own money on TV ads, even though neither seemed interested in debating or spelling out his beliefs very clearly on paper. If you have enough money, they seemed to think, you can just buy enough TV coverage to drown out any meaningful questions about your qualifications.

Fortunately, voters proved these millionaires wrong; all of them lost in the primaries. But perhaps it's only a matter of time before such blatant tactics start working. Money-driven campaigns that are only slightly more subtle have already landed many candidates in office. The millions spent in some campaigns shut out potential candidates—decent, everyday people who don't earn six- and seven-figure salaries—who either lack rich friends or are unwilling to make such connections. And without these ordinary citizens among our elected officials, the politicians and their wealthy supporters start looking awfully similar: rich, male, probably white, and probably not very ethical.

Press coverage of campaign finance and its reform doesn't give much immediate hope for a solution. The *New York Times* article "Campaign Finance: The Lateral Pass" explains the curious phenomenon of how members of Congress can talk about reform without actually getting anything achieved. Here's how it's worked eight times in the last 19 years: Every couple of years, one chamber (either the Senate or the House) will pass a campaign finance reform bill with the tacit understanding that the other chamber will defeat it (Clymer 6). This has occurred under both Democratic- and Republican-controlled congresses. This way, political parties can claim that they "passed finance reform" without having to turn it into a law.

There are certainly many groups working behind the scenes on both sides. As I looked over reform efforts, Common Cause was the first to catch my eye, probably because it makes the most noise in the media. It is a citizen's lobby, financed solely by individual contributions of its 250,000 members. It has no party affiliation and does not back specific candidates. Its Web site shows its work as a watchdog and as a state advocate for various bills seeking greater candidate accountability and greater controls on "soft money," or the largely unregulated contributions that corporations and special interest groups can make directly to political parties. At the state level, this has been achieved through supporting proreform legislation and voter initiatives, and serving as a watchdog for bad political behavior. Its Web site provides e-mail addresses for various senators so that you can write them about your support for the latest version of such reform ("Common Cause: Take Action").

Passing reform—any reform at all—would slow the waves of money crashing into political campaigns. But the weakness to this approach lies in the resistance of Congress to passing such laws; neither side is interested in cutting off their donors, and so they persist in passing such bills in only one chamber of Congress. You can send all the e-mails you want to your senator, but it still isn't in their personal interest to change these laws. And even if such a bill were passed, it would be challenged by free-speech advocates like the American Civil Liberties Union (ACLU).

But Jim Knox, the executive director of California Common Cause, points out that federal reform—which relies on Congress and the Supreme Court—differs from state reform, which can be citizen driven. "My experience has been that there's virtually no chance of the [state] legislature passing meaningful campaign finance reform. All the campaign reforms in California, back to Prop 9 in 1974, have been through state initiatives." These initiatives have to be carefully worded; winning propositions in 1988 and 1996 were struck down in court.

The ACLU acts as a gatekeeper among reformers in this debate. The ACLU remains opposed to limits on spending because it sees them as a limit on free speech ("Support Constitutional Campaign Finance Reform"). While the ACLU offers no solution to campaign finance, it makes clear that it *doesn't* like limits on fund raising, different mail or broadcast rates for Clean Money candidates, required record keeping of small contributions (e.g., $20), the ability of the Federal Elections Commission to contest campaigns during an election, and any ban or restriction on PACs ("February 20, 1997 Letter … ").

The ACLU's stand has the advantage of constitutional purity: *if* one defines money as equivalent to speech, these objections insure that speech would be unhindered. That's a big if. The ACLU's stand also leaves us where we started: in a system of "might is right," where the candidate with the most money usually wins.

This view is seconded by the Web sites for the conservative Cato Institute and the Heritage Foundation, both of which include papers on campaign finance. The Cato Institute's papers feature the work of Bradley Smith. He argues that the separation of "soft" and "hard" money is working well, and has the advantage of not infringing on the First Amendment. In fact, he claims the existing limits on hard money ($1,000 by individuals to a candidate, $5,000 to a PAC) hurt because they force politicians to campaign longer and discourage those who lack the stamina to chase "small" amounts. Smith also attacks federal financing as supportive of "extremist" candidates, thus "forcing citizens to pay for others to express opposing opinions" ("Campaign Finance Reform"). Smith goes on to argue elsewhere that "Contrary to the assumption that large contributions are undemocratic is the reality that most challenges to the status quo and most working-class political movements have been financed by wealthy donors" ("Campaign Finance Regulation").

The Cato Institute's arguments presume that campaign funds flow to the best candidates, rather than to candidates who grants favors to wealthy donors—though in the view of the wealthy, perhaps that's exactly who the best candidate is. The complaint about the public funding of opposing views misapprehends the nature of elections. Voters are liable to change their minds at any point—otherwise, why campaign or debate at all? Anyone's stance is liable to be opposing, at least in retrospect, and we can only know that a view opposes ours after our vote is cast. Finally, Smith's contention that the wealthy are the best friends of working-class movements is hard to believe. But like the ACLU, Smith's approach has the advantage of a laissez-faire simplicity and of not clashing with the Constitution.

A similar argument is raised through the Heritage Foundation by Lamar Alexander. In his 1996 run for president, he claims, donation limits forced him to attend fundraisers daily: "I became acquainted with a great many good Americans capable of giving $1000 (who probably represent a cross section of about one percent of all the people in the country.)" His implication is that had he been able to get this fundraising out of the way with a few unlimited donations, he'd have had more time to mingle with working people. Furthermore, limits favor incumbents who already have donors at hand, and wealthy individuals who can ignore limits by simply using their personal fortune ("Off With the Limits").

Alexander's argument seems reasonable, as attending fundraisers does sound like a drain on candidates. Even Common Cause's Jim Knox admits that there may be a "kernel of truth" to Lamar Alexander's contention that unlimited contributions would free him up to spend more time with the citizenry. But as Knox points out, the smaller the contributions, the broader the base of support a candidate needs—an argument that also points to more contact between candidates and voters.

Will a well-connected incumbent's advantage of a donor list evaporate with a lifting of limits? Now, instead of being $1 million or $2 million ahead of a challenger, they can be $10 million or $20 million ahead. The stakes will be raised on both sides, but the uneven ratio remains the same. And as for the contention that time away from the wealthy at fundraisers will be spent with working-class people instead—it's a nice thought, but I've yet to see a politician who wouldn't rather spend their free time with their well-educated and well-fed peers.

We are not the only country to grapple with these issues. In 1995, British Columbia's Election Act created a system of nomination, advertising, and financing. Candidates there may be nominated by collecting 25 signatures and making a deposit of $100 (about U.S. $75) ("Guide to the Election Act"). This prevents flippant candidacies, but is still within the reach of someone willing to stake a little money and spend an afternoon out with a clipboard to collect the necessary signatures.

To advertise their positions, candidates can buy advertising at the lowest commercial rate on TV and radio, and in print. They cannot spend more than $50,000, although the limit can be raised for larger voting districts. Parties are limited in their budgets, with a ceiling of $1.25 per registered voter per electoral district ("Guide to the Election Act"). A "third-party" advertiser (e.g., interest groups, corporations, unions) has to register with the province's Chief Electoral Officer, and is then restrained to a $5,000 budget ("Media Obligations").

For candidates, political parties, and third parties alike, the identity of contributors of more than $250 has to be disclosed publicly. Anonymous contributions are limited to $50; political parties can accept a total of up to $10,000 in anonymous donations, while individual candidates are limited to $3,000 ("Guide to the Election Act").

British Columbia's system does have advantages. It does not restrict speech, just the spending of large quantities of money to broadcast speech. This forces candidates to use debates, interviews, and in-person appearances to convey their views to the public, rather than the bludgeoning power of TV ads. While parties can gather some funds to get their message across, they can't overwhelm others.

The law's fiscal limits are admittedly arbitrary: There's nothing magic about the $1.25 or $10,000. What's more, there's no indication of indexing for inflation. I suspect that a few years from now there will be a debate over the adjustment of this figure. With this adjustment comes the possibility of a grab by hungry politicians for a much higher figure.

The more serious problem facing such models in our country is that fiscal limitations would come under fire as a restriction of free speech, because the

Supreme Court's *Buckley* ruling equates political spending at some level with free speech. As Common Cause's Jim Knox notes:

> Canada is not constrained by *Buckley*, whereas we've historically tried to address campaign finance reform within the framework of *Buckley*. Our political assessment is that it's probably not a good idea to challenge *Buckley* head on, because we might lose ground in the current Supreme Court.

It should be noted that, after my interview with Jim Knox, the Court did in fact rule favorably on just such a challenge; that is, it "reaffirmed that limits can be placed on the amount of money individuals contribute to political candidates" (Richey 1). It may turn out that the Canadian system is a more viable model for the United States than previously thought.

Even within our own borders there is cause for hope. Knox points to the partial public funding of presidential elections as one of the movement's success stories. But without a scandal on the scale of Watergate—when this last round of reforms occurred—it seems unlikely that federal reforms will be pursued further. "We got close in 1996, but it takes a lot of public pressure for Congress to do what it is naturally inclined not to do."

With this in mind, I believe our best hope for foreseeable reform is at the local and state level through model legislation developed by the reform group Public Campaign. It painstakingly worded their "Model Legislation for Clean Money Campaign Reform" to anticipate the ACLU's concerns, thus lessening the chance that it would encounter that group's opposition.

The bill provides that:

1. Candidates using government funds cannot also use private or personal funds.
2. After raising enough seed money in $5 amounts from individuals, candidates qualify for government Clean Money funding.
3. If their opponent persists in raising "dirty" money from private sources, then the Clean Money candidate can receive matching funds to stay competitive ("Clean Money Campaign Reform").

Because candidates are not forced to use Clean Money, it would pass muster under the Supreme Court rulings that equate campaign spending with free speech. Clean Money leaves candidates free to finance their campaigns with their own or contributor's money. It does ban so-called soft money, but that's only used for party-building activities, and doesn't impact any individual candidate's campaign. Clean Money merely provides incentives, not penalties, for candidates to campaign under its guidelines. It is designed to provide funds at a level sufficient for candidates to run ads and make public appearances, only now they won't have to resort to tacit favors for wealthy contributors.

This system works, and versions of it are already in use in Vermont and Maine. Maine's Clean Election Act provides full financing for candidates who collect a sufficient number of $5 donations. Candidates collect 50 (House) or 150 (Senate) $5 checks before a March 16 deadline. Once they have advanced to the general election, candidates then can spend state funds up to $12,000 in House races and $40,000 for the Senate. In the 2000 election, 115 of the state's 374 registered candidates took this clean money option (Goldberg A1). And while such plans do cost some money—a nationwide total of about $1.3 billion per 2-year election cycle, by Public Campaign's estimate—the government spends more than that on a single B-2 bomber. It works out to about $3 a year for every American ("Just the FAQs").

Clean Money is a bargain in more ways than one. Clean Money allows individual citizens to express their support of a candidate through a $5 donation—enough money to prevent a frivolous vote, but not so much that you couldn't pull it from your wallet for a campaign volunteer out on Main Street. These contributions can help offset some of the cost of Clean Money. Most of the money for this system will come through indirect savings, though. When senators approve bombers and cargo planes that the Pentagon never asked for, or fund highways that no one particularly wanted—will it surprise any of us if businesses and unions have been filling their campaign chests? With politicians no longer in the back pocket of powerful labor and industry PACs, a lot of pork will vanish from the federal budget.

What's more, Clean Money keeps costs under control by capping its funding. If a very wealthy candidate decides to pour an enormous sum of money into a race, then at some point the opponent's Clean Money matching funds would stop. This helps prevent the system from being bankrupted by one or two exceptionally expensive races, freeing it to fund the many races that do not have such candidates.

Of course, not everyone will be happy with this legislation. Though $650 million a year is chump change compared other expenditures, it's enough money that a senator might score points by cutting it from the budget. There would be an ulterior motive to this, too. Incumbents, with their longstanding contacts with various PACs and wealthy donors, will no longer have an unfair advantage in fundraising over the new, equally funded opponents that they'll be facing. Now incumbents will have to win elections by virtue of their abilities and ideas, and not simply because they have a fat bankroll to wave around.

Industry, unions, and pressure groups probably won't like it, either. They may even argue that PACs represent "you and me," the workers of America. But can a donation from a union PAC truly represent the wide range of beliefs among its members on the social, foreign, and domestic issues that a political candidate has to deal with? Business PACs have even less claim to mainstream legitimacy, because they represent the interest of their executives and major stockholders, and that's hardly a cross section of American society.

We've all lived for years with politicians whose moneygrubbing has kept them from mingling with and understanding the concerns of common citizens. No democracy can function without fair elections involving all the people, and the Clean Money proposal will restore that fairness to our country.

Works Cited

Alexander, Lamar. "Off With the Limits: What I Learned About Money and Politics When I Ran for President." Heritage Foundation. 26 May 1996. 13

Apr. 2000. <http://www.heritage.org/library/categories/govern/lect568.html>.

"Clean Money Campaign Reform." Public Campaign. 13 Apr. 2000. <http://www.publiccampaign.org/cleanmoney.html>.

Clymer, Adam. "Campaign Finance: The Lateral Pass." *New York Times*. 9 Aug 1998: Review 6

"Common Cause: Take Action." Common Cause. 19 Apr. 2000. <http://www.commoncause.org/get_involved/action.htm>.

Goldberg, Carey. "Mainers Try a Donation-Free Campaign." *New York Times*. 1 Apr. 2000: A1

Gora, Joel. "February 20, 1997 Letter to Senator McConnell on the Bipartisan Campaign Finance Reform Act of 1997." American Civil Liberties Union. 20 Feb. 1997. 13 Apr. 2000. <http://www.aclu.org/congress/ls022097a.html>.

"Guide to the Election Act." Elections British Columbia. 1 Jun. 1999. 19 Apr. 2000. <http://www.elections.bc.ca/guidebooks/p855_toc.html>.

"Just the FAQs." Public Campaign. 17 Apr. 2000. <http://www.publiccampaign.org/DA.html>.

Knox, Jim. Telephone interview. 23 Dec. 1998

Loewenberg, Ted. Personal interview. 21 Dec. 1998

"Media Obligations Under the New Election Act." Elections British Columbia. 1 Jun. 1999. 19 Apr. 2000. <http://www.elections.bc.ca/guidebook/p862_toc.html>.

"Public Campaign: Real Campaign Finance Reform." Public Campaign. 13 Apr. 2000. 13 Apr. 2000. <http://www.publiccampaign.org>.

Richey, Warren. "Court Affirms Campaign Finance Limits." *Christian Science Monitor*. 25 Jan. 2000: 1

Smith, Bradley. "Campaign Finance Reform: Soft Money and the Presidential System." Cato Institute. 14 May 1997. 13 Apr. 2000. <http://www.cato.org/testimony/ct-bs051497.html>.

———."Campaign Finance Regulation." Cato Institute. 13 Sept. 1995. 13 Apr. 2000. <http://www.cato.org/pubs/pas/pa238.html>.

"Support Constitutional Campaign Finance Reform." American Civil Liberties Union. 13 Apr. 2000. <http://www.aclu.org/congress/campaignfinance.html>.

"Voter Turnout Drops in 1998 Primaries." *New York Times*. 30 Jun. 1998: A18

Focus On: Dick Falkenbury

With its booming computer industry, scenic waterfront, and famous grunge and café cultures, Seattle is one of America's fastest-growing cities. But with this growth has come traffic congestion, along with a rise in pollution and delays. While funds have been poured into new tunnels, light rail, and roads, they're often one step behind the growing city's needs.

Enter Dick Falkenbury. A 44-year-old cabdriver, Dick had a flash of insight while stuck in traffic. Why not build a rail system *over* the roads? There would be no delays, no collisions with vehicles or pedestrians, and no costly tunneling. Unlike a subway, it could easily run uphill. All you had to do was look at the one profit-making transit system in the country, right there in Seattle: the monorail built for the World's Fair in 1962.

Falkenbury drew up plans on his kitchen table for a 40-mile monorail that covered every corner of the city, and in 1992 he set about gathering voter signatures to place his plan on the city ballot. Although he failed that time, he learned valuable lessons about persuasion. The next time around, in 1996, he was prepared. He had maps to show passersby, and pictures of existing monorail systems; with these visual aids, the idea no longer seemed as abstract or pie-in-the-sky. He also armed himself with an impressive array of facts and statistics: that cities around the world successfully used monorail systems; that there had never been a fatality in a century of monorail use; and that the Kobe, Japan, monorail was one of the few transit services still running after that city's massive earthquake. In fact, the first monorail, built in Wuppertal, Germany, still runs today—almost a century later!

Politicians and pundits across Seattle scoffed at Falkenbury's plan, as much because it was written by a cabbie as anything else. When the press covered the story, it was as the whimsical quest of one off-kilter man. Opponents sniffed (erroneously) that the only places that bothered to use monorails were amusement parks and casinos, while most cities relied on light rail. Fine for the casinos, Falkenbury shot back, but "When you build with your own money, you build a monorail. When you build with other people's money, you build rail."

On less than $3,000 and through word of mouth, Falkenbury got his Seattle Monorail Initiative on the 1997 ballot. Politicians ignored or ridiculed the measure; eight out of nine City Council members weighed in against it. News accounts paid more attention to them than to transit advocates, daily commuters, or monorail manufacturers. On election eve, a *Seattle Times* editorial dismissed the initiative as "charming but unsound."

But on election day that November, to the surprise of nearly everyone, it won. Over 52 percent of ballots cast were in favor of the system, leaving "experts" in the city sputtering for words—and opponents rushing to block the voters' decision. But Falkenbury, it turned out, had also included a clause to withhold City Council salaries if they impeded the project. Debate soon turned from whether the plan would be adopted to how it would be adopted.

Within a month, as directed by the initiative, an Elevated Transportation Corporation was formed, and official appointments and plans were being drawn up. When the ETC unveils its 40-mile monorail network, it will be largely thanks to one man: a half-broke cabdriver with a good idea, an armful of signatures, and an informed community on his side.

Sources

Daniels, Stephen F. "Monorail Proposal Glides Onto Seattle's Transportation Agenda." *Engineering News-Record*. 8 Dec. 1997: 21

Egan, Timothy. "'Or Else' Gives Seattle Voters the Last Laugh." *New York Times*. 7 Dec. 1997: 1

"Friends of the (Seattle) Monorail." Friends of the Monorail. 12 Jan. 2000. <http://www.monorail.org>.

Godden, Jean. "Monorail Promoter a New Hero." *Seattle Times*. 21 Nov. 1997: 1

"The Monorail Initiative, Seattle Washington." Whatrain WWW Services. 12 Jan. 2000. <http://www.whatrain.com/monorail/>.

Seven, Richard. "Northwest People: One Track Mind." *Seattle Times*, 22 Feb. 1998. 12 Jan. 2000. <http://archives.seattletimes.com/web/>.

Schaefer, David. "Monorail's Back on Track." *Seattle Times*. 4 Dec. 1997: 1

Questions to Consider

1. How did Falkenbury, as a newcomer to transportation policy and politics, make himself credible to Seattle voters?

2. What methods of getting the word out helped Falkenbury in his task?

3. Outline the process by which Falkenbury went from irritation over a problem to the adoption of a solution. How applicable is this process to the issue that you're studying?

PEER READING

> **In Class:** Read and respond to the papers written by your classmates. Review the peer reading instructions for paper #1 and organize your reading groups in the same manner. Note: Due to the longer length of these papers, you may want to form smaller groups.

Peer Reading Worksheet for the Final Paper

Writer:

Partner:

Are there any parts that you found confusing or insufficiently explained? Why?

Does the paper read as a unified whole? Are there jarring transitions between materials combined from previous papers? Are old introductions or conclusions stranded in the middle of this longer paper?

Who is quoted in the paper? Is there anything else you might you want to ask them? What other sources or points of view could the writer include?

Did the writer provide enough evidence or examples to show why their solution is needed? What would make their essay more convincing to you?

Overall, how might the writer improve this paper?

REVISING THE FINAL PAPER

> **Assignment:** Revise and print out a new version of the paper. Then add it to a folder that includes your first draft, your peer reading worksheet, and the shorter assignments.

Revising for Appearance

Page design—that is, the visual appearance of your paper—is the least of your worries when writing a research paper. Good design won't save poor writing, nor will bad design doom a well-written paper. But papers that are easier to read are likely to receive more attention from readers, so it's worth knowing the basics of good design. The seven elements of design to be aware of are: *fonts, style, size, chunking, layout, materials,* and *graphics.*

Fonts

Use Serif Fonts for Your Text. A font (or typeface) is the design of the letters that you use. There are two basic categories of fonts: serif and sans serif. Serif fonts are what you see in books and magazine articles. This paragraph is written in a serif font. Their letters have little "feet" that make it easier for the eye to jump from one letter to the next. The most common serif fonts include Palatino, Courier, Times, and Bookman.

Sans serif fonts are clean, rounded designs like Geneva, Chicago, Helvetica, and Futura. This paragraph is written in a sans serif font. They are good for titles and headlines, but are not very effective for the actual body of a document.

While you may want to mix sans serif headlines with serif text, you should not use more than two or three fonts in a research paper.

Avoid Novelty Fonts. It's hard not to play with the dozens of odd fonts available on most computers. But many of them— such as "old-fashioned" fonts, handwritten fonts, and script fonts—simply don't print very legibly. While they may be useful for posters, brochures, and announcements, they are a distraction to the reader and don't work in a research paper.

Style

Boldface, *italic,* and <u>underlined</u> text are the three most common style changes that you can make to plain text. Although you may have to use them in your citations (for example, when underlining a book title), you can also use these styles to emphasize a word or phrase within your paper. Use them sparingly, because they are the written equivalent of raising your voice. If you keep raising your voice, a listener will simply tune you out.

Size

The size of letters (expressed in typography as "points") is important, because text that is too small can render a paper nearly unreadable. Your best bet is to stay with the 12-point text, and 12- or 14-point headlines. Ten-point text, while recommended by some textbooks, is a headache to read; it's only useful for graphics, captions, and page numbering.

Some fonts, even when they are the same size, are much bigger or more compact than others. If you change your font from Palatino to Times, for example, the length of your paper will shrink. If you change it from Palatino to Geneva, though, it will grow. Palatino is your best bet, because it is generally accepted as the most readable of the common fonts.

Chunking

Chunking refers to the separating of text into reader-friendly chunks, as opposed to an impenetrable wall of text. This is achieved through borders, subheads, and lists. These allow the reader to take a breath before moving on to the next section of a paper, or to easily absorb a series of facts.

Borders are the simplest way to separate two different sections of a paper. Some word processors can easily insert a line or some other visual flourish across the page; lacking that, you can always simply type in a few centered asterisks:

* * * * *

Subheads are headlines in the text that describe a specific section. They're used in magazine articles and newspaper features. The word "CHUNKING" that heads this section is a subhead.

Lists are useful for getting across a series of steps or for emphasizing a few basic points. They stand out in the text, especially when centered, and are easier for a reader to absorb, and easier to find again if they want to refer back to your text. When the order of the list is important, you should number each item. When the order isn't important, you can either let the text stand alone or insert "bullets" (a * or •) next to each item. For example, the basic points of this paragraph can be summed in this bulleted list:

- Lists stand out in a text

- They're easy to read

- They're easy to find

- Use bullets for nonordered lists

- Use numbers with ordered lists

Layout

Layout is the way blocks of text are arranged on the page. For a pamphlet, designing layout can take as much time as writing. For a research paper, though, a few general rules suffice:

Use Ragged Justification. Ragged justification is when each line of text ends at a different point on the right side of the page, giving the right side of your copy a "ragged" appearance. Forced justification, often used in newspaper columns and books, makes each line exactly the same length. Forced justification is too distracting for research papers, though, because it can force odd spaces and hyphens between words.

Avoid Cutoffs and Stranded Lines. These are sometimes referred to (in word processors) as *widows* and *orphans*. A paragraph can be cut off, or widowed, at the bottom of the page just as it begins or just before it ends. A stranded line, or orphan, results when the last line of a paragraph is printed at the top of the next page. An orphaned concluding paragraph is worth avoiding, because it will leave you with a last page with only one line on it. This can be avoided by editing your paragraph to a slightly shorter length, or by using your word processor to insert a page break after the previous paragraph.

Preview Your Work. Before you print out a copy of your paper to hand in, take a moment to look it over. Many word processors have a "Print Preview" function that will show you on screen how the document will print out; this is especially useful for discovering accidental gaps, cutoffs, and stranded lines. Even without this function, you can still print out a draft copy on paper and look for any layout and design glitches that need fixing.

Materials

Paper. Print double-spaced text on one side of letter-size white paper.

Staple. Staple the upper left corner. Don't use paper clips.

Folder. Your instructor may want a portfolio of your work in a folder or binder. Avoid plastic folders or covers; they are slippery and difficult to stack.

Using Charts And Graphics

Most computer word processing programs can add charts, photos, or other art to your writing. (There's always scissors and glue, too). These illustrations can be useful aids to your presentation, but remember that they are only aids. A graph is not self-explanatory: you must explain why it is significant, who provided the information, and what conditions (method of polling, margin of error) apply. In other words, you must interpret visual data as fully as any other data that your paper provides. A three-page paper padded out with two pages of uninterpreted graphics is still really just a three-page paper.

A photo, whether used on the cover of a paper or within the text, can add a visual impact that words alone can't convey. But make sure that the photo does in fact have an impact on the reader's understanding; if it's merely cute or filling space, then it will make your paper look less serious. A caption is essential for all photos used in research papers, because you can't assume that readers will know exactly what they're seeing. And if the picture was taken by someone other than yourself, you should also identify the photographer or your source.

Numbering your charts and graphics (Figure 1, Figure 2, etc.) will make it easier for you to refer the reader back to them later in the text. If these graphics are derived from some other source, then cite the source just as you would with any other kind of quotation or paraphrase. This will also make your figures easier for a reader to believe or verify.

Finally, it's easy to get caught up with fonts, sizing, and other intricacies of graphic design. Don't let it drag you down; you should be spending much more time on your research than on getting the paper to look "just right." In your research you've probably already come across slickly produced articles and brochures where it seems like more time was spent worrying about the artwork and fonts than about what was actually being said. Don't let your paper end up like this.

Focus On: Helen Hill

Sometimes you don't have to seek out a cause—the cause finds you. That was certainly the case for adoption rights activist Helen Hill: Had it not been for a chance discovery when she was 10 years old, Helen Hill might never have become the prime mover in a 1998 Oregon ballot measure. Growing up in Kansas City in the late 1960s, she was poking around her parents' room when she discovered adoption manuals behind the bed. When she confronted her parents, they admitted that, yes, she had indeed been adopted. "The seeds of this whole ballot measure," Hill later told the *New York Times*, "were probably sown right there."

In 1998 Hill led the successful fight for Measure 58, a state proposition that allows adoptees to see their own birth certificates. Since birth certificates typically include the name of the birth mother and father, the measure in effect gives adoptees access to records that, in some states at least, were long closed to them. But the road to this victory was a long one. Hill first spent decades and thousands of dollars finding her parents. The experience of being denied basic information about her own identity led her to the adoption rights group Bastard Nation, and to considering how adoptees might get the access they felt they deserved. She had many allies in her fight, including fellow adoptee Curtis Endicott. Endicott, like Hill, had a moment of epiphany while dealing with an adoption case worker. "All of a sudden it hit me," Endicott told *Newsweek* magazine. "This stranger was sitting there looking at the names of my parents, and I had no right to see them."

It was these kinds of frustrations that caused Hill to lead the fight toward creating and publicizing Measure 58. Hill spent about $90,000 of her own money to mount a campaign that featured ads with a golden retriever and the provocative tag line of "Max has his papers. We want ours." In the November 1998 election, Oregon voters approved Measure 58. But, like many controversial state propositions, it had to survive court challenges to take effect. Six birth mothers challenged the measure. The case went all the way to the U.S. Supreme Court, which on May 30, 2000, refused to hear an appeal of a ruling for Measure 58. This was a go-ahead for the measure to be enforced.

It may seem at first glance that nobody could sensibly oppose greater access, but the issue turned out to be more complicated than that. Many birth mothers had been assured by the state that their identities would always be kept a secret. Especially in an earlier era, when the stigma of unplanned or out of wedlock births was much greater, many birth mothers felt that their families and later marriages might be imperiled by the discovery of such children; they wanted no contact with the children they had given up for adoption. On the other side were adoptees who contended that the state's promises of secrecy were not legally enforceable, because they were promises that no state could ethically make.

Considering how important family histories and genetics are in modern medicine, one could argue that denying adoptees information on their parentage might be life threatening. And, in fact, Curtis Endicott died tragically from a heart ailment before ever getting a chance to use Measure 58 to discover his parentage—or his family's heart history. In the end, courts decided the stigma to birth mothers was outweighed by the possibility of harm to their children. But at a more basic level, Helen Hill says, "This is about civil rights. There is no reason we should be denied a basic right."

Measure 58 is a good example of how well-intentioned people on both side of an issue can have compelling arguments, and how in some issues it is simply not possible to please everyone involved. It is easy to see how birth mothers feel betrayed by the state, and yet it is just as easy to see the point of Helen Hill and her fellow adoptees. Hill's fight in winning Measure 58 shows just how much one individual can achieve, and yet it also shows what individuals often can't achieve. Reasoned argument is vital to addressing community issues, but in some issues you just cannot please or convince everyone, no matter how well constructed your arguments are. Research and arguments need to be constructed along rational lines, but the reactions that people have to them will not necessarily work the same way.

Sources

Clemetson, Lynette. "Haunted by a Painful History." *Newsweek.* 22 Feb. 1999: 46–47

Graves, Bill. "Oregon Live 9-14-99: Advocate for Adoptees Dies at Age 51." 14 Sept. 1999. 6 Jun. 2000. *The Oregonian.* <http://www.oregonlive.com/news/99/09/st091406.html>.

"Online News Hour: Opening the Records." PBS: News Hour with Jim Lehrer. 2 March 1999. 6 Jun. 2000. <http://www.pbs.org/newshour/bb/law/jan-june99/adopt_3-22.html>.

"Talk of the Nation Features Helen Hill and Oregon Open Records Bill." Mail-Archive.Com 18 Jun. 1999. 6 Jun. 2000. <http://www.mail-archive.com/adoptionconnection%40onelist.com/msg00119.html>.

Verhovek, Sam Howe. "An Adoptee-Rights Hero Who Knows All the Arguments." *New York Times.* 3 Jun. 2000: A7

———."Anonymous Mothers Lose Long Court Fight." *New York Times.* 31 May 2000: A1

Questions to Consider

1. Think about the issue that you have been researching. Might anyone be unshakably opposed to your solution, no matter how well you argue it? Why?

2. Do you agree with Measure 58? Why or why not? How could birth mothers opposing it have made a more convincing case to the public?

3. How might you overcome resistance to your solution, that is, get around or over those who simply will not be convinced by your arguments? What potential allies would you need to place your solution in motion?

THE NEXT STEP:
WORKING IN THE COMMUNITY

This textbook has two goals: to help you become a better writer, and to help you become a more active citizen. Now that you're nearing the end of this book, you may be wondering: What do I do now? Your school probably has a good idea of how it would like you to continue work on your writing skills. Knowing where to turn in order to be an active citizen can be a bit harder, though.

You may already be familiar with a number of local organizations from your research this semester, and they may be just the people to help you become more involved. You can also try checking in your local phone book or in the *Encyclopedia of Associations*; both are available as library reference books.

Many schools have also started *service learning* programs that allow you to combine learning with community service. This textbook, in fact, was designed to give you the civic and rhetorical awareness needed to embark upon service learning. Even in schools that don't have such programs, there are still ways to find out how you can get involved in your community. We'll be going over both in this chapter, as well as giving names and numbers of organizations that are eager for volunteers to help them work toward making better communities.

Service Learning

Service learning is increasingly popular in schools; it sees community service as only one part of the larger context of analysis and long-term action. It acts locally but thinks globally. Service learners not only ladle out soup in a shelter, they also consider: How did this situation come to pass? What action has been taken? What action might still be taken? How can I work with others to effect these changes?

Ask your subject major department or dean's office if your college has a service learning program that you can join. Even if your school doesn't have such a program, they probably have a person or office responsible for community outreach. Student government representatives are another potentially knowledgeable source of information on student organizations and volunteer programs.

Youth and College Groups

A number of organizations specialize in assisting community volunteers from colleges and high schools. Youth Ventures works with college and high school students alike, while COOL has a presence on many college campuses. Do Something, cofounded by actor Andrew Shue, pays particular attention to social and political issues that affect younger citizens.

Youth Ventures: Young People Changing Communities
1700 Moore St., Suite 1920
Arlington VA 22209

(703) 527-8300
www.youthventure.org

COOL (Campus Outreach Opportunity League)
1511 K St. NW, Suite 307
Washington DC 20005
(202) 637-7004
www.cool2serve.org

Do Something
423 W 55th St., 8th Fl.
New York NY 10019
(212) 523-1175
www.DoSomething.org

Nationwide Service Agencies

There are a number of nationally recognized organizations that work with volunteers in the community; the most prominent of these include the United Way and Project America.

United Way
Local branches listed in the phone book
National toll-free number: (800) 895-2822
www.unitedway.org

Project America
310 S. Boulevard
Richmond VA 23220
(800) 880-3352
www.project.org

Government-Affiliated Service Organizations

One of the largest providers of community outreach is, of course, the federal government. The Corporation for National Service includes such programs as Americorps, which offers college aid in return for community service; Learn and Serve for high school service; the Senior Corps; and a number of service-based scholarships. For an even more serious commitment to helping others, the Peace Corps offers the opportunity to work at bettering communities around the world.

Corporation for National Service
1201 New York Ave. NW
Washington DC 20525
www.cns.gov

Peace Corps
1990 K St. NW

Washington DC 20526
(800) 424-8580
www.peaceCorps.gov

Community Service Web Sites

There are many Web sites devoted to hooking up potential volunteers with community activists. Action Without Borders covers such efforts both domestically and internationally. Impact Online has an excellent database that lets you enter your zip code to learn about events you can begin attending today. You can search among thousands of "Youth Development Internships" in The National Assembly database, which draws from over 500 organizations nationwide.

Action Without Borders
www.idealist.org

Impact OnLine
www.impactonline.org

The National Assembly
www.nassembly.org

Free inquiry and civic responsibility helped form our country's past. By learning and working through these community organizations, you can help insure that this spirit remains alive in our future.

Focus On: Alexis de Tocqueville

Alexis de Tocqueville was a writer more often invoked than understood. The young French nobleman visited the United States in 1831, concerned with what America's great experiment in democracy augured for his own country. His travels over the next nine months were informal, but the book they produced has proved remarkably prophetic. *Democracy in America* (1835) is not an endorsement of democracy, but rather a cool appraisal of the strengths and weaknesses inherent in both monarchies and democracies.

Tocqueville feared what he called democracy's "tyranny of the majority," as well as the coarseness of unbridled public discourse. These are problems we grapple with today in debates on proportional representation and censorship. But Tocqueville also sensed the dynamic nature of democracy—the powerful current of American opportunity that runs through his work like an electric charge. It is in conveying this sense of boundless possibility that Tocqueville is often the most eloquent spokesman for American democracy, even as he is one of its sternest critics.

He was particularly fascinated by the freedom and enthusiasm among Americans for organizing activist groups of every variety, ranging from volunteer charities to entire political parties. "There is," he marveled, "no end which the human will despairs of attaining through the combined powers of individuals united into a society" (Tocqueville 192). To him, this liberty of association—of concerned citizens discussing issues and working together to address them—was the essence of a workable democracy:

> At the present time the liberty of association has become a necessary guarantee against the tyranny of the majority. In the United States, as soon as a party has become dominant, all public authority passes into its hands .... There are no countries in which associations are more needed to prevent the despotism of a faction or the arbitrary will of a prince than those which are democratically constituted .... [otherwise] a great people may be oppressed with impunity by a small faction or a single individual (194–195).

While the majority might deserve the most power, the ability of determined minorities to get the public ear would insure that their needs were not altogether forgotten. It could be a messy and argumentative way to run the country—and yet in the end, Tocqueville mused, still quite possibly the best way.

Sources

Brogan, Hugh. "Tocqueville From the Heart." *Times Literary Supplement*. 2 Oct. 1998: 40

Commager, Henry Steele. *Commager on Tocqueville*. Columbia: University of Missouri Press, 1993.

"C-SPAN Tocqueville Project." C-SPAN. Http://www.tocqueville.org (Accessed 4 Jan. 2000)

"Democracy in America." American Studies at the University of Virginia. 4 Jan. 2000. <http://xroads.virgnia.edu/~Hyper/DETOC/home.html>.

Tocqueville, Alexis de. *Democracy in America*. Trans. Henry Reeve. New York: Vintage Books, 1990.

Questions to Consider

1. Are there any national issues on which your opinion differs from the majority? How could this majority be persuaded to change their view, or at least to give more time to yours?

2. What rights do we enjoy today that were once believed in or argued for by only a small minority of the public?

3. What kind of small activist groups observed by Tocqueville are in your community today? (If you cannot think of any, which groups should be in your community?) Which might you agree with, or even want to join? Why?

Appendix 1:
Further Readings

Although this is a writing textbook, it also grew out of a concern with understanding the media, community activism, persuasive rhetoric, and experience-based learning. If you're interested in learning more about any of these subjects, the books below are a fine place to start.

Understanding the Media

Annotations: A Guide to the Independent Critical Press. San Francisco: Independent Press Association, 2000

Bagdikian, Ben. *Media Monopoly*. 5th ed. Boston: Beacon Press, 1997

Chomsky, Noam. *Manufacturing Consent*. New York: Pantheon Books, 1988

Cogswell, David. *Chomsky for Beginners*. New York: Writers and Readers, 1996

McChesney, Robert. *Corporate Media and the Threat to Democracy*. New York: Seven Stories Press, 1997

Phillips, Peter (ed.) and Project Censored. *Censored 1999: The News That Didn't Make the News*. New York: Seven Stories Press, 1999

Pilger, John. *Hidden Agendas*. New York: New Press, 1999

Postman, Neil. *Amusing Ourselves to Death*. New York: Viking Press, 1986

——— and Steve Powers. *How to Watch TV News*. New York: Penguin Books, 1992

Rosen, Jay. *What Are Journalists for?* New Haven, CT: Yale University Press, 1999

Scheuer, Jeffrey and James Lieber. *The Sound Bite Society: Television and the American Mind*. New York: Four Walls Eight Windows, 1999

Underwood, Doug. *When MBAs Rule the Newsroom*. New York: Columbia University Press, 1995.

Media Activism

Branwyn, Gareth. *Jamming the Media: A Citizen's Guide to Fighting for Media Democracy*. San Francisco: Chronicle Books, 1997

179

Kalmar, Veronika. *Start Your Own Zine*. New York: Hyperion, 1997
Project Censored. *The Progressive Guide to Alternative Media and Activism*. New York: Seven Stories Press, 1999
Ryan, Charlotte and William Gamson. *Prime Time Activism: Media Strategies for Organizing*. Cambridge, MA: South End Press, 1990
Salzman, Jason and Jack Salzman. *Making the News: A Guide for Nonprofits and Activists*. Boulder, CO: Westview Press, 1998
Winokur, Julie (ed.). *We the Media: A Citizen's Guide to Fighting for Media Democracy*. New York: New Press, 1997

Community Activism

Center for Public Integrity. *Citizen Muckraking: How to Investigate and Right Wrongs In Your Community*. Monroe, ME: Common Courage Press, 2000
Hill, Kevin and John Hughes. *Cyberpolitics: Citizen Activism in the Age of the Internet*. Lanham, MD: Rowman and Littlefield, 1998
Kryzanek, Michael. *Angry, Bored, Confused: A Citizen Handbook on American Politics*. Boulder, CO: Westview Press, 1999
Rubin, Barry. *A Citizen's Guide to Politics in America: How the System Works and How to Work the System*. M. E. Sharpe, 1997
Seo, Danny. *Generation React: Activism for Beginners*. New York: Ballatine Books, 1997
Shaw, Randy. *The Activist's Handbook: A Primer for the 1990s and Beyond*. Berkeley: University of California Press, 1996
———.*Reclaiming America: Nike, Clean Air, and the National Activism*. Berkeley: University of California Press, 1999
Thoreau, Henry David. *Civil Disobedience and Other Essays*. New York: Dover Publications, 1993

Persuasion

Asher, Herbert. *Polling and the Public: What Every Citizen Should Know*. Washington, DC: Congressional Quarterly Books, 1998
Cialdini, Robert. *Influence: The Psychology of Persuasion*. New York: Quill, 1993
Ewen, Stuart. *PR!: A Social History of Spin*. New York: Basic Books, 1996
Frank, Thomas. *The Conquest of Cool: Business Culture, Counterculture, and the Rise of Hip Consumerism*. Chicago: University of Chicago Press, 1997
Paulos, John Allen. *A Mathematician Reads the Newspaper*. New York: Anchor Books, 1996
Stauber, John. *Toxic Sludge Is Good for You!: Lies, Damn Lies, and the Public Relations Industry*. Monroe, ME: Common Courage Press, 1995

Writing Guides

Gibaldi, Joseph and Phyllis Franklin. *MLA Handbook for Writers of Research Papers*. 5th ed. New York: Modern Language Association, 1999
Maloy, Timothy. *The Internet Research Guide*. Rev. ed. New York: Watson-Guptill, 1999

O'Conner, Patricia. *Woe Is I: A Grammarphobe's Guide to Better English in Plain English*. New York: Riverhead Books, 1998

Strunk Jr., William and E. B. White. *Elements of Style*. 4th ed. Boston: Allyn & Bacon, 1999

Weston, Anthony. *A Rulebook for Arguments*. 2nd ed. Indianapolis, IN: Hackett Publishing Co., 1992

Experience-Based Learning

Dewey, John. *Experience and Education*. New York: MacMillan, 1997

Freire, Paulo. *Pedagogy of the Oppressed*. Continuum Publishing Group, 1995

James, William. *Pragmatism*. New York: Dover Publications, 1995

Menand, Louis (ed.). *Pragmatism: A Reader*. New York: Vintage Books, 1997

Appendix 2:
Using The Freedom
Of Information Act

Using the Freedom of Information Act (FOIA) can be a lengthy process, and it's probably too slow to be useful within the confines of a semester. All government agencies are required to respond in 2 weeks to FOIA inquiries, though they are often lax in meeting this requirement. But if you're pursuing longer-term research on your subject, then a FOIA request may be very useful. Be aware, though, that FOIA searches are notoriously uneven: Some agency searches will turn up nothing but a form letter, while others will unexpectedly land boxes of documents on your doorstep.

Copying fees may run 10 to 25 cents per page. These fees, if any, can be waived for noncommercial purposes, so make it clear in your letter that you're a student or researcher.

The following standard letter should work well for a FOIA search:

Date

Freedom of Information Officer
Name of Agency
Address of Agency
City, State, Zip Code

Dear FOIA Officer:

This is a request under the Freedom of Information Act (5 U.S.C. §552). I request that a copy of the following documents [or documents containing the following information] be provided to me: [Identify as specifically as possible.]

In order to help you determine my status to assess fees, you should know that I am [insert description of requester and purpose of request, such as "a student at Blank University researching this issue … "], and this request is made as part of news gathering/research and not for commercial use. [You may also offer to pay fees, up to a certain amount, or request a fee waiver.]

Thank you for your consideration of this request.

Remember to write "Freedom of Information Request" on both the envelope and the letter.

Follow up your request in a couple of weeks with a call, especially if there's a delay. If your initial request doesn't work, call the agency and ask for the freedom of information officer. Also be prepared to rewrite your letter with a more specific request, or write to a different agency altogether.

You can appeal if your request is denied. Consult FOIA books or your local American Civil Liberties Union chapter for more information. You can also check online resources for more information on how to use the Freedom of Information Act:

Society of Professional Journalists, FOIA Web site: (www.spj.org/foia/). An excellent how-to resource on all aspects of FOIA and its uses.

The American Civil Liberties Union maintains a simpler but useful Web site at www.aclu.org/library/foia.html

Appendix 3:
Citing Your Sources
In The MLA Format

This appendix provides only a brief summary of the MLA (Modern Language Association) style of citation; the most complete reference work on the subject is the *MLA Handbook for Writers of Research Papers*. It's available in bookstores and at the reference desk of most libraries.

Citing Sources Within Your Paper

The following (entirely fictitious) paragraph shows how to cite a paraphrase from a web page, a quote, and a quote where you've already mentioned the author's name. (In this last case, you previously cited Zimmerman's article.)

> The owners of the Plunket Company avoided takeover by offering to buy shares from any and all shareholders (Plunket Company Page). They knew that the philosophy behind the Widget Company's growth has been described as "the voracious and unceasing acquisition of competitors" (Zimmerman C2). At least one financial analyst believes that "the Plunket family lost itself more money in this 'rescue' than the takeover would have cost them" (C2).

If the author's name is given in the sentence, only the page number is needed in the parenthetical citation. For example:

> As historian Frederick Turner saw it, "The existence of an area of free land, its continuous recession, and the advance of American settlement westward, explain American development" (28).

If no author is listed, give the title or beginning of the title plus the page number.

If using more than one work by the same author, include the title in the citation. For example:

184

"The 'family' concept is at work at many local stations. The anchors will probably be a couple, male and female, both goodlooking and in the same relative age bracket as husband–wife .... " (Postman, *How to Watch TV News* 91).

If you're using a quote that your source quoted from somewhere else, explain in your sentence where it originally came from. For example:

After aviation pioneer Otto Lilienthal took a fatal dive in a glider in 1896, his last words were that "sacrifices must be made" (qtd. in Hart-Davis 52).

Citing a quote with two authors: (Reeves and Mortimer 41).
Citing a work with four or more authors: (Reeves et al. 78).
For an interview or a lecture, simply note the person's name in parentheses.
For a quote from multiple pages: (Reeves 114–115).

The Works Cited Page

Now that you've made your citations, you also need to give information on your sources in a separate Works Cited page at the end of your paper. Note that the entries are listed in alphabetical order by their last names. Here are what the entries would look like for a web page, a book, a magazine article, a book with two authors, a personal interview, a phone interview, and a newspaper article:

Works Cited

Carvell, Tim. "I Was Alan Greenspan's Roadie." *Timothy McSweeney's Worldwide Fondness*. 6 Jan. 2000. Timothy McSweeney's. 11 Apr. 2000 <http://www.mcsweeneys.net/2000/01/06greenspan.html>.
Eggers, Dave. *A Heartbreaking Work of Staggering Genius*. New York: Simon and Schuster, 2000
Friedman, Robert I. "Land of the Stupid." *New Yorker*. 10 Apr. 2000: 40–49
Lake, Brian and Russell Ash. *Bizarre Books*. London: Pavilion Books, 1998
Vowell, Sarah. Personal interview. 30 Jun. 2000
Wallace, David Foster. Telephone interview. 24 Jun. 2000
Weber, Bruce. "Plan Your Family Reunion in Rehab." *New York Times*. 11 Apr. 2000: B1

OTHER TYPES OF WORKS CITED LISTINGS

CD-ROM Periodical Indexes

Shearson Lehman Brothers, Inc. "Widgets International Company Report." 14 Aug. 2000. *General Business File*. CD-ROM. Information Access.

CD-ROM Reference

The Oxford English Dictionary. 3rd ed. CD-ROM. New York: Oxford University Press, 2000

E-mail

Richards, John. <jrichards@ucdavis.edu> "Mass Transit in Northern California." 15 Feb. 1999. Personal e-mail. (16 Feb. 1999)

Online Database

"Acme Products, Inc.: Sales Summary, 1999." *Disclosure/Worldscape*. Online. Lexis. 12 Mar. 2000

Usenet Posting

Coldon, Joe. <joco@squirrel.net> "Ringo's Drumming." 15 Feb. 1998. <alt.fan.beatles> (20 Feb. 1999)

Four or More Authors

Smith, William, et al. *1998 Widget Report*. Chicago: Pointless Press, 1999
More Than One Entry by the Same Author
Jerome, Jerome K. *Three Men in a Boat*. London: Penguin Books, 1994.
————. *Three Men on the Bummel*. London: Penguin Books, 1994.

If there is no author listed for the book, place the Works Cited entry alphabetically in the list by the first word in its title (disregarding *The, A,* or *An*):

Essay or Chapter in an Edited Book

Peirce, Charles. "The Rules of Philosophy." *The American Pragmatists*. Eds. Milton Konvitz and Gail Kennedy. New York: Meridian Books, 1962, 80–82

Collection or Anthology

Gates, Henry Louis Jr. (ed.). *The Classic Slave Narratives*. New York: Mentor Books, 1987

Institutional or Corporate Author

Dominican College. *Undergraduate Catalog, 2000–2001*. San Rafael, CA: Dominican College, 2000

Government Documents

U.S. Bureau of the Census. *Statistical Abstract of the United States*. Washington, DC: GPO, 2000

Personal Letter

Tovar, Chris. Letter to the author. 22 Apr. 2000

Index

H